BEACON
BIBLE
EXPOSITIONS

BEACON BIBLE EXPOSITIONS

BEACON BIBLE EXPOSITIONS

VOLUME **12**

JOHN
JUDE
REVELATION

by

T. E. MARTIN

Editor
WILLIAM M. GREATHOUSE

BEACON HILL PRESS OF KANSAS CITY
Kansas City, Missouri

Copyright 1983
by Beacon Hill Press of Kansas City

ISBN: 0-8341-0809-7

Library of Congress Catalog Card No. 74-78052

Printed in the
United States of America

Contents

Editor's Preface

No Christian preacher or teacher has been more aware of the creating and sustaining power of the Word of God than the Apostle Paul. As a stratagem in his missionary endeavors, he sought out synagogues in the major cities where he knew Jews would gather to hear the Old Testament. No doubt he calculated that he would be invited to expound the Scriptures and so he would have a golden opportunity to preach Christ. That peripatetic preacher was confident that valid Christian experience and living could not be enjoyed apart from the Word of God, whether preached or written. To the Thessalonians he wrote: "And we also thank God constantly for this, that when you received the word of God which you heard from us, you accepted it not as the word of men but as what it really is, the word of God, which is at work in you believers" (1 Thess. 2:13, RSV). Strong Christians, and more broadly, strong churches, are born of, and nurtured on, authentic and winsome exposition of the Bible.

Beacon Bible Expositions provide a systematic, devotional Bible study program for laymen and a fresh, homiletical resource for preachers. All the benefits of the best biblical scholarship are found in them, but nontechnical language is used in the composition. A determined effort is made to relate the clarified truth to life today. The writers, Wesleyan in theological perspective, seek to interpret the gospel, pointing to the Living Word, Christ, who is the primary Subject of all scripture, the Mediator of redemption, and the Norm of Christian living.

The publication of this series is a prayerful invitation to both laymen and ministers to set out on a lifelong, systematic study of the Bible. Hopefully these studies will supply the initial impetus.

—William M. Greathouse, *Editor*

Introduction

1, 2, 3 John; Jude; Revelation

This volume includes the last five books of the New Testament. They speak to events and issues of the early Christian church as she moved westward. These Christians are the fruit of the missionary thrust under the leadership of the Apostle Paul. The other leaders had a part in it as well. Their guidance and personal presence was very much a part of the growth of the churches which Paul and his associates established. As he himself wrote earlier to the church at Corinth, the spread of the gospel was not by any means a one-man effort. One man sows, he said, another man waters but God gives the increase (2 Cor. 3:1-9).

These five books together with the two Epistles of Peter, the general Epistle of James, and possibly Hebrews bear witness to the involvement of the other church leaders in the development of the community of Christian faith.

By the time these books were written, it had become clear that Christians had to face up to the challenge of their times. The early expectation of the Jerusalem disciples that Jesus would return immediately had to be revised. Many of them who had sold all they had and pooled it to live on had grown old and died. The continuing community was increasingly made up of people who knew nothing of Palestine and Galilee. Their only knowledge of the events was what had been told them. There were very few left who could say that they had seen Jesus in His earthly presence.

New enemies had appeared in the meantime. The church now found it necessary to defend its faith both against foes without and within. Christians were identified by Rome as followers of a foreign faith. She would not tolerate any competition to either her rule or emperor worship. The list of martyrs was rapidly increasing. To accept Christ had come to mean one was committed to imprisonment and even death itself.

But also within the body of believers many were being confused and misguided by concepts which dissipated their purity and strength. Theological divergence from the original teaching gave rise to many heretical doctrines. The bottom line of such teaching was the embracing of a way of life that contradicted the gospel and was in fact anti-Christ. Thus John could say, "Even now are there many antichrists . . . they went out from us, but they were not of us; for if they had been of us, they would no doubt have continued with us: but they went out, that it might be made manifest that they were not all of us" (1 John 2:18-19).

Both of these foes, external and internal, are the subject of these final books of the scripture. The heresy is exposed, and the faithful are exhorted to endure any hardship to be true to the faith once delivered unto the saints. Though they are brief, they are intense. The violence of the struggle can be sensed in the stringency of the language as the battle lines are drawn. They are not desperation harangues, however. Over and underneath it all is the Christian hope still strong and undiminished by the seeming delay of the Lord's return. To be sure, much of the symbolism that had originally seemed literal had now become spiritualized. But this had meant no loss in commitment or determination to overcome. The promise was that they who followed the Lamb should triumph. They were increasingly willing to let God keep His timetable and to concentrate on the gospel being preached to every creature.

Since this series of volumes is designed to be expositions rather than commentaries, the critical questions of authorship, date, etc., have not been addressed. Tradition had held that the John of the Epistles and the Revelation was the "beloved disciple" of the Gospels. He and James are called the sons of Zebedee. They were fishermen in Galilee before they met Jesus. This designation has not been challenged here.

The material in the five books has been considered in the light of its preaching potential. There are many ways of interpreting them, especially the Revelation. Many books have been written and will be written with a view to explaining the symbols in the light of current events. So no particular point of view suffers from this volume which seeks to explore only how these books can be used in preaching today.

In general this volume has sought to address the questions of what the writer was saying to his times and what his words say to ours. These two questions do not necessarily call for differing emphases. It is often surprising how much of the spiritual problems of mankind have remained the same for all the change of the times. Well did James Russell Lowell write, "For mankind are one in spirit, and an instinct bears along round the earth's electric circle, the swift flash of right or wrong" (The Present Crisis).

A reader with an interest in prophetic study will be either disappointed or pleased with the expositions of Revelation. He will be disappointed if he expects any discussion at all of the prophetic significance of the visions that John relates. He will be pleased, perhaps, that no attempt is made to support or challenge any of the prolific interpretations extant. The symbolic and poetic beauty of the book offers much for preaching by those who do not wish to become entangled in theories about the future. Too many ministers have avoided the book altogether because of the problems of literal interpretation. Hopefully this volume will lure them into the rich potential of John's visions.

J. B. Phillips in his introduction to his translation of the book quotes Martin Luther to say that this book is "neither apostolic nor prophetic," that "everyone thinks of the book whatever his spirit suggests." Phillips goes on to express a view that this writer shares and was guided by in the exposition:

The poetic impact of the book carries us away to a realm where the pedestrian rules of grammar no longer apply—we are dealing with celestial poetry and not with earthly prose. To be literally minded and studiously analytical in such a work is to kill its poetic truth. Dissection is not infrequently the death of beauty. J. B. Phillips. *The Book of the Revelation* (The Macmillan Co., 1957), p. xiii.

The First Epistle of
JOHN

Topical Outline of 1 John

Prologue: To Be in Christ Is to Be Free from Sin (1:1-4)

Christian Fellowship Requires Walking in the Light
(1:5—2:27)
Walking in the Light Means Cleansing from Sin (1:5-10)
Walking in the Light Means Christlikeness (2:1-8)
Walking in the Light Means Loving One's Brother (2:9-14)
Walking in the Light Is Walking Away from the World
(2:15-17)
Walking in the Light Has a Deadline (2:18-27)

The Marks of Birth into the Fellowship (2:28—4:6)
The Children of God and the Second Coming of Christ
(2:28—3:3)
To Be Born Again Is to Not Sin (3:4-10)
To Be Born Again Is to Love the Brethren (3:11-18)
To Be Born Again Is to Have Confidence Before God
(3:19-24)
To Be Born Again Is to Try the Spirits (4:1-6)

Christian Assurance and Fellowship (4:7—5:12)
Assurance and Fellowship in God's Love (4:7-12)
The Presence of the Holy Spirit (4:13-16)
Christian Boldness: The Fruit of Assurance and
Characteristic of Fellowship (4:17-21)
Christian Assurance in the Family of God (5:1-5)
The Witness of the Spirit (5:6-10)
The Assurance of Life in the Son (5:11-12)

Epilogue: Benefits of Christian Fellowship (5:13-21)
The Purpose of the Letter Reaffirmed (5:13)
Prayer Is a Benefit of Christian Fellowship (5:14-16)
The World Is in Sin (5:17-19)
Understanding Is a Benefit of the Christian Fellowship
(5:20)
A Parting Word of Advice (5:21)

To Be in Christ Is to Be Free from Sin
Prologue
1 John 1:1-4

1 JOHN 1

The Fellowship of Eternal Life in Christ

1 John 1:1-4

> 1 That which was from the beginning, which we have heard, which we have seen with our eyes, which we have looked upon, and our hands have handled, of the Word of life;
> 2 (For the life was manifested, and we have seen it, and bear witness, and shew unto you that eternal life, which was with the Father, and was manifested unto us;)
> 3 That which we have seen and heard declare we unto you, that ye also may have fellowship with us: and truly our fellowship is with the Father, and with his Son Jesus Christ.
> 4 And these things write we unto you, that your joy may be full.

The disciple "whom Jesus loved" (cf. John 21:7, 20) wrote in his latter years to the churches in Asia Minor. It was a time of ideological controversy. The Gnostics, with elaborate concepts of supernatural beings and denial of the deity of Jesus, had torn the churches apart.[1] Christians needed to be reassured of the basic truths of the Christian faith and life.

John had been an eyewitness of the Word of Life. He had touched Him and experienced His presence. He had heard Him speak of the truths of God. He could challenge the contentions of those who spoke of Him as only "seeming" to be divine. He had walked and talked with Him.

He had seen the miracles. He watched Him die on a cross. He had seen the empty tomb and the graveclothes lying in such a way as to convince him that Jesus had risen from the dead. He was with the other disciples when the risen Lord had suddenly appeared and spoken peace to them. He had shared the joy of that moment as they saw the scars in His hands and side. His answer, then, to those who built their fanciful theory and twisted explanation was that he had seen and known the Word of Life. He spoke from personal experience.

1. The central conviction of those who were with Jesus was that God was in Him. They found in Him life that was of God and which was made evident to them. It was not a secret reserved for a special few. Whether everyone accepted it or not, the life of God was displayed in Christ and was known as eternal life. What John means by that term, *eternal life,* has more to do with endlessness than with timelessness. Those who believed on Christ received life that never ends. It was in the beginning in God. He sent that life to the world in Jesus. The Cross and the Resurrection made that endless life available to every man who would receive it. The distinction between *endless* and *timeless* is important because the Christian heritage is not a quality that is received after this life but here and now. It exists after death because it is endless, and nothing can separate the Christian from this life.[2]

Eternal life is the point of fellowship between the Father and the Son. The Christian who receives it is brought into this fellowship. This also means that this life brings all who have received it into a community of faith and fellowship. It is the life of God manifested in Jesus Christ and experienced by all who believe on Him. The *we* of John in this letter is probably in part editorial in the sense in which he is testifying that he personally has experienced the eternal life of God through Christ. It also refers to the company of the disciples who shared for nearly three years with Jesus and experienced the life of God in

Him as they walked and talked with Him. But in its fullest sense the *we* includes the whole of the Christian community from the disciples to the reader of the letter. We all have this basis of fellowship, that we have experienced eternal life through Christ. The fellowship of this life in Christ is not of our own making. It is the work of the Holy Spirit. This "fellowship of kindred minds" is not only "like to that above" but in fact is the very life of eternity known and experienced and lived in this world.

2. The story of man that is called history is a story of man seeking for life. He has constantly striven for the fuller and richer life. To his disappointment, when he thought he had found the secret of it, he often experienced only failure. In Christ alone there is the answer to man's deepest longing. He came that man might have life and have it more abundantly (John 10:10). The fellowship of those who have entered into this life is the true community of man. Lloyd Ogilvie, in a recent book titled *When God First Thought of You,* sees the fellowship of eternal life in Christ as God's original intention for man. It is, he says, what God had in mind when He created the world, and is also what God has in mind for each person.[3]

3. As it was for the disciples the first Easter evening, the fellowship of eternal life in Christ is the source of joy. John says he wrote the letter so that the joy of the readers might be full. It is the joy of entering into the full life, the joy of realizing that for which we were made. In a reverent sense it is the joy of doing and being one's own thing. To those who question the reality of life in Christ, the Christian responds that the joy of having found His life is real and satisfying.

There are many ways of expressing joy, such as singing, shouting, smiling, or wholehearted participation in whatever one is doing. The mode of this expression is not as important as the joy it is expressing. Paul and Silas sang songs at midnight (Acts 16:25). The disciples after Pentecost continued "daily with one accord in the temple, and breaking bread from house to house, [eating] their meat with gladness and singleness of heart" (Acts 2:46). The Macedonian brethren in a great trial of affliction though poor gave liberally with great joy for the church at Jerusalem, after first giving themselves to the Lord (2 Cor. 8:2, 5). The Galilean followers of Jesus shouted, "Hosanna," as they accompanied Him into the city. We are told in Luke 1:44 that the unborn baby John the Baptist leaped for joy in his mother's womb when she greeted Mary, the mother-to-be of Jesus. The writer of Hebrews states that Jesus endured the Cross for the joy that was set before Him (Heb. 12:2). Jesus, in His farewell address to the disciples, tells that obedience to His commandments will result in His joy remaining in them (John 15:11).

The Christian life is one of joy. It is a joy that comes when one is born again, and it lasts through every experience. Sometimes it is effervescent and bursts into song or praise. Sometimes it is still and deep. But always it grows with the passing days. It is climaxed when the Lord returns and says to the faithful on His right hand, "Enter thou into the joy of thy lord" (Matt. 25:21).

Christian Fellowship Requires Walking in the Light

1 John 1:5—2:27

Walking in the Light Means Cleansing from Sin

1 John 1:5-10

> 5 This then is the message which we have heard of him, and declare unto you, that God is light, and in him is no darkness at all.
> 6 If we say that we have fellowship with him, and walk in darkness, we lie, and do not the truth:
> 7 But if we walk in the light, as he is in the light, we have fellowship one with another, and the blood of Jesus Christ his Son cleanseth us from all sin.

8 If we say that we have no sin, we deceive ourselves, and the truth is not in us.
9 If we confess our sins, he is faithful and just to forgive us our sins, and to cleanse us from all unrighteousness.
10 If we say that we have not sinned, we make him a liar, and his word is not in us.

1. The Christian message begins with the premise that God is light. There is no darkness in Him. In the vision of the Holy City which John saw, there was no sun, for the Lord God was the light of it (Rev. 21:23). Light symbolizes illumination and revelation. It also means healing, security, and joy. By early Christian times light had become a symbol of ethical purity. The Essenes divided men into the children of light and the children of darkness. The Dead Sea Scrolls have much to say about the conflict between those groups. The Teacher of Righteousness is the leader of the children of light.

God brings truth and meaning to the world He has created. The people who respond in holy living are described as walking in the light. They are children of light. To say that one has fellowship with God but does not obey His commandments or do His will is to lie, says John. But to walk in the light is to confess one's sin under the moral judgment of God. It is to ask for and receive His forgiveness. It is to submit to His cleansing. To walk in darkness is to deceive oneself and in pride to deny one has sin. It is to make the truth of God a lie.

Like the sun, God sheds the light of His truth everywhere. All who will accept it see themselves and their need. Fellowship with Him means forgiveness and cleansing by the blood of Jesus from all sin. It also means fellowship with all who likewise walk in the light. Cleansing follows confession. Jesus at one time, when talking about the entrance of light through the eye, remarked, "If . . . the light that is in thee be darkness, how great is that darkness!" (Matt. 6:23).

2. The children of light walk in it and are cleansed; the children of darkness hide from it. They deceive them-

selves, denying truth, and their darkness intensifies. There is no middle ground. There is no way to avoid the demands of the light. It will not retreat or dim; it reveals things as they are. There is no use to argue with or rationalize its judgment. One either accepts its evaluation or sets out upon a course of self-deception which ends in moral confusion and distortion until blindness shuts one in a dark closet of denial. Truth becomes untruth and God a liar. How great is that darkness!

3. Walking in the light is synonymous with Christian victory. If God is light, then walking in the light is walking with God. It is keeping step with all who are likewise walking with Him. It is facing every flaw and need in the joyous knowledge that, as one confesses, the blood of Jesus cleanses. It also implies an upward progress. Fellowship with God means the realization of potential. The truth of God is not just to make us admit what we are but it is, as we are willing to receive it, the revelation of what He intends us to be. It is in Ogilvie's word becoming the person we were when God first thought of us.[4]

Walking in the light is the assumption that God wants His best for us. He does not face us with our sin to put us down but to bring us up. The Light invites us. It is, as the song puts it, "the beautiful light of God." The cleansing means "feeling at home in His presence." It is also feeling at home with all who walk with us in His light.

To the first readers of this letter the affirmation of forgiveness and cleansing of sin as tests of walking in the light was especially relevant. There were people who claimed to walk in the light but lived sinful lives. John says they are fooling only themselves. For if one walks in the light, his life shows it in the moral and ethical behavior which results. It is relevant today as well. While the popular thing seems to be boasting of one's sinfulness and calling it liberation, there are many who talk about being born again, yet their lives show no steps toward purity. They fail the test John asserts.

Walking in the Light Means Christlikeness

1 John 2:1-8

1 My little children, these things write I unto you, that ye sin not. And if any man sin, we have an advocate with the Father, Jesus Christ the righteous:

2 And he is the propitiation for our sins: and not for ours only, but also for the sins of the whole world.

3 And hereby we do know that we know him, if we keep his commandments.

4 He that saith, I know him, and keepeth not his commandments, is a liar, and the truth is not in him.

5 But whoso keepeth his word, in him verily is the love of God perfected: hereby know we that we are in him.

6 He that saith he abideth in him ought himself also so to walk, even as he walked.

7 Brethren, I write no new commandment unto you, but an old commandment which ye had from the beginning. The old commandment is the word which ye have heard from the beginning.

8 Again, a new commandment I write unto you, which thing is true in him and in you: because the darkness is past, and the true light now shineth.

1. The term *sinning Christians* is an anomaly. The purpose of following Christ is not to sin. The definition of a Christian as a follower of Christ is to have left a life of sin and by His grace to have begun a new life. It is Christ's will that His followers do not sin. He told the woman convicted of adultery, "Go, and sin no more" (John 8:11). To the man healed after 38 years of affliction, He said, "Behold, thou art made whole: sin no more, lest a worse thing come unto thee" (5:14).

But if any man sin, there is a sure remedy in Christ. Jesus is the Christian's Advocate before God. He is not there to excuse sin. Rather, when one tries but fails to do the right thing, he has a helper. The Advocate is in touch with the Judge of All. He will plead for all who fall short. The writer of Hebrews reminds us that He has lived in the world and in the days of His flesh learned the strength of man's trials. He was tempted in all points as men are tempted, yet did not sin (Heb. 5:7-10; 4:15). He knows and understands. One does not need even to explain to Him how or why. All the extenuating circumstances He knows. No one could better present whatever case he has than Christ.

2. Not only does He understand, but also He is the One who has paid the penalty for sin. He took the sins of the whole world, for all time, in His body on the Cross. There is no sin that ever was or ever will be committed that was not included in the load He bore. He loved the world and gave himself for it. His death is an eternal testimony to His love and the efficacy of His expiation of sin.

His life, too, was a part of that expiation. He set the example that we should follow His steps (1 Pet. 2:21-25). While His life stands in judgment on us, for so often we do not do what He did in a similar circumstance, yet He forgives and calls to us, "Follow Me." To the disciples who grew discouraged when they could not do what they knew He wanted them to, He promised the Spirit to help them. He told them that the works which He did they would do, and greater works, because He was going to the Father and would send the Paraclete to them (John 14:12, 16).

This full and ongoing solution to the problem of sin is for all the world. No one is left out. What Christ did for any He does for all. And history has borne this out. Wherever people have heard the Good News and believed on Him, they have found Christ a full and adequate answer to sin. If culture has given them varying concepts of what constitutes sins, the forgiveness and cleansing has not been different. No one has come to the Savior in vain.

3. As some claim to walk in the light but really walk in darkness, there are some who claim to know the Savior but do not live according to His commandments. The reality of Christ's answer for sin is found in one's obedience to His will and way. These commandments are not the laws that men have enacted. They are God's Word revealed in the moral law. There are many rules and regulations that men have made in order to demonstrate how the obedience

to the laws of God operate. They have a certain force, to be sure. But it is a force that must depend upon the inner knowledge of God's will. Jesus gave us the tersest and yet fullest summary when He said that we should love God with all the heart, soul, mind, and strength, and our neighbors as ourselves. He declared that on these two commandments hang all the law and the prophets (cf. Matt. 22:37-40).

No matter what one claims, unless obedience to the moral law is seen, his claim is false. It is as simple and awesome as that—he lies. The truth is not in him when his life does not measure up to his claim. However one may rationalize his concept of salvation, he is wrong if he talks about fellowship with God and lives in sin.

4. To know the Savior in His forgiveness and cleansing is to walk with Him. The love of God ripens in his life. The best test of His presence is the perfecting of this love as the days go by. The perfection of God's love is the inevitable outcome of trusting Christ for salvation. This is why He died for us. It is His purpose that the love of God should be perfected in us. Paul wrote to the saints at Thessalonica, "This is the will of God, even your sanctification" (1 Thess. 4:3). He later in the same letter explained that the God who had called us to holiness was faithful and would accomplish it. When it happens or as it is happening, the Christian is assured that he is in Christ. For this is what should occur, that the love of Christ be brought to its fullest measure in the believer.

The perfecting of love is an inner condition that is expressed in a Christlike walk: The bottom line of sanctification is to walk as Jesus walked. It is no more or no less than that. From the very beginning of one's birth into the Kingdom this is the sum total of life's demand. One follows by his very nature the One who loved him and gave him birth. Even when one is the farthest from Him, there is the desire to be like Him. That one may have felt and said that it could never be. Yet the longing would not go away.

When one is forgiven and his heart cleansed, the new life in him reaches out to walk as He walked. The demand is not new; it is as old as life itself.

With every new day and situation the demand to walk as Christ walked is renewed. In this sense it is an ever new demand. One can never reach a point at which he boasts, "I have arrived!" Every achievement reveals new possibilities. Christ is forever going further. He is with us and in front of us, forever beckoning us on. In this sense His commandment is ever new. The old commandment which was ours from the beginning becomes the new commandment. The light shines "far down the future's broadening way." The wise man put it, "The path of the just is as the shining light, that shineth more and more unto the perfect day" (Prov. 4:18). Walking in the light is walking as Christ walked. The light is shining, revealing things both true and new. The path it illumines leads ever forward in Christlikeness.

Progress in Christlikeness is an infallible test of walking in the light. If one looks ahead, he may feel he has a long way to go. But if he looks behind to where he started, he sees how far Christ has already brought him. He will say as another did, "In this business of being a Christian, I find I have a long way to go, but I find the going good."

Walking in the Light Means Loving One's Brother

1 John 2:9-14

> 9 He that saith he is in the light, and hateth his brother, is in darkness even until now.
> 10 He that loveth his brother abideth in the light, and there is none occasion of stumbling in him.
> 11 But he that hateth his brother is in darkness. and walketh in darkness, and knoweth not wither he goeth, because that darkness hath blinded his eyes.
> 12 I write unto you, little children, because your sins are forgiven you for his name's sake.
> 13 I write unto you, fathers, because ye have known him that is from the beginning. I write unto you, young men, because ye have overcome the wicked one. I write unto you, little children, because ye have known the father.
> 14 I have written unto you, fathers, because ye have known him that is from the beginning. I have written unto you, young men, because

ye are strong, and the word of God abideth in you, and ye have overcome the wicked one.

1. A third characteristic of walking in the light and having
fellowship with the Father is to have love for one's brother.
This is to be contrasted with the person who says he loves
God but hates his brother. Such a person is in darkness.
It is not only the darkness of self-deception but also the
darkness of consuming and destructive hate. His eyes are
blinded. He stumbles on, and the hate which he directs to
his brother eats him up. It is like one who holds a nuclear
weapon to destroy his brother only to find that the radia-
tion is destroying him.

On the other hand so certainly is love for one's brother
a fruit of walking in the light that he can know he is doing
so by the love he feels for his brother. Beyond knowing
that he is in the light, the landscape and perspective become clear to him. While the blind, hating one stumbles,
he walks surefooted and confident. He strengthens the
family of God about him with his outgoing love. Others
are at ease around him. They are warmed by his love and
set free to realize their potential in Christ.

2. The family of God is made up of all ages. There are newborn babes, there are growing young people, and there are
mature fathers. All are experiencing in one form or another
the love of God being perfected in them. They all have
something to give in love to others and something they
need to get. This is the binding love of the family. Everyone in it needs both to be nourished and to nourish.

The love of Christians for each other is both a giving
and receiving love. The youngest are the nearest to the
bounding joy of sins forgiven. The mature are the most
confident in the love that lasts. The growing are in the
midst of the conflict with darkness and sing the songs of
victory. The mature reassure the babes the joy will last.
They encourage the growing by sharing the story of their
struggle and victory in Christ. Babes in their excitement
keep the growing and the mature from losing the freshness

of first love. They help them to remember. Many a mature Christian who has shared the moment that new life in Christ has come to another have felt just like having it happen over again for them. All who share the testimony of their victory encourage others who are in the midst of conflict.

People do not mature in all directions equally. Our lives are more pear-shaped than circular. Christians grow in grace in this same fashion. All make great progress in a few things and are painfully slow in others. Everyone needs to minister out of his maturity and be ministered to in his immaturity. Love for one's brother is the key to this inter-action which gives the community of the people of God meaning and strength. The Spirit enables the Christian to understand his needs and accept the nurture of others. It also pushes him to draw on his strengths to nurture others who need him. Love for one's brother is the mood in which Christians can appreciate how much they need each other.

3. There is a sense in which each of us has the character-istics of all three groups John addresses. We can live in the freshness of a new beginning every day. Grace should never be taken for granted. We are never through growing. The longer we walk with Christ, the more we realize how far we have yet to go. Yet from the very first moment of our life in Christ we can have the sense of a full relationship, mature and solid. Each characteristic gives us added occasion for reaching out and sharing the life and love of fellow Christians.

Christians walk in the light together. They help and sustain each other. The slow teach patience and discipline to those who race madly in all directions. The fast set goals and teach the challenge of the long look. The strong sup-port the weak. The weak show the warmth and satisfaction of true gratitude. The love they have received from Christ finds expression in concern for every other fellow traveller. Like Judah's plea to Joseph they seem to say, "For how shall I go up to my father, and the lad be not with me?" (Gen. 44:34a). It is this love that makes all men know they are Christ's disciples and are truly walking in the light.

Walking in the Light Is Walking Away from the World

1 John 2:15-17

> 15 Love not the world, neither the things that are in the world. If any love the world, the love of the Father is not in him.
> 16 For all that is in the world, the lust of the flesh, and the lust of the eyes, and the pride of life, is not of the Father, but is of the world.
> 17 And the world passeth away, and the lust thereof: but he that doeth the will of God abideth for ever.

1. Walking in the light is walking toward God. He is the Source of the light that is shining. It is a beckoning light, and those who walk in it walk toward Him and away from the world. The *world* as John uses it is not the created order only but the world that has fallen through the disobedience of man.[5] It includes God's creation, but it is that creation separated from Him and seeking its own purposes. The world is good when it fulfills the purpose for which it was created. When it becomes something other than that, it is a rival of God. Too frequently men worship the creation rather than the Creator. To that extent the good becomes evil. God loves the world, for it is His work and His footstool. But man must not love the world in the sense of preferring it to God. The Creator is greater than His creation, and it is He that man must worship and love.

The world is in the control of the evil one. To love it is to turn one's back on God. Jesus said, "Ye cannot serve God and mammon" (Matt. 6:24). John puts it plainly, *If any man love the world, the love of the Father is not in him.*

2. To walk in the light is to bid the world good-bye. Its attitudes are abandoned. The things that are in it are forsaken. The people and things which make up the world are only seen in their true worth when one gives God first place in his affection. We were made for God, and there is

no peace until we turn toward Him and walk in the light. When we do,

> *The things of earth will grow strangely dim*
> *In the light of His glory and grace.*

The people and things of the world have value for us only as they enrich our view of God and His will for us.

The world as evil is left behind. It is a world of evil desire. It uses the best for the worst ends. The devil has it in his control when the lowest passions provide the impulse for thought and action. John places all that is evil in the world in three categories: *the lust of the flesh, and the lust of the eyes, and the pride of life.* These are enemies of love for God.

a. The lust of the flesh does not mean the natural physical appetites. The evil is in the lust. Jesus came in the flesh and did not sin. Flesh of itself is not inherently evil. It is the distortion of natural appetites to sinful satisfaction that is lust. Sinful man is deceived. He finds certain desires with which he is born. These desires demand satisfaction. He hungers for such satisfaction. The devil, the great deceiver, convinces him that satisfaction comes in sin. Man discovers, often too late, that there is no real satisfaction, only gratification, when he gives way to evil passions and lust. The momentary achievement of his pleasure leaves him with a deeper hunger.

There is a right way for every natural desire to find fulfilment. It is not to be found in secular humanism, which makes gain and pleasure the prime goal of living. If this generation has learned anything, it is that to be better off is not to be better. Like the inflation that destroys the economy, the rush for sensual satisfaction has resulted in an explosion of sex, alcoholism, and obesity. People eat too much and have to run it off. They drink too much and have to go to special institutions to "dry out." They abandon discipline and wind up with broken homes and empty lives. They wear themselves out to get money only to have it devalued. This is the lust of the flesh. One turns his back on it when he walks in the light.

b. *The lust of the eyes* involves the imagination. It is seeing things not as they are but as we want them to be. It begins in the glittering and showy and descends to the pornographic. Jesus taught that immorality began with the look of lust (Matt. 5:27). Under the guise of "art for art's sake" the things of beauty become the idols of passion. God condemned Israel in these words, "Then said I unto them, Cast ye away every man the abominations of his eyes, and defile not yourselves with the idols of Egypt: I am the Lord your God. But they rebelled against me, and would not hearken unto me: they did not every man cast away the abominations of their eyes, neither did they forsake the idols of Egypt: then I said, I will pour out my fury upon them, to accomplish my anger against them in the midst of the land of Egypt" (Ezek. 20:7-8). Lot's wife was commanded not to look back as they left the sinful city of Sodom. The Christian, too, must keep his eyes on God if he will walk in the light.

c. *The pride of life* is the egotistical notion that one is better and deserves better things. It is more than an idea of "keeping up with the Joneses"; it is keeping ahead of them. It is taking all one can get and claiming it is earned. For many people Thanksgiving Day has become an occasion of thanking themselves instead of the God who made them and has given them all things. This is the pride of life which boasts, "My power and the might of my hand hath gotten me this wealth" (Deut. 8:17, ASV). Pride is an exacting master. It drives one to ever more gaudy display. It thrusts one in the center of attention no matter how boring it is for others. Pride incites strife and war. It destroys relationships and refuses to admit responsibility for failure. It isolates one from the affection so desperately needed. James asks, "From whence come wars and fightings among you? come they not hence, even of your lusts that war in your members? Ye lust, and have not: ye kill, and desire to have, and cannot obtain: ye fight and war, yet ye have not, because ye ask not" (Jas. 4:1-2).

All that the lust of the flesh and eyes and the pride of life seek for, even if obtained, soon pass away.

> *The Worldly Hope men set their Hearts upon*
> *Turns ashes—or it prospers; and anon,*
> *Like Snow upon the Desert's dusty face*
> *Lighting a little Hour or two—is gone.*
> —*Omar Khayyám,* 1st ed., stanza 14[6]

What seems so important is gone so soon. But he that does the will of God abides forever. Walking in the light is leaving the passing for the eternal.

Walking in the Light Has a Deadline

1 John 2:18-27

> 18 Little children, it is the last time: and as ye have heard that antichrist shall come, even now are there many antichrists; whereby we know that it is the last time.
> 19 They went out from us, but they were not of us: for if they had been of us, they would no doubt have continued with us: but they went out, that they might be made manifest that they were not all of us.
> 20 But ye have an unction from the Holy One and ye know all things.
> 21 I have not written unto you because ye know not the truth, but because ye know it, and that no lie is of the truth.
> 22 Who is a liar but he that denieth that Jesus is the Christ? He is antichrist, that denieth the Father and the Son.
> 23 Whosoever denieth the Son, the same hath not the Father: [but] he that acknowledgeth the Son hath the Father also.
> 24 Let that therefore abide in you, which ye have heard from the beginning. If that which ye have heard from the beginning shall remain in you, ye also shall continue in the Son, and in the Father.
> 25 And this is the promise that he hath promised us, even eternal life.
> 26 These things have I written unto you concerning them that seduce you.
> 27 But the anointing which ye have received of him abideth in you, and ye need not that any man teach you: but as the same anointing teacheth you of all things, and is truth, and is no lie, and even as it hath taught you, ye shall abide in him.

There is an urgency in walking in the light. The end time is upon the Christian. It is beside the point to argue that every generation of Christians has felt they were living in the last days. That sense of urgency was given the disciples by the Lord himself. The essential elements of the end time are always with us. We know we have today; we do not know about tomorrow. The Judge is always at the door. The words Jesus put in the mouth of a rich man, "I will say to my soul, Soul, thou hast much goods laid up for many years," were answered by God, "Thou fool, this night thy soul shall be required of thee: then whose shall those things be, which thou hast provided?" (Luke 12:19-20).

1. The Antichrist will come in the end time. But John says that even in his time there were *many antichrists* among the Christians. Evil forces move to climactic showdowns in every generation. While the Christian walks in the light, there come also those who deny Christ and the gospel. They represent untruth, and they demand showdowns. The Christian knows that the conflicts against these antichrists must be resolved. Toynbee defines an antichrist as one who opposes Christ in the guise of Christ. He cannot be tolerated or ignored. Whenever he appears, it is a crisis time until the issue be resolved in the power of the eternal God.

It is the antichrists that John says went out from the fellowship. They were not and could not be a part of it. They turn away from walking in the light. What they are becomes known, and the break must be clear.

2. The Christian has a weapon against them. The Spirit of God is the Teacher and Defender of truth. He brings the things of Christ to the Christian's remembrance. He provides insight that reassures and guides the Christian along the way of truth. There need be no fear of showdowns about truth. The unction of the Holy One guards the Christian in his conflict with untruth and antichrists.

The point at issue is Christ. To deny Him is to deny the Father. Christ is reality. All that He has said is true; time and eternity bear it out. Whether the testing period is short or long, the secret of being ready when the climax comes is to live every day and moment in fellowship with Christ.[7] The continuing relationship with God is the vital thing. It is abiding in the Son and the Father that is eternal life. John writes that if we stay on course, that is, let what we *have heard from the beginning . . . abide* in us, we have an antidote to the evil about us and the assurance of victory.

3. It seems difficult for us to understand how anyone could call himself a Christian and deny that Jesus is the Christ. But there are many who do. Even in John's day they had to distinguish between the "Christ of faith" and the Jesus of history. They taught that Christ had come, not as a person but a mythical symbol of a spiritual reality. They saw Jesus only as an example of that philosophical abstraction. For those who had walked and talked with Him, this was not only ridiculous but blasphemous. What they learned of Him by physical presence, the Holy Spirit made clear by His revelation. For all the others this same Holy Spirit has brought the reality of Christ's presence to them by bringing them into spiritual fellowship with Jesus. Through the ministry of the Holy Spirit, Jesus is real to all who will believe on Him. They can sing:

> *You ask me how I know He lives?*
> *He lives within my heart.*

This personal experience of Jesus John calls the "anointing from the Holy One" (v. 20, ASV). It is an abiding experience. One does not have to live in the memory of the initial experience as though Christ came once to touch him and then is gone. As He promised, Christ comes to stay. Through the days and nights in every situation and event of the believer's life He is always there. This is better than argument or polemics. While those who deny His deity—and there are many who call themselves Christians today who do—make their assertions and spin their theological fantasies, doing the work of antichrist, the Christian carries on in this fellowship and walks in the light. Deadlines only keep him up-to-date in his relationship with Christ.

The Marks of Birth into the Fellowship
1 John 2:28—4:6

The Children of God and the Second Coming of Christ
1 John 2:28—3:3

> 28 And now, little children, abide in him; that, when he shall appear, we may have confidence, and not be ashamed before him at his coming.
>
> 29 If ye know that he is righteous, ye know that every one that doeth righteousness is born of him.
>
> 1 Behold, what manner of love the Father hath bestowed upon us, that we should be called the sons of God: therefore the world knoweth us not, because it knew him not.
>
> 2 Beloved, now are we the sons of God, and it doth not yet appear what we shall be: but we know that, when he shall appear, we shall be like him; for we shall see him as he is.
>
> 3 And every man that hath this hope in him purifieth himself, even as he is pure.

When one is born again, he becomes a child of God. He is a new person. "Old things are passed away; [and] all things are become new" (2 Cor. 5:17). This relationship is a growing and personal one. As a child of God he possesses the nature of God. He enters into a new kind of humanity. The world does not know this kind of humanity. The reality of it is taught by the Holy Spirit. His witness to the newborn Christian is clear and unmistakable. He knows that he has been born again and is in the family of God.

This inner witness gives the Christian confidence as he awaits the second coming of Christ. He will not be ashamed when his Lord appears. Since Christ is righteous, all who are born again in Him must live righteously. This is a mark of the new life in Christ—right living. It is an almost inconceivable thing that sinful man can be so changed that he can be called a child of God. It is only because of the great love of God that it happens.

1 JOHN 3

1. The Christian can never quite get over it. To be called a child of God is either a horrible mistake and reflection on God, or it is a miracle of His love and grace. The warm witness of the Holy Spirit teaches him that it is the latter. The world of wicked men cannot understand his joy and are amused or angered by his claim. Since they have not been born again, they do not know the reality of the new humanity which was instituted at the Cross. The world did not know Christ; He was crucified as a criminal. They wagged their heads in derision and cried, "He saved others; himself he cannot save" (Matt. 27:42).

While the Christian has overwhelming joy in this new relationship in the family of God, he also has the pain of not being understood by those who are not in the family; often some are of his own flesh and blood. He is known of God but not known of the world. The pain is assuaged by the wonder that he is a child of God. The ties he has to the family of God are much greater than any other. The most meaningful fact of life for the born-again Christian is that now he is a child of God.

2. This would be sufficient in itself, but there is more. We do not know what all we shall be. There is an exciting uncertainty about being a child of God. It is that we are becoming. What we are as we experience Christ's presence and our relationship to Him is wonderful. But it is not all; He is not through with us yet. We are being changed from glory to glory (2 Cor. 3:18). We know what the final outcome will be: we shall be like Christ. We know when that will be: when He appears in His second coming.

Christ is the goal of human history. His first coming

was in Galilee long ago. His second coming may be at any moment. The time in between has been called "the blessed interlude."[8] It is the time of the Christian fellowship—the Church. It is a time of birth and growth into the likeness of Christ. Wherever men will receive Him through the Holy Spirit, they are given the power to become the children of God. Whenever Christians surrender to the control and obedience of the Holy Spirit, they are being made into the image of Christ. While the timetable is not revealed, the outcome has been promised and will not fail.

3. The obligation the Christian has in all this is to purify himself. This he cannot do of himself. It is accomplished by the cleansing of the blood of Christ which occurs when he walks in the light. His nature is purified by the fiery baptism of the Holy Spirit which occurs when he consecrates his all to Christ. These works of grace, the latter subsequent to the former, are the provision of purification God has willed for all His children (1 Thess. 4:2-8). It does not lead to spiritual pride as some have claimed, for it is the supernatural work of God. It is wrought by faith in Jesus who loved men and gave himself for them. Man's only part is his choice to appropriate the blessings offered him.

To Be Born Again Is to Not Sin

1 John 3:4-10

> 4 Whosoever committeth sin transgresseth also the law: for sin is the transgression of the law.
> 5 And ye know that he was manifested to take away our sins; and in him is no sin.
> 6 Whosoever abideth in him sinneth not: whosoever sinneth hath not seen him, neither known him.
> 7 Little children, let no man deceive you: he that doeth righteousness is righteous, even as he is righteous.
> 8 He that committeth sin is of the devil; for the devil sinneth from the beginning. For this purpose the Son of God was manifested, that he might destroy the works of the devil.
> 9 Whosoever is born of God doth not commit sin; for his seed remaineth in him: and he cannot sin, because he is born of God.
> 10 In this the children of God are manifest, and the children of the devil: whosoever doeth not righteousness is not of God, neither he that loveth not his brother.

1. There are in the final analysis two kinds of people in the world. There are those who do right and those who do not. The people who live righteously are the children of God. The people who do evil are the children of the devil. The devil sinned from the beginning. He is the author of evil. He enticed the first parents to sin and thereby established a sinfulness to the whole human family. Christ did not sin. He came to establish a new race of people who would be like Him and do right. To enter this family of God, one must be born anew (John 3:5-7). The contrast between these two kinds of people is self-evident. Consequently one can lay down this universal rule: *He that doeth righteousness is righteous . . . He that committeth sin is of the devil.*

To understand this rule, one must know what sin is. It is, John says, the transgression of the law; it is lawlessness. This is a universe of moral law. In spite of the claim of situation ethics, there are moral absolutes. God is a God of order. He is good and holy. His order is one of moral law. Whoever commits sin is a lawbreaker. Sin is more than an isolated act; it is an expression of disposition or nature that will not accept the moral law. Man is not a sinner because he sins. He sins because he is a sinner. He has the disposition of lawlessness.

2. The Christian does not sin. He has been born into a new humanity. John says that he is a child of God and has God's seed in him, and so cannot sin (9). What he means, of course, is that he cannot sin and remain a child of God. There is no such thing as a "sinning saint." If he violates the law of God unwittingly or inadvertently, he has an Advocate who is the propitiation for sin. He cleanses from all sin. The fullness of the Holy Spirit in the Christian's life enables one to live a life of victory over sin. This was the purpose of Jesus Christ's coming into the world—to destroy the works of the devil and bring all men who will into sonship with God and right living.

There are two kinds of people in the world, and one

can tell them apart by how they live and what they do. It is a sad day when, if it is true, there is not enough difference between people who are in the church and those who are not. It means that the church has ceased to be the family of God. Whatever else may be said about the people who have been born again, it must be that they are different. That difference is that they live righteously. Anyone who lives a sinful or unrighteous life is not a child of God. He is rather a child of the devil, for one of the marks of being born again is that one does not sin.

3. There are sins of omission as well as commission. Sinning may be doing the wrong things or may be not doing the right things. To know to do right and not do it is sin. John Wesley distinguished between what he called "sin properly so called" and "improperly so called." He insisted that sin was a willful violation of a known law of God. If one willfully does what God has forbidden, he sins as did Adam and Eve in the garden. If he fails to do what God has instructed him to do, he sins as did King Saul in the conquest of Amalek. If one claims that any falling short of the perfect standard is sin, then, of course, the test John puts of a mark of being born again is invalid. Thus it is a dangerous thing so to define sin as to make untrue the inspired Word of God. Once one starts down that road of definition to fit one's argument or rationalize his lack of faith, there is no stopping short of unbelief; and, like the devil, one becomes the accuser of the brethren.

The test is a clear and God-given one. The devil is the father of all who sin. The children of God do right because Christ is righteous and abides in them. They do not do their own will but His. They are not troubled by legalism because they live by the law of their new nature in Christ. As He lived righteously in this world, so do they in His power and grace. This is why holiness of life is not an option for the Christian. It is the mark of his belonging to Christ. As He who has called him from darkness to light is holy, so the born again follows after that holiness and finds it in the fullness of the Holy Spirit.

To Be Born Again Is to Love the Brethren

1 John 3:11-18

> 11 For this is the message that ye heard from the beginning, that we should love one another.
> 12 Not as Cain, who was of that wicked one, and slew his brother. And wherefore slew he him? Because his own works were evil, and his brother's righteous.
> 13 Marvel not, my brethren, if the world hate you.
> 14 We know that we have passed from death unto life, because we love the brethren. He that loveth not his brother abideth in death.
> 15 Whosoever hateth his brother is a murderer: and ye know that no murderer hath eternal life abiding in him.
> 16 Hereby perceive we the love of God, because he laid down his life for us: and we ought to lay down our lives for the brethren.
> 17 But whoso hath this world's good, and seeth his brother have need, and shutteth up his bowels of compassion from him, how dwelleth the love of God in him?
> 18 My little children, let us not love in word, neither in tongue; but in deed and in truth.

1. The two kinds of people in the world may also be distinguished by those who love one another and those who do not. As righteousness and sin provide a testing contrast, so do love and hate. Those who love are like Christ who gave himself for others. Those who do not are like Cain, who hated his brother and killed him. Love gives and enriches; hate destroys. Those people who are motivated by love have been born again. It is a test which has been valid from the beginning. To love one another is not a late commandment given after the example of Jesus on the Cross. It has been the moral law of God since the creation of the universe.

Cain was evil, and he hated his brother Abel who was righteous. At the very beginning of human history God told Cain that if he would live righteously, he would be accepted. John states that Cain hated his brother. His not being accepted of God gave the excuse to destroy Abel. It did not relieve Cain. He complained that his punishment was more than he could bear. The hatred which he had directed toward his brother did not let him go once the act was completed. It had fastened on him and drove him from the presence of his family. It would have made him a pariah everywhere he went were it not for the mercy of God which restrained anyone from adding to his despair. The destructiveness of his own hate was enough.

2. The story of Cain should explain to the born-again Christian why he is hated by men who have not accepted the love of God in their lives. As Cain hated Abel because sin had control of him, so evil people hate the Christian. They speak of "being born again" in derision and suggest it is some sort of weird religious bigotry. So the child of God should not be surprised or think himself mistreated because the world hates him. It is because the world is evil that it hates. What other people think of him is not important. What counts is whether his heart has been captured by the love of God which flows outward to his brother and eventually to all men. To love is to abide in life; to hate is to abide in death. In Christ is life; in Cain is death. Love of the brethren is the proof of being in Christ.

3. The evidence of love is Jesus on the Cross. Jesus himself had said that greater love no man can have than to lay down his life for his friend (John 15:13). This is not the sum total of the meaning of the Cross, to be sure, but it is a vital part of it. It was not the nails but His love that bound Him to the Cross (10:18). The songwriter put it:

> *See, from His head, His hands, His feet,*
> *Sorrow and love flow mingled down.*
> *Did e'er such love and sorrow meet,*
> *Or thorns compose so rich a crown?*

Our way of knowing that God loves us is that He sent Jesus to die in our stead. To see Him is to testify with Paul that He "loved me, and gave himself for me" (Gal. 2:20).

4. John sees something else in the Cross, however. It does say that we are loved by the greatest love humans can know. It also shows us how to love and whom we should love. We are tempted to make it a little circle of recipro-

cal love. We love Him who loved us. John sees the love of God as an ongoing stream. The true response to God's love is not only to love God but to love others who have been created in the likeness of God. This may be what Paul meant when he said the children should not save up for the parents but parents for the children (2 Cor. 12:14). He was not talking as much about social security as he was saying that the way children return the love of parents is to love their own children. We sing:

> Oh, dearly, dearly has He loved,
> And we must love Him, too;
> And trust in His redeeming blood,
> And try His works to do.

If He so loved us, we should love the brethren. It is the mark of realization that Christ redeemed us in love. He forgives us freely our sins; He asks that we freely forgive others. He gave of himself to us; He asks that we give of ourselves to our brethren.

All of this may be easy to say, yet it must be done to be true. Love is not just saying so; it is doing acts of love to one another. John touches here on a very human weakness in the child of God. It is easier to talk than to do. Let us love, he exhorts, not in word only but in deed. If one says that he loves his brother but, seeing him in need, does not minister to him, he is not telling the truth. How, he asks, can the love of God dwell in one who shuts up his compassion from an unfortunate brother?

There is the lighthearted story of the young man who wrote his girl friend of his love. He said he would climb the highest mountain or cross the widest sea to be with her. Nothing could stop him, he claimed, from being with his dearly beloved. Then he added the P.S., "I will be over to see you Wednesday night if it does not rain." Real love may be lavish in its words, but it is nonetheless extravagant in its deeds. Children of God love in truth and in deed.

To Be Born Again Is to Have Confidence Before God

1 John 3:19-24

19 And hereby we know that we are of the truth, and shall assure our hearts before him.
20 For if our heart condemn us, God is greater than our heart, and knoweth all things.
21 Beloved, if our heart condemn us not, then have we confidence toward God.
22 And whatsoever we ask, we receive of him, because we keep his commandments, and do those things that are pleasing in his sight.
23 And this is his commandment, That we should believe on the name of his Son Jesus Christ, and love one another, as he gave us commandment.
24 And he that keepeth his commandments dwelleth in him, and he in him. And hereby we know that he abideth in us, by the Spirit which he hath given us.

1. A child of God knows that he is one. It is not something that he assumes. He is assured by the truth of God. Whatever may be the feeling of his heart, the truth of God is greater. His confidence is not in what he is but in what God is. It seems too good to be true. He may be so tempted by the awareness of his faults and failings as to question that he is really a child of God. But the truth of God rests not upon one's feeling but His Word. He is the Source of truth; one's heart is not.

2. The condemnation that John writes of here is not one of guilt. It is not that one is in rebellion against God. It is one of worth. There are times when the Christian feels himself unworthy to be called a child of God. He cannot understand how the Heavenly Father would stoop to acknowledge him. The wonder of grace can be both exhilarating and frightening. That God should love one who deserves only condemnation is almost beyond imagination. That it may be just that, imagination, is a temptation one could face. If he does, he is reminded that, hard as it is to fathom, it is nonetheless true. God does not lie. He is true to His promise and His Word. If one abides in God, he is assured by the reality of that relationship. It may not seem possible, but it is. The assurance of it rests in God. He is great enough and loving enough to look beyond one's faults

and see one's need. He knows better than one's heart the depth of grace and the extent of divine love.

3. The very heights of joy and praise that so often are the experience of the child of God can cause him to despair when for any reason they abate. Many Christians have acknowledged emotional letdowns often so severe as to cause darkness. In the "dark night of the soul" introspection can lead to self-condemnation. In such times the Christian must rest upon the unchanging Word of God. He knows everything and can understand much better than the despondent one the reason for the darkness. Assurance of sonship rests not on the feelings of one's heart. It rests on the faithfulness of the Father.

Our Lord on the Cross cried, "My God, why hast thou forsaken me?" (Matt. 27:46; Mark 15:34). They were the words of the Psalmist who called out in the dark night of his soul the condemnation of his own heart. In that 22nd psalm he searches his heart and the situation around him and then looks toward God and finds reassurance in Him. His heart was convinced of despair, but God was there; and when he looked to Him, he was reassured. If in that moment on the Cross Jesus knew the terribleness of sensing estrangement from the Father, He also knew that the Heavenly Father was there. The psalm He quoted says, "I will declare thy name unto my brethren; in the midst of the congregation will I praise thee. . . . For he hath not despised nor abhorred the affliction of the afflicted; neither hath he hid his face from him; but when he cried unto him, he heard" (Ps. 22:22, 24). The last words of Jesus were not the cry of dereliction but, "Father, into thy hands I commend my spirit" (Luke 23:46).

If Jesus knew the dark night of a heart that feels separated from the Father and found confidence when He cried to Him, so can all who follow Him. *God is greater than our heart, and knoweth all things.*

Such an experience may be widely known but is not the frequent day-by-day experience of the born again.

They know the assurance of a heart that rests in the knowledge that it is abiding in God. When our hearts do not condemn us, we have confidence toward God, John assures us. There is an ongoing relationship with Him. The child receives from the Father the things he asks as he keeps the Father's commandments and does that which is pleasing in His sight. This is far from saying that prayer commands God or that His children are "spoiled brats" that can have anything they want. It is saying that as the child lives in obedience to the Heavenly Father's will and has His approval, his prayers are answered. That is partly because he only asks those things he knows that the Father wills. It is also because the very prayer of his heart is in response to the prompting of the Holy Spirit who makes intercession for him (Rom. 8:26).

4. This confidence that we are the children of God is based on three important conditions in our hearts. First, we must believe on the name of the Lord Jesus. "For with the heart man believeth unto righteousness." Paul summarized the apostolic teaching in these words: "If thou shalt confess with thy mouth the Lord Jesus, and shalt believe in thine heart that God hath raised him from the dead, thou shalt be saved" (Rom. 10:9-10*a*). To believe on Jesus brings the assurance that the believer is a child of God, that he has been born again.

Second, we must love one another. Jesus said this was the evidence to all men that we are His followers and children of God. God is love. All who are born of Him love one another. Later in this letter John will tell us that to say we love God is to love men. The more we surrender ourselves to God's love and direct it outward to others, the greater is our confidence that we are God's. We know enough about ourselves to know that we could not do it unless He had changed us.

Third, we have the Holy Spirit dwelling in us. John says we know that God is abiding with us by the Holy Spirit that He has given us. His presence and power gives us the confidence that we are God's children. The more we learn to trust the Spirit and follow His direction, the greater our confidence. The moment comes, sooner or later, when the child learns the limits of his own strength and wisdom and gives himself irrevocably and fully to the life in the Spirit. Like the first day of His outpouring, the Spirit then fills the heart and life with the fullness of His power and the love of God. In other sections John refers to this being filled with the Spirit as being perfected in love. It is the moment when the heart of the Christian is brought fully into the love of God. It does not mean that the Christian is perfect. It does mean that the fullness of God's love fills his heart and motivates his actions. He may not always do the best or wisest thing, but what he does is out of love for God who has redeemed him and for his fellowmen who have been made in the likeness of God.

1 JOHN 4

To Be Born Again Is to Try the Spirits

1 John 4:1-6

> 1 Beloved, believe not every spirit, but try the spirits whether they are of God: because many false prophets are gone out into the world.
> 2 Hereby know ye the Spirit of God: Every spirit that confesseth that Jesus Christ is come in the flesh is of God:
> 3 And every spirit that confesseth not that Jesus Christ is come in the flesh is not of God: and this is that spirit of antichrist, whereof ye have heard that it should come; and even now already is it in the world.
> 4 Ye are of God, little children, and have overcome them: because greater is he that is in you, than he that is in the world.
> 5 They are of the world: therefore speak they of the world, and the world heareth them.
> 6 We are of God: he that knoweth God heareth us; he that is not of God heareth not us. Hereby know we the spirit of truth, and the spirit of error.

1. When one lives a life in the Spirit, he must accept the responsibility of trying the spirits which offer him guid-

ance and advice. The spirit world is not free from error. There are many false and deceptive spiritual suggestions and ideas which confront the Christian. If the devil cannot get him to go into sinful acts, he tries to divert the believer's best purposes into fruitless or harmful paths. The devil will try to get the Christian to do the right thing in the wrong way. Or even worse he will tempt him to do the wrong thing with the right purpose. Either one is counterproductive to the kingdom of God and the spiritual life of the Christian. Jesus warned the disciples that the time would come when men would kill them and think they did God service (John 16:2). In Matthew 7 He tells of people in the Judgment who will insist that they are children of God. They will recount how much they have done for Christ and for His name's sake. They will hear the reply, "I never knew you: depart from me" (v. 23).

It is shocking to realize that one could go all his life thinking he was a child of God and doing His work and wake up too late to discover that he was not. How does one know he is on the right team? Certainly fervency is not the best test, nor is inner conviction. One could be so strongly of the opinion that he was right that he would die for it and become a martyr to the cause and find at the last that he wasted his pains and was off the track all the time. Do we have to wait until the Last Judgment to find out if we were right or wrong? Is there a litmus test we can apply now?

Yes, says John the elder, there is a way to know in every moment whether one is a child of God. There is a way to try the spirits which seem so right and may not be. That test is Jesus. If the spirit confesses Jesus as God come in the flesh, he is of God. The Man of Galilee in His earthly life and ministry is the true way. Whatever conforms to the record He left is true. Whatever does not is antichrist and untrue.

This is one reason why the Bible is so much a groundwork to all the Christian believes and does. God inspired its writing by the Spirit so that we could have from eye-witnesses the accurate and valid record of what is true both in ideas and actions. God was in Christ, showing the way to live, the things which are eternally important, and what we may know of Him. This is why Paul says that God will judge the world by Jesus (Rom. 2:16). He means the standard by which the rightness or wrongness of thought, word, action, and motive can be evaluated is by the example we have in Jesus. Peter says that Christ left us the example that we should follow His steps (1 Pet. 2:21).

2. The Christian need not feel that he is alone as he tries the spirit. God who is greater is in the Christian and gives him the victory. Spirits can offer deceptive suggestions, but they cannot overcome the Christian except as he allows them entrance into his motives. As has often been said concerning evil thoughts, We cannot keep the birds from flying over our heads, but we can keep them from building nests in our hair. False ideas and erroneous spirits confront the child of God. He overcomes them because greater is He that is in him than he that is in the world. It is not a misfortune that error should tempt him. For the warmest kind of confidence comes to him as he, by the Spirit of God, identifies the error and rejects it. The fellowship and communion with God that the Christian has as he faces the temptation of false spirits is worth the effort. The test gives him renewed assurance that he is born again as he identifies truth and sides with it. In a sense he welcomes the confrontation, for he knows when it is resolved he will be the stronger. The way, the truth, and the life in Christ become more meaningful as they are tested against the spurious options.

The little girl replied to her Sunday School teacher's question about what she wanted to be when she grew up, "I'd like to be a returned missionary!" As humorous as it seems, there is a confidence born of struggle that is deep and rewarding. To be challenged with the untrue, see its error, and stand for truth brings the assurance of sonship ever so stronger to one's heart.

They passed thro' toils and trials,
And, though the strife was long,
They share the victor's conquest,
And sing the victor's song.[9]

Popularity is not an adequate test of truth. It is tempting to worship at the shrine of success. One sees those prospering who use the truth of God to their own ends. They build great cathedrals; they enjoy wide listening and viewing audiences. Millions of dollars flow in to support their projects, rescuing them from the ever-recurring emergencies. And one concludes this must be of God, for they enjoy such blessing. This is not necessarily so, says John. The world responds to them because they are of the world. They have been caught in the world's way of evaluating worth. They talk the language of the world. The truth is not determined by what receives the widest support but by what is true to the words of the "Stranger of Galilee." The world does not hear Him because they do not know Him. The born again do.

Christian Assurance and Fellowship
1 John 4:7—5:12

Assurance and Fellowship in God's Love
1 John 4:7-12

> 7 Beloved, let us love one another: for love is of God; and every one that loveth is born of God, and knoweth God.
> 8 He that loveth not knoweth not God; for God is love.
> 9 In this was manifested the love of God toward us, because that God sent his only begotten Son into the world, that we might live through him.
> 10 Herein is love, not that we loved God, but that he loved us, and sent his Son to be the propitiation for our sins.
> 11 Beloved, if God so loved us, we ought also to love one another.

12 No man hath seen God at any time. If we love one another, God
dwelleth in us, and his love is perfected in us.

1. The basic foundation of Christian experience and relationship is to be found in the love of God. God is love. It is the sum total of His being. Everything God is and does is an expression of His love. So when Christians are urged to love one another, it is important for them to remember that love is of God. He is the Source of it. When God's life is born in the Christian, he loves. His loving is a signal that he knows God, from whom the love came.

In some ways it seems unfortunate that the English word *love* is used with such a wide range of meaning. It is used for the highest expression of God we can contemplate all the way down through affection for others or for things to whims and at last physical and/or sexual pleasure. What John is saying is that love in its loftiest sense describes the nature of God and what it is that the born again share of their Father's nature.

2. This lofty love was made clear to the world in Jesus. He was the Son of God who was sent into the world to reveal to men the love of their Heavenly Father. This love of God is redeeming. It lifts men from sin and brings them into fellowship with God. It restores the relationship God had in mind when He thought of creating them. It not only demonstrates God's outreach to men but also brings life unending to all who receive it. Death had descended on the world of men because of sin. The soul that sins must die—this is the rule by which the universe is governed. The love of God was displayed in Jesus, who died the death that all men should die. His death and resurrection brought resurrection power to all who would receive Him before they die. He showed the love of God, that men might live through Him.

3. The initiative is on God's part. Christian assurance and fellowship come in response to the prior love of God. God's love is seen in the fact that He first loved men. The love that brings assurance and fellowship to the Christian is not

something of the Christian's own making. It is something that God first had for him. *Herein is love, not that we loved God, but that he loved us.* These words of John are most profound. The Christian does not have to develop a way to love God or others. He is already the object of God's love through Jesus Christ. He needs only to respond to that love to come into a right relationship with God and a right relationship to others.

The whole process begins with the good news of God's love. If one tries to begin by seeking to corral his wayward heart, to strip from it every other love, and make it turn its love toward God, he is going at it in the wrong way. The Christian experience is not a matter of disciplining ourselves to love God and Him alone. For too long, too many have tried, only to weary themselves without finding the door. All men have been loved beyond measure and been shown that love in Jesus. He became the propitiation for sin. He cleared the way for the love which God has for men to be fully known. The depth of this love is to love God. The way is provided. All the sinner has to do is accept the love so freely proffered. He discovers then that he is so strongly loved that he never can love anything else. He loves God who first loved both him and his fellowman made in the image of God.

4. It follows simply, then, *if God so loved us, we ought also to love one another.* Jesus illustrated this in the story of one who owed a debt too large for him to ever repay. But wonder of wonders, the one to whom he owed the debt freely forgave him. Yet when the one whose debt had been cancelled came upon one who owed a small amount, he was unyielding in his demand for repayment. The lesson is clear. To be forgiven much is freely to forgive the little. To have been loved much is to love as much as one is able.

5. Not being able to see God, we can love Him to as full an extent as our faith will permit. One step on the way to fully loving Him whom we have not seen is to love those we do see: our fellowmen made in His image. If that circle is too

large, we can start with loving those who are a part of the fellowship of believers. However, it must not end there. Jesus told the disciples that if they loved only those who loved them, they would have no reward (Matt. 5:46). He had just said that the children of the Heavenly Father should love even their enemies and do good to those that persecuted them. If this seems too much for us, we should remember the Cross and His prayer of forgiveness for those who were crucifying Him.

Loving others, even our enemies, is not so tall an order when we see the activity of God in us. The love we have for God and others comes from the indwelling presence of God. God dwells in those who love Him, and His love is perfected in them. The perfect love which John Wesley taught is the work of God in the heart of the believer. It is not only the nature of God to love, but it is also the nature of God to bring that love to perfection or fulfillment. Christian holiness is the fruit of the love relationship with God. It is what He intends for everyone born again of the Spirit. To resist holiness is to resist the very purpose for which Christ died. It is not an option for those who want to be superreligious. It is rather God's will for every child of His, and He will accomplish it.

The initiative is God's. We do not perfect His love in us; He does. When we open our hearts to the love of God, we are at one with the purpose for which we were created. We are "at home." The realization of that purpose begins to work within all we are and do. We begin to be what we were intended to be. That intention is brought to fulfillment as His love is perfected in us. That is the outcome of God's dwelling in us. If that does not happen, He is not dwelling there. It is His presence which accomplishes and guarantees it. One can see God having this perfection of love. Jesus said, "Blessed are the pure in heart: for they shall see God" (Matt. 5:8). God is seen in the outflow of His love from hearts that are filled with it. It is an unselfish and giving love that does not love for return but finds its joy in the giving.

The Presence of the Holy Spirit

1 John 4:13-16

> 13 Hereby know we that we dwell in him, and he in us, because he hath given us of his Spirit.
>
> 14 And we have seen and do testify that the Father sent the Son to be the Saviour of the world.
>
> 15 Whosoever shall confess that Jesus is the Son of God, God dwelleth in him, and he in God.
>
> 16 And we have known and believed the love that God hath to us. God is love; and he that dwelleth in love dwelleth in God, and God in him.

1. The source of the Christian's assurance is the presence of the Holy Spirit. When Jesus told the disciples He would be leaving them and they would see Him no more, He urged them not to be sad. He told them it was the best thing for them that He was going. He would be gone, but He would send the Holy Spirit. Jesus had been with them; the Holy Spirit would be in them. The Holy Spirit would keep Christ and His words ever before them. The world would be convicted of sin as the disciples witnessed to the life and teaching of Jesus. The Holy Spirit faces men with the choice of believing or not believing on Christ. The Holy Spirit would also demonstrate to the world the way of right living. Jesus would be gone, but the Holy Spirit would enable the followers of Jesus to be models of God's love (John 16:4-11). The Holy Spirit brings victory to the Christian because the devil has been judged, and all who trust God share in the victory over evil.[10]

The Holy Spirit is the Christian's proof of acceptance. His presence enables him to know that he dwells in God and God in him. He is the evidence of the fellowship of the community of Christ's Body, because all experience the same presence. While the Holy Spirit respects and enhances each one's individuality, there is a oneness about His presence that assures each member of a common fellowship through Him. That oneness is the unity of their faith in Jesus Christ, the Son of God who has been sent into the world to become the Savior of the world. This united confession of Jesus is prompted by the indwelling Spirit and is the evidence of His presence.

The characteristic of the Holy Spirit's presence is His self-effacement. He does not call attention to himself; He centers attention on Jesus. It would be a little more accurate when speaking of the Spirit's presence to say that one senses Christ's presence. Of course, we understand what is meant when we hear people say they feel the Spirit. But, if we are faithful to His prompting, we would be more aware of Christ when the Holy Spirit makes His presence known.

2. Christian fellowship centers around this shared confession of Christ's saving action. This confession has two parts. It is the testimony to what has been the individual's experience of Christ's saving action. It is also the proclamation to all that there is salvation in Christ for all who will confess His name. What He has done for us He wants to do for others. His salvation is for all men. This is the message of the redeemed. The gift of the Holy Spirit brings the living confirmation of salvation to everyone who believes on Jesus.

The Holy Spirit further prompts and enables the Christian's testimony to the world. It is the reality and awareness of the redemption in Christ that motivates the evangelistic and missionary thrust of the church. We are so grateful for what Christ has done for us and are so filled with His love that we want everyone to share in the life of God experienced in Jesus Christ. The church must not be like the leprous men in Israel who on a venture found the camp of the besiegers empty. At first they rushed in to get all they could for themselves until they acknowledged to one another, "We do not well: this day is a day of good tidings, and we hold our peace" (2 Kings 7:9). Good things are to be shared. If this was the tardy reaction on the part of grateful men before the Christian era, how much more will it result in those who have received the Holy Spirit.

In this experience of the Holy Spirit's presence, the

current believer becomes one with the Apostolic Church and all that are in between. From the Day of Pentecost on, all who have received the Holy Spirit have shared in the same joy and thrust into Christlikeness. In every time with all the changes time brings, there remains this continuity that *God is love; and he that dwelleth in love dwelleth in God, and God in him.*

Christian Boldness: The Fruit of Assurance and Characteristic of Fellowship

1 John 4:17-21

> 17 Herein is our love made perfect, that we may have boldness in the day of judgment: because as he is, so are we in this world.
> 18 There is no fear in love; but perfect love casteth out fear: because fear hath torment. He that feareth is not made perfect in love.
> 19 We love him, because he first loved us.
> 20 If a man say, I love God, and hateth his brother, he is a liar: for he that loveth not his brother whom he hath seen, how can he love God whom he hath not seen?
> 21 And this commandment have we from him, That he who loveth God love his brother also.

1. To live in the love of God and have it flow out of us to others bears fruit in holy boldness. The fear of judgment fades. The writer of Hebrews expresses a nearly universal anxiety of mankind when he says that all men must die and after this face judgment (9:27). Whether that judgment be the Great White Throne Judgment (Rev. 20:11-15), or the judgment of consequences in this life, it is a fearful thing. The apocalyptic writers all portray a panic and overwhelming fear upon all who face the judgments of God in the end time. All of us have known or seen the terror in men when the mountains crumble or the earth trembles.

The love of God in a person's heart brings a boldness because the person knows the Judge of All is working out His purpose in his life. When the same One who administers judgment dwells in a person and His love fills him, fear is gone, and boldness—a loving boldness—takes over. This boldness comes because that one is becoming like

Christ, the standard by which men are judged. *As he is, so are we in this world.* What will be asked of the believer at the last is occurring through the cleansing and empowering love of God in the heart and life of the child of God. The judgment becomes for the Christian not a time of fearsome disclosure but of loving affirmation.

Some Christians look at the end time as frightening. They try desperately to interpret the prophecies so that they can predict the probable dates when the events will take place. They almost frantically seek an understanding that will remove them from the scene. John sees the love of God as making one comfortable with His judgment since it is an expression of His love. What judgment is all about is that which is happening in the person in whom the love of God is perfected. The perfection of love is the grasp of God's purpose in the individual and in history in such a way as to welcome all that has come and will come in the assurance and boldness that his times are in God's hands.

2. This *boldness in the day of judgment* is not limited to that event or relationship only. It applies to every tormenting fear. *Perfect love casteth out fear.* The fears that beset people are their tormentors. They distort perspective; they disrupt relationships; they retard growth; they inhibit development. They blind moral judgment and enflame passions. The writer of Hebrews describes the power of the devil to be subjecting to bondage people who fear death (2:14-15). It would be mind-boggling to sum up the colossal amount of money and time and energy that is expended to attempt to escape the fears of life. Love is the best antidote. Fully realized and mature love casts out fear like Jesus cast out devils. Love and fear cannot survive together. Either fear undercuts and destroys love, or love casts out fear. "There is no fear in love; . . . and he that feareth is not made perfect in love" (v. 18, ASV). It is as simple and profound as that. These are contradicting forces. Love is positive; fear is negative. They are mutually

exclusive. The more one loves, the less he fears. The more he fears, the less he loves.

Some rationalize fears. They believe some fear is normal and necessary. They argue that without a healthy fear one might easily and quickly be the victim of the pitfalls and dangers of life. They say that fear keeps one alert and on the defensive. To some degree such rationalizing appears valid. But there is nothing that fear does for us in a constructive way that love and confidence will not do better. So Jesus calls to the fearful, "Come unto me, all ye that labour and are heavy laden, and I will give you rest. Take my yoke upon you, and learn of me; for I am meek and lowly in heart: and ye shall find rest unto your souls. For my yoke is easy, and my burden is light" (Matt. 11:28-30). His love helps us accept each day and all that comes.

If the things we fear are not real, we waste ourselves fearing them. If they are real, they have a place in the purpose of Him who loves us and dwells with us through the Holy Spirit. This kind of boldness strengthens us to live every moment to the full and in love. Like Faithful in Bunyan's story, we can call back across the wave, "Have no fear, for I have felt the bottom, and it is sound."[11] Over and over again Jesus reached out to His companions with this word. Whatever came, they were not to fear. His love takes care of every eventuality.

3. If someone adds, "Well, I trust God and believe He wills me good, but I'm not sure of my fellowman," the Christian fellowship provides a setting in which one can and should find release from such fear. It brings him into a community of trust and love. The best way to see or understand God is to see Him at work in the lives of those who have Him in them. No man has ever seen God. If he talks about loving God whom he hasn't seen and does not love his Christian brother whom he has seen, he is not truthful. The Christian fellowship is a community of love. They are people who have responded to the love of God and love

Him and each other. For not only do they need each other for the full development of their personalities, but they also find each other to be opportunities to express the love of God.

It is true that a person under the slavery of sin may not be trusted in the same way as a brother in Christ. This is not to excuse the Christian from loving him, however. The Christian loves because he has been loved. The motivation of his love for the sinner is not the lovableness of the sinner but the love Christ had for him. The sinner is one for whom He died. The Christian reaches out to him for Christ's sake. So the Christian who has been loved of God loves Him in return and his brother as well, whether that brother is a member of the Christian fellowship or one that the love of Christ is still seeking.

Like their Savior, the Christian fellowship reaches out in love, desiring that all men would come to repentance and faith in the Lord Jesus. Like the sinner the Christian fellowship has been loved of God through Christ. Like the sinner the Christian fellowship does not deserve this love. Still it flows to them unabated. Aware of the wondrous grace that made them an object of Christ's love, the Christian fellowship tries to repay its debt of love by loving the unlovely and reaching out to the unworthy as Christ reached out to them. In the feeling and doing of this, they are not blind to the scorn they often receive as being "softies" or "do-gooders." They are reinforced in the knowledge that to this degree they are like their Lord. They share His suffering and His joy.

Christian Assurance in the Family of God

1 John 5:1-5

> 1 Whosoever believeth that Jesus is the Christ is born of God: and every one that loveth him that begat loveth him also that is begotten of him.
> 2 By this we know that we love the children of God, when we love God, and keep his commandments.
> 3 For this is the love of God, that we keep his commandments: and his commandments are not grievous.
> 4 For whatsoever is born of God overcometh the world: and this is the victory that overcometh the world, even our faith.
> 5 Who is he that overcometh the world, but he that believeth that Jesus is the Son of God?

1. John has insisted that loving others is the way in which Christians express their love for God. He supports this position with three reasons: first, because no one has ever seen God, and the only way to love Him is to love men whom we have seen; second, because the Christian has been commanded to do so by Christ; and third, because to be born of God is to belong to His family. Families are held together by love. Everyone who loves the parent loves the child. Christians love each other because they have been born into the family of God and are one with each other. Everyone who believes that Jesus is the Christ is born of God.

Faith in Jesus means the acceptance of the solidarity of the family of God. Jesus asserted that entrance into the Kingdom meant the leaving of father and mother to follow Him. The Kingdom is the new relationship into which the Christian is born. This new family is an eternal one. Christians love each other because they are part of each other in Christ.

There is an orderliness about life in the family of God. The family has rules. They are the commandments of Jesus. All who are in the family carry out these commandments. They live as He has taught them to do. In contrast to the law of Moses the Christian commandments are not burdensome. When Peter was addressing the council at Jerusalem and pleading for freedom in Christ, he said, "God, which knoweth the hearts, bare them witness, giving them the Holy Ghost, even as he did unto us; and put no difference between us and them, purifying their hearts by faith. Now therefore why tempt ye God, to put a yoke upon the neck of the disciples, which neither our fathers nor we were able to bear? But we believe that through the grace of the Lord Jesus Christ we shall be saved, even as they" (Acts 15:8-11).

It is not hard to love one another in the fellowship of the family. This is a commandment that is easy because it is the natural thing to do. The new nature into which the Christian is born makes it a joy to do Christ's will. The born-again child of God does not want to do anything else. The commandments of Christ become the joyous pattern of his life. The Christian joins his Lord in declaring, "I delight to do thy will, O my God" (Ps. 40:8).[12] Christians do not love each other because they have to do so. They want to live in this kind of relationship because they are family.

2. To be born into the family of God is to share His power and victory. In every situation the child of God can withstand the world and be victor over its assaults. When sin and doubt assail him, he is victor through Christ. Christ met every temptation which is common to man and did not sin. He defeated the devil and shares this victory with all who are in Him. It is a victory of faith.

This victory is experienced here and now. The faith that brings it is not just the belief that all will be well in the next world. It is the confidence that in this present world one can live victoriously. All that God has promised is available to the one who will believe. It is not a denial of sin and trouble. The Christian knows only too well the wickedness and woe of the world. It is the confidence that in all these things he is more than conqueror. It is not the victory of *avoiding* difficulty, for the Christian has his share and more of it. It is the victory of *overcoming* difficulty. It is the victory of finding God's way out of temptation. It is not the victory of never meeting the devil or struggling with him. It is the victory of the standard raised against him when he comes in like a flood (Isa. 59:19).

It is a victory that witnesses. Sometimes Christians are perplexed when they seem to have received more than their share of trouble. They ask God to heal them or remove the pain, and nothing happens. They see no redemptive value in what is happening. But there is such value, for the victory that comes testifies to the grace of God. It tells the world that this is the way Christians overcome. He who bore affliction and even death for us came through exclaiming, "All power is given unto me in heaven and in earth" (Matt. 28:18). He then promised to be with His disciples always, even unto the end of the world (v. 20).

3. This is the assurance the Christian has as he realizes his place in the family of God. He that believes that Jesus is the Christ experiences a new birth. He finds he has been born into a family made of all the followers of Christ of all time. It is quite a family, not for its size but because it is bound together in a common tie of love. All the members love their Father and His children, their brothers in Christ. The new believer learns that life in this family is according to the rules of Christ.

Life in the Son is dependent on this obedience. There is nothing threatening in this, however, for *his commandments are not grievous.* They are, in fact, a joy to carry out. The new nature loves to do Christ's will. There is nothing else the Christian could want to do than it. This life in the family of God brings both confidence and fellowship because it is an overcoming one. It is not a sheltered life in which the child of God lives in a glass house. It is rather a victorious one in which nothing that does or can happen to him is too much for him. In all the things his life encounters he is more than conqueror. Such a life says to men overwhelmed by the woes of life, Christ can make you victor; have faith in Him.

The Witness of the Spirit

1 John 5:6-10

> 6 This is he that came by water and blood, even Jesus Christ; not by water only, but by water and blood. And it is the Spirit that beareth witness, because the Spirit is truth.
> 7 For there are three that bear record in heaven, the Father, the Word, and the Holy Ghost: and these three are one.
> 8 And there are three that bear witness in earth, the spirit, and the water, and the blood: and these three agree in one.
> 9 If we receive the witness of men, the witness of God is greater: for this is the witness of God which he hath testified of his Son.
> 10 He that believeth on the Son of God hath the witness in himself: he that believeth not God hath made him a liar; because he believeth not the record that God gave of his Son.

1. The Holy Spirit, as Jesus promised, has come to bear witness of Him (John 15:26). He does so in the awareness of Christ's presence that He brings to the believers. He does so in the life of the fellowship of believers, the Church, as she affirms the incarnation of Christ both in the faithful record of the Scriptures and the formulation of the creed. First, the Holy Scriptures are the true Word of God written by men under the inspiration of the Holy Spirit. They witness to the plan of salvation: prophesied in the dealing of God with His people Israel; fulfilled in the life and death and resurrection of Jesus; and lived out in the life of the Church. The Scriptures have been gathered from many writings which claimed inspiration and then put together under the guidance of the Holy Spirit; and this phase, the formulation of the canon, is perhaps as vital as the writing itself. Second, the Holy Spirit through the Church has formulated the creed. This statement of doctrine puts in orderly fashion the things believed by Christians.

Central to the creed is the historical fact that Jesus of Nazareth *came by water and blood.* He came by *water:* He was baptized by John the Baptist in the river Jordan. A descending dove and a voice from heaven affirmed that

He was indeed God's Son; and He lived in the presence and power of the Spirit. He came by *blood:* He was crucified by Pontius Pilate and died; the shedding of His blood was for the remission of sin. The Christian follows his Lord's example by being baptized and remembers His death by partaking of the Communion. Jesus is the Revealer as He gives the light of truth by the Holy Spirit. He is the Redeemer as He cleanses from all sin by His blood.

The Spirit and water and the Blood are three witnesses, and their witness is one. Jesus was God incarnate— God in the flesh. He came to show men how to live. He died that men might have the power to become the sons of God and live as He lived. He rose again from the dead that He through the Holy Spirit might forever be with every follower and head their fellowship, the Church. This is the one witness of the Spirit, the water, and the Blood.

2. Another threefold testimony is: the testimony of men, the testimony of God, and the testimony of inner experience.[13]

a. From the first disciples until the present moment *men* have heard the good news of the gospel. The testimony of those who have believed on it is that it is true. The songwriter penned:

> *I heard the voice of Jesus say,*
> *"Come unto Me and rest.*
> *Lay down, thou weary one, lay down*
> *Thy head upon My breast!"*
>
> *I came to Jesus as I was,*
> *Weary, and worn, and sad;*
> *I found in Him a resting-place,*
> *And He has made me glad.*[14]

In this and many other similar words and word pictures men who have trusted Christ for salvation have witnessed that He keeps His word and that His promises are true. Nearly two millennia have gone by and, still men testify in a far different world and life-style from those who first saw and heard Him but with the same affirmation. His words are true; He keeps His promise.

b. The second kind of testimony is the testimony of *God.* Several times He spoke from the skies during the earthly life of our Lord, that this was His Beloved Son in whom He was well pleased. God shaped into His dealing with His people Israel the pattern of Christ's sacrifice for sin. By the miraculous acts of the Virgin Birth, the Incarnation, the miracles Jesus did, the unique events surrounding His death, and the Resurrection, God has borne witness that Jesus truly was the Son of God. The centurion said as much at the Cross. God established His testimony in history so that, no matter how man disbelieves, he cannot escape the facts. One way or another all men must come to terms with them. E. Stanley Jones used to say that no man breaks the law of God; rather, he breaks himself over it. No man destroys the witness of God; he destroys himself if he rejects it.

c. The third kind of testimony is the *inward experience of the believer.* The reality of being cleansed and knowing Christ in one's heart is the final and best testimony. Charles Colson, in *Born Again,* tells how in prison after he had been converted he found himself drifting into the same pattern of life that had led him to become involved in the Watergate scandal. As he sought to understand what was happening and what was the solution, he learned about the promise of the Holy Spirit. One day in the prison Bible study he heard the teacher affirm the inward witness through the Holy Spirit. He told the little group they could receive the Holy Spirit if they would but ask. Colson did, and his heart was filled. He says this about the inward experience, "It was an incredible thing to have one's spirit washed clean."[15]

The witness of men is most convincing and is added

to with each generation. The witness of God is greater because He is Truth. But the most convincing witness of all is the witness of the Spirit in the inner life. Men can deny the testimony of others and disbelieve the testimony of God. The inner witness, however, comes only to those who believe. So true and real is this experience that one could only deny it by setting oneself against truth. He makes himself a liar because he looks truth in the face or feels it in his heart and says it is not so. And when one makes truth a lie, there is no hope or light for him forever.

Who has not felt the power of this inward witness when on an Easter morning he joined with the fellowship of the believers to sing, "You ask me how I know He lives? / He lives within my heart." In the last analysis it is not belief in a doctrine but a relationship with the Person that establishes the inner witness. It is because He walks with the Christian and His presence fills the waking and sleeping hours that the believer knows He is real and true. It is after a long night of darkness when he awakens to find Jesus is still with him that the Christian declares, "I will not fear what man shall do unto me" (Heb. 13:6).

There is a story going the rounds of church newsletters which tells of one who at the end of life is talking with the Savior, saying to Him, "As I look back over my life and walk with You, I see our footprints side by side." Then puzzled, he goes on, "But in the deepest valleys there are only single footprints. Why did You let me go through the shadows alone?" To which the Master replied, "It was in those deep, dark valleys that I felt you could not walk, *and I carried you.*" The story is beautiful and reminds one of the faithfulness of his Companion in the ways of life. However, the Christian does not ask even a question, for he feels His presence all the more in the loneliest moments. Like Paul, on a storm-tossed sea when all the experienced sailors had given up hope, the Christian can say, "The Lord I love stands with me and assures me" (cf. Acts 27:21-25).

The Assurance of Life in the Son

1 John 5:11-12

11 And this is the record, that God hath given to us eternal life, and this life is in his Son.
12 He that hath the Son hath life; and he that hath not the Son of God hath not life.

The whole matter of assurance and fellowship can be summed up in the proposition that the life of the Son is given to all who believe. God has given eternal life to all men who will have it. It is given in His Son. This personal relationship is the proof positive. To have Christ in one's heart is to have eternal life. It is not simply that he will have it after he dies. He has it now in the indwelling presence of the Holy Spirit. If this personal relationship does not exist, then one does not have eternal life.

The most important question is "Do you have the Son?" Many questions can be asked about belief and practice of the Christian faith, but they all lead to the bottom line of personal relationship. "Is Christ living in your heart?" is the all-important one. To be born again is the way it all begins. To live the life given in Christ is the way it is evidenced. It is not even enough just to know one has been born of the Spirit. The final test is whether that life born in one continues in the fullness of its promise. One may testify that he has been born again, but if he does not have the Son abiding in him, he does not have eternal life. *He that hath the Son hath life; and he that hath not the Son of God hath not life.*

This is the unity of the fellowship of believers. They all have life. The Holy Spirit dwells in and among them. The life of God in His Son is theirs both individually and in common. They are all one in Him, however they may appear to differ.

Epilogue

Benefits of Christian Fellowship

1 John 5:13-21

The Purpose of the Letter Reaffirmed

1 John 5:13

> 13 These things have I written unto you that believe on the name of the Son of God; that ye may know that ye have eternal life, and that ye may believe on the name of the Son of God.

This letter has been written to Christian believers to reassure them in their faith. It was written in the midst of the controversies with the so-called Gnostics who claimed to know the hidden things. They were dogmatic in their assertion of many antichristian ideas. John wanted the believers to know that they had eternal life. The source of knowledge is God. He has revealed himself in Jesus Christ. He who knows the Son knows the Father. Entrance into this knowledge is by faith. He who believes on Jesus, walks in the light, and loves his brothers knows by these activities that he has eternal life.

There is no higher purpose for any communication. Human beings were made for eternity. They seek the full life. The serpent in the garden trapped the first couple into sin by telling them that to eat of the forbidden fruit would not be to die, as God had warned, but rather to know the full meaning of life. Life is what the heart longs for. If one can know that he has eternal life, it answers his deepest longings. St. Augustine prayed, "Thou hast made us for Thyself, and our hearts are restless until they rest in Thee."[16] This restlessness is the thirsting after the full and unending life.

Rest is one of the things God had in mind for everyone when He first thought of us. We were made to live forever with Him and each other. We have capabilities to adjust to and exploit the values of new relationships. We cannot be happy without them. We can expand our fellowship. We are less than fulfilled without it. Life must be satisfying and growing. The span of threescore and 10 is too short for all the potential that the soul enjoys. It is the forever forward look that life must have which is to be found in the gospel. Jesus came that we might have life and have it more abundantly (John 10:10). This letter was written to show that is what happens when one believes on Him.

Prayer Is a Benefit of Christian Fellowship

1 John 5:14-16

> 14 And this is the confidence that we have in him, that, if we ask any thing according to his will, he heareth us:
> 15 And if we know that he hear us, whatsoever we ask, we know that we have the petitions that we desired of him.
> 16 If any man see his brother sin a sin which is not unto death, he shall ask, and he shall give him life for them that sin not unto death. There is a sin unto death: I do not say that he shall pray for it.

1. Eternal life in the fellowship with God and His people includes the confidence that prayer accomplishes things. Prayer is a means of communication in the fellowship. It is sharing with God the desires of one's heart. The confidence the believer has is that, if he asks anything according to God's will, he is heard. Of course, this is quite different from saying that everything the Christian prays for he gets. Prayer must be within the will of God. It is unreasonable to suppose that God will do something He does not want to do just because a Christian asks for it. What is promised is, first, that He hears the prayer of all who are in the fellowship of life unending. What is heard is what was asked for in His will. He hears the Christian sharing in His purpose for the person or events that are the object of the petition. If one asks in His will, He hears in His will.

It is when the prayer is heard within His will that God answers it by giving the request that was asked. The late Dr. U. E. Harding used to say that God can see better than He can hear. What he meant was that God heard what the Christian asked and also saw his heart and what it really wanted and answered more in response to the heart than the mouth. He would illustrate his point by pointing to Elijah under the juniper tree following his victory at Mount Carmel. He had fled there because Jezebel was threatening to kill him. Under the tree the prophet asked to die. He really did not want to, Harding would say, for if that was what he really wanted, Jezebel was glad to accommodate him.

Augustine's mother prayed all night that God would keep her son from going to Italy. In the morning he went. But later after his conversion she concluded that God had answered her prayer far better with a no than a yes. This is often the case. The Christian with his limited knowledge projects a solution in prayer that is not God's way. God does not and will not change His mind because the Christian thinks he has a better idea. God will not do evil or unnecessarily harmful things. This is why prayer may often be prolonged and a struggle. It was for Jacob at Jabbok. It is when the petitioner comes to accord with the will of God in prayer that God hears him. It is when the petitioner knows that God has heard that he knows he has what he asked.

2. This is not to suggest that fellowship with God is a continual struggle between His will and ours. Paul says in Romans that often we do not know what to pray for. We are troubled about situations or needs and do not know even what to ask for. The Holy Spirit, he says, helps us (Rom. 8:26). To live in fellowship with God is to embrace His will. The more one lives within this fellowship, the more the very promptings to prayer are at the initiative of God through the Holy Spirit. Fellowship with God and others is to become ever more sensitive to His purposes in one's own life and in that of others.

A good example is to be found in the prayer for a Christian brother. If one sees a brother sin a sin that is not mortal, he can pray for him to receive forgiveness and restoration, and his prayer will be answered. This is Christian love in action. It is willing an unbroken relationship between ourselves and others and between them and God. Paul says it is the responsibility of those who make up the spiritual community to restore a fallen brother (Gal. 6:1). Jesus seems to have this in mind when He said He would give to the disciples the keys to the Kingdom. Those whom they prayed for and loved would be loosed, and those they did not would be bound (Matt. 16:19). It is safe to assume that the one restored wanted to be. One cannot imagine anyone being in the Kingdom who wanted out.

3. There is much that is both encouraging and frightening about this illustration. It is encouraging to realize the power of intercessory prayer. No member of the fellowship need ever be lost. It is frightening to ponder on how many there have been who would not have needed to be lost if a Christian brother interceded. The statistics of church membership contain too many dropouts. It may be true that many were never really in the Body of Christ. But accounting for that, we still have not done too well at implementing the privilege cited in this letter.

It is easy and fatal to be judgmental of another's problem. The deep concern for holiness of life does and should motivate the Christian to uphold the standard himself and pray that others will. The response to falling short in ourselves is to remember that in the Lord Jesus Christ we have an Advocate with the Father. He is faithful to forgive and cleanse. Our response to another's failure is to intercede in prayer, knowing that God will give us life for them who do not commit mortal sin. This suggestion of degrees in sinning will be discussed in the next section. Intercession means outflowing love and vicarious suffering. To be judgmental is to fall into the devil's well-disguised trap of spiritual pride. In the verse cited above concerning the spiritual restoration of a fallen brother, Paul reminds us it must be done in the spirit of meekness and in the awareness of how easily the intercessor himself could fall.

4. Love for one another will do just what is illustrated here. Unselfish concern will view another's sin as though it were his own. It will not enjoy salvation for oneself if his brother in Christ is lost. The fellowship of believers is the forgiven forgiving. It is the loved loving. It is the saved restoring. It is the cleansed interceding. It is the holy healing. It is praying for others because others have prayed for them. It is sharing our mutual woes before the God we love. It is carrying one another's burden with tear-stained eyes. It is every man looking not on his own things but on the things of others. It is in lowliness of mind, each esteeming others better than himself (Phil. 2:3-4).

There is an example of this in the account of our Lord's conversation with Peter on the night that He was arrested and that Peter denied Him. Jesus said to Peter that Satan was out to destroy the fellowship, but that He had prayed for Peter. He then admonished Peter that when he had been restored, he should channel the love and gratitude for his restoration into strengthening his brothers (Luke 22:31-32).

The World Is in Sin

1 John 5:17-19

> 17 All unrighteousness is sin: and there is a sin not unto death.
> 18 We know that whosoever is born of God sinneth not; but he that is begotten of God keepeth himself, and that wicked one toucheth him not.
> 19 And we know that we are of God, and the whole world lieth in wickedness.

In the previous section John has differentiated between sin that is mortal and sin that is not mortal. He is very confident that intercessory prayer can expunge in a brother the guilt of sin that is not mortal. He is not so sure about the sin that is mortal. He does not say it will not be forgiven. He just says that he is not suggesting that it should be prayed for in the same context. Jesus said that all sin will be forgiven except blasphemy against the Holy Ghost. Perhaps it will not be forgiven because to blaspheme against Him is to reveal a mind-set that will not ever ask forgiveness. It is to shut the door against one's last and best hope, according to Dr. Olin Curtis.[17]

1. The difference in this passage is between sin that is inadvertent and unintentional and sin that is deliberate and willful. Mortal sin seems to be sin that is committed because one wants to do so and knows while doing it that he is doing wrong. The former is something that happens all unexpected and unwanted. The latter implies a way of life that is in rebellion to the law of God. If one misses the mark because he was rushed in his taking aim, that is one thing. If he misses because he aimed in another direction, that is quite another.

All wrongdoing is sin. The only remedy for sin is divine forgiveness. If one imagines that he can escape the need of forgiveness by narrowing his definition for sin, he borders on dangerous rationalization. One risks spiritual pride to claim there is nothing for which one needs to be forgiven. It may be helpful to define sin so as to exclude mistakes and faults. But if mistakes or faults result in wrongdoing, they, too, need to be forgiven. It is safer to admit that one always needs the forgiveness of Christ's Blood.

The argument about what is sin and what is not is important in the building of true Christian doctrine,[18] but it is not so important in the appropriation of Christ's forgiveness and cleansing. God has provided a full and adequate remedy for sin so that His children may be victors over it. That remedy needs to be ever present and fully applied.

2. The Christian lives in a world that is under the power of

sin. It is God's will that he live in it without sin. For he that is born of God does not commit sin. He belongs to Christ, and Christ keeps him from the wicked one. When He prayed for His disciples, Jesus did not ask that they be taken out of the world but that they be kept from the evil one (John 17:15). That prayer was answered by the gift of the Holy Spirit. The Holy Spirit teaches the Christian what is God's will. The Spirit also brings the Christian to appropriate the cleansing of his heart so that the disposition to sin which he inherited is removed. Furthermore, He enables the Christian to obey God's commands. And again, the Holy Spirit empowers the Christian to share in the victory over the wicked one accomplished by his Lord. When temptation comes, as inevitably it will, the Holy Spirit provides the way of escape.

The Christian is in the world but not of it. He is confronted by sin but victor over it. He is warned that the sea of evil about him could engulf him. He is also reassured that Jesus has promised to bring him through. Christ does not belittle the danger, because He himself has faced it. By that very fact He is able to deliver the Christian. When Christ showed His hands and side to the disciples, He seemed to say, "See, I have the scars of battle." He also has the trophy of victory which He described as all power in heaven and earth. The world enslaved in wickedness may appear such an overwhelming threat that one would be tempted to ask, "Who can be saved?" The one who believes on Jesus, though he were the weakest of all men, has put himself in an invulnerable position. "That soul, though all hell should endeavor to shake," Jesus has said He will not ever forsake.

This letter does not deny the reality of sin or its scope. To do so would be to fly from the truth. John fully accepts the fact of sin's presense and power. He responds with the assurance that "greater is he that is in [the Christian], than he that is in the world" (4:4). Sin is all around, but the Savior also is here.

Understanding Is a Benefit of the Christian Fellowship

1 John 5:20

> 20 And we know that the Son of God is come, and hath given us an understanding, that we may know him that is true, and we are in him that is true, even in his Son Jesus Christ. This is the true God, and eternal life.

The coming of the Son of God means for all who will receive Him the ability to grasp truth. Christian truth is founded on the Incarnation. The Christian knowledge of God is based on His revelation of himself in Jesus. To know Jesus is to know God. This knowledge is a gift to the believer. Spiritual things are spiritually discerned (1 Cor. 2:14-15). While the Gnostics had boastfully claimed to be "in the know," the Christian had spiritual insight. This understanding is sometimes called the "anointing from the Holy One" (2:20, ASV), referring to the insight the Holy Spirit brings to the person who is born anew in Christ Jesus.

The two disciples who walked with the risen Lord on the road to Emmaus saw the Scriptures in a new light under His tutoring. They understood how what seemed a tragic end of the short ministry of Jesus was in fact God's plan and the great promised victory over sin and death. They testified that their hearts burned as they received the understanding that He gave them.

This understanding makes clear the fact that Jesus, the Son of God, is true. One believes on Him and is saved. He then understands that his faith was not in vain. Jesus was and is truly the Son of God. It is knowledge confirmed by experience. It is "inside" knowledge, for the Christian knows that he is in Christ as well. These two truths are the heart of Christian knowledge—that Jesus of Nazareth is the Son of God and that all who will accept Him as Savior are in Him. By perceiving that He is the Son of God, the Christian understands that He is the true God. By perceiving that he is in Him, the Christian understands that he has eternal life.

Not all of his questions are answered by any means. But the child of God in Christ has come to understand the very Source of life and truth and entered into its meaning. He has found a relationship with God and his fellowmen that is deeply satisfying and unending. He can humbly proclaim, "I have found it." Or better yet, "He has found me!"

A Parting Word of Advice

1 John 5:21

> 21 Little children, keep yourselves from idols. Amen.

The elder closes the letter with a warm but strange word of advice, *Little children, keep yourselves from idols.* At first glance the admonition seems out of place. The whole Epistle has been about truth and love in Christ. It has been a testimony more than an argument. Again and again there has been the phrase, "We know." It has not been so much a plea for the reader to accept the truth as to confirm its reality. The exhortation has been to rejoice in the knowledge that he has been born from above into an unending life and fellowship. To end this suddenly with the cryptic command to keep oneself from idols is puzzling.

1. It could be that the advice was a common comment with which a conversation is closed. We often use the secular benediction, "Take care of yourself," or "Have a good day." Even the word "Good-bye" is in the same category. For the Jew the worst thing he could do was to worship idols. Throughout the Scriptures idolatry is called spiritual immorality or adultery. So when one is warned against the worst, he is warned against idols. So frequent had the inroads of idol worship been in the history of God's people that the abhorrence of it was basic to any attempt to live righteously. One can imagine that the exhortation against it became so common as to be a form for closing every

conversation: "Whatever you do, keep yourself from idols."

2. However, throughout the Epistle the dualism of right and wrong, light and darkness, truth and lie, love and hate, life and death, has been described. Perhaps the writer has this in mind. His previous sentence was "This is the true God, and eternal life." The opposite would be idols. The worship of the true God is to believe in Christ. The rejection is to worship idols. So he adds another dualism to the list, God and idols. Such an interpretation has considerable appeal.

3. A third and perhaps more logical explanation would be to say that the reference to idols is a summary of the error of the heretics that formerly John has called antichrists. The Gnostics and their boastful claim of knowledge is really idolatry, he affirms. They cannot be considered just optional ideas or different ways of looking at things. They are wrong, as wrong as idols. Keep yourselves from them and remain in the truth.

The parting word reminds us that living in the fellowship of God's people is not an automatic thing. If one would keep himself from idols, he must keep himself in the love of God. All that has been said about the reality and joy of life in Christ is true. It is hard to suppose anyone would be careless about it. Yet the advice is timely. For one must be constantly on guard against being caught in a current which takes him from the truth. The lie of the devil is deceptive. The appeal of idols is never to be taken lightly. Far better to keep oneself from them. The tragic truth is that what one abhors he may come to tolerate; and what one tolerates he may at last embrace.[19]

The Second Epistle of
JOHN

Topical Outline of 2 John

The Ages Speak to the Hours

The Lady Is the Church (vv. 1-3)

Her Children Should Love One Another (vv. 4-6)

Don't Lose What You Have Worked For (vv. 7-11)

Face-to-face Talk Is the Best (vv. 12-13)

The Ages Speak to the Hours

The Lady Is the Church

2 John 1-3

> 1 The elder unto the elect lady and her children, whom I love in the truth; and not I only, but also all they that have known the truth;
> 2 For the truth's sake, which dwelleth in us, and shall be with us for ever.
> 3 Grace be with you, mercy, and peace, from God the Father, and from the Lord Jesus Christ, the Son of the Father, in truth and love.

1. This short letter is about the length of one page or sheet of papyrus. The form is somewhat artificial in the sense that it is obviously a general Epistle to the whole Church. The writer calls himself *the elder*. This may be an official title for in the Early Church the office of elder was recognized. It seems more likely that the term is descriptive of this having been either one of the apostles or acquainted with them. Traditionally this letter has been attributed to John the Beloved. The similarities with the content of 1 John and the Gospel make such a designation likely.

The fact that the *lady* in this letter is a title for the Church should please the feminists.[1] So much of the Bible uses the male pronouns and characteristics that modern feminists have protested. They wonder why God must always be described in male terms. It is true that there are female traits ascribed to Him. "As one whom his mother comforteth, so will I comfort you" (Isa. 66:13). But these are few. However, the Church is nearly always given female pronouns and designations (cf. Gal. 4:26; Rev. 21:2, 9). If the elder had been addressing a particular lady he probably would have given her name. The letter itself soon makes it clear that "she" is a church. Her sister would refer to a neighboring congregation, and her children would be the members of the churches.

This interpretation makes his expression of affection a testimony to the depth of the Christian fellowship. *Whom I love in the truth* is beautifully pictured in the hymn "I Love Thy Kingdom, Lord," especially the verse:

> *For her my tears shall fall;*
> *For her my pray'rs ascend;*
> *To her my cares and toils be giv'n*
> *Till toils and cares shall end.*

Such gifts can be given to the church by those who love her. Grace, mercy, and peace come to her from God the Father and the Lord Jesus Christ. They are gifts that He can and will give.

2. It is the power of motherhood to bring forth new life that has made the designation *thy children* meaningful. The language of childbirth has been used to picture the love and pain involved in bringing children into the world. The relationship of mother to children and children to mother all correspond very well to the relationships in the Kingdom. The giving and receiving, the nurture, and dependence of Christian fellowship, are descriptive of the home. The love of a mother for her child and the child for his mother is not different from love in the Church.

3. Thus, one who has known the Kingdom from its beginning writes to the Church out of his years and experience. It was Emerson who suggested that every generation should listen to what the ages have to say to the hours. He said, "The years teach much which the days never know."[2] Out of the teaching of the years the elder now addresses his fellow Christians with advice for the days. It is tempting to feel that each day is a new day and that the truths of yesterday may not now apply. It is true as Lowell wrote:

> *New occasions teach new duties,*
> *Time makes ancient good uncouth.*

Yet there is timelessness to the ways of God in the world that each new day must learn and use.

His letter is motivated by the love of truth. It is truth that surpasses both time and place. It will be, he writes, forever with us. Scenes change and situations differ; but truth does not. The fellowship that Christians have in love and truth transcends the changing times and is anchored in eternity. What made our yesterdays bright has meaning for today and hope for tomorrow. This is what is meant in Heb. 13:7-8. Each new generation should remember their yesterdays and the lives of those who have gone before them. They must take this faith into their todays. Because the purpose of their yesterdays was Jesus Christ, that purpose should remain the same yesterday, today, and tomorrow. It is following a faith in the future with the "outcome of their way of life" (NASB) remaining always the same.

> *Change and decay in all around I see;*
> *O Thou who changest not, abide with me!*[3]

Her Children Should Love One Another

2 John 4-6

> 4 I rejoiced greatly that I found of thy children walking in truth, as we have received a commandment from the Father.
> 5 And now I beseech thee, lady, not as though I wrote a new commandment unto thee, but that which we had from the beginning, that we love one another.
> 6 And this is love, that we walk after his commandments. This is the commandment, That, as ye have heard from the beginning, ye should walk in it.

1. It was a joy to the elder to see that some of the members of the church were walking in the truth. Not all were, to be sure. One could wish that all who named the name of Christ walked with Him, but alas, they do not. With a true pastor's heart the elder finds consolation and hope in the fact that some do. Nothing is said of those things which seem most popular today: the amount of money raised, the statistics of attendance, the abundance of programs. After all, the church's first business is the growth in

the life and grace of its congregation. This is what makes the Church the Church. The great superchurches of our time are encouraging. The atmosphere of success which pervades all they do is most commendable. But what is really vital is how well their children walk in truth. This has more to do with growth than numbers.

2. The advice of the years to the days is to honor the commandment to love one another. It has not been worn out. It is as new as the sunrise each morning. People have not and will not outgrow their need for love. That need is twofold: it is the need to love someone or something and the need to be loved by someone. There are no problems which arise or will arise that cannot be solved if the solutions are made in love. Jesus commanded love of one another because it is vital to the life of the community. He also commanded such love because it is basic to Christian witness. It was the love binding His Body, the Church, together which would enable all men to know that the witness was authentic.

3. Our times demand authenticity. This generation is quick to spot phonies. The emphasis on realism and freedom requires that people be what they say they are. To say that one belongs to Christ demands that His love be seen in his relationships with others. It is Christ's commandment. Not only does our world require it, but also He, our Savior, expects it of us. His name is at stake. He is not ashamed to acknowledge us if we are true in our claim of Him. Jesus suggested that He would confess before God those who confessed Him before men.

To love one another is to fulfill the expectation of a watching world. It is to bring the Christian into obedience to the commandment of His Lord. A third merit of such love is that it places the Christian in conformity with the basic characteristic of the Body of believers through the ages. They have in their best moments been a community of those who love one another. To respond to the plea of the elder is to join the hosts of those who have followed

Christ like a mighty army from His coming to the world as a babe in Bethlehem to the present moment. It will be their way of life until He comes again in power and great glory. The kingdom of Christ is a kingdom of love. And Christians that love one another can joyfully say they are "one of them."[4]

Loving one another is more than the experienced advice of the elder who has walked with Christ for years. It is the earnest plea of one who demonstrates that he does what he asks by the very asking. His heart is wrapped up in what he is asking. He cannot be objective or uninvolved. He loves the Church and her children too much to be casual. He has watched them with love and care so that everyone who walked in truth brought joy to his heart. Now he begs them, whatever they do and whatever comes to them, to live in truth and Christlike love for one another. This is the only way they can keep walking together and arrive where Christ would lead them. This is the only way the fellowship of which he is a member and which he deeply needs can be sustained.

4. One can feel the shadow of approaching trouble in the earnestness of his language as he appeals for love of each other to be enhanced. He does not want to discourage them, and yet he knows he must talk to them about the dangers which are pressing in. So before he ever mentions the dangers, he begs for their obedience to the request of their Lord that they continue in their love of each other no matter what may come. All Christians are aware that the world lies in wickedness (1 John 5:19). They cannot escape this reality. They may be able to change it somewhat by their example and witness. Their strength, however, comes not in their successful stamping out of evil but in their warm, mutual love.

Don't Lose What You Have Worked For

2 John 7-11

7 For many deceivers are entered into the world, who confess not

that Jesus Christ is come in the flesh. This is a deceiver and an anti-christ.

8 Look to yourselves, that we lose not those things which we have wrought, but that we receive a full reward.

9 Whosoever transgresseth, and abideth not in the doctrine of Christ, hath not God. He that abideth in the doctrine of Christ, he hath both the Father and the Son.

10 If there come any unto you, and bring not this doctrine, receive him not into your house, neither bid him God speed:

11 For he that biddeth him God speed is partaker of his evil deeds.

The danger that gave rise to the elder's plea was the existence of antichrists in the world, full, he says, of deceivers who do not confess *that Jesus Christ is come in the flesh.* They do not believe that God has revealed himself in the Lord Jesus. They are against Christ and His teaching. They do not obey His commandments. They endeavor to get Christians to abandon the way of truth and life. If they are listened to and followed, the Christian individual and the Christian community could lose everything it has worked for through the years. All the time and labor would be in vain if the deceivers are successful in beguiling the children of God.

1. In the first place they, the Christians, must look to themselves (v. 8). Of course, he does not mean by this that Christians prevail in their own strength. What he is saying is that there is sufficient power in the love of Christ shed abroad in their hearts by the Holy Ghost to keep them in the truth. There is a power that works in the heart of the believer and in the midst of the Church that is able to do exceedingly abundantly more than all they can ask or think (Eph. 3:20). The Christian is not a pawn in the struggle between good and evil. He is a combatant. He has his part to play and a reward to receive. He must trust as though all depended on God, and work as though all depended on himself.

God is faithful. There is no chance that He will fail. He can be depended upon though everyone and everything else prove false. The only uncertainty is the Christian himself and his resolve. That uncertainty lies not in his ability, for when he is weak, by God's grace he is strong. The uncertainty, if there is any, lies in his will. Jesus said, "He that endureth to the end shall be saved" (Matt. 10:22). Paul encouraged the young Christian, Timothy, to endure hardness as a good soldier (2 Tim. 2:3). James suggests that happiness is the reward for those who endure (Jas. 1:12). The Christian can win against the deceivers if he will. The choice is his.

2. In the second place John warns against getting ahead of the plan of God (v. 9). If the devil cannot get the Christian to give up, he will endeavor to get him to run ahead. Timing is important to God. His plan requires that His people keep step with Him. It is not that God is always to be associated with the old or traditional ways. He is often in the forefront and moves ever forward. But there is reckless progressivism which plays into the hands of the enemy because it does not stay within the commandments of the Lord. The so-called thrust to move forward that is caused by the restlessness of one outside the will of God is really rebellion. God takes His people forward fast enough. It keeps them pushing to keep up. The true forward progress of the Church is in following her Lord, not in irresponsibly running ahead.

There are those who run ahead because they are unwilling to fulfill their task where they are. In Dante's vision of paradise he found angels out in the far reaches of heaven. He asked them if it did not bother them to be so far removed from the throne. They replied, "You don't understand. He placed us here, and in His will is our peace" (*Paradiso*, 3.85). The reward of the Christian is happiness and peace. To keep God's commandments is to walk with Him and with Christ. It will get us to our destination safely and on time. The Christian must walk at His pace, not behind or ahead. He must stay when God says stay and go when He says go. In His will is the Christian's peace.

3. The Christian will not be without suggestions, some of

which will not be good advice. The test of the advice is whether it corresponds with the will of God (vv. 10-11). If it does not, the suggestion should not be entertained. However glamorous or personally rewarding it may appear, it should be quickly put out. All kinds of ideas and suggestions will come to mind. They are not one's until he adopts them. It is not sinful for wrong thoughts to come; it is sinful for one to entertain them. When one welcomes them or wishes them Godspeed, he wills them and becomes partaker of their evil. Wrong actions begin with wrong thoughts in one's mind. If they are not rejected there, one has already begun the process that involves him in the guilt of the deed whether he finally does it or not.

It is true that the elder may have in mind the false prophets and erroneous evangelists that were on the move in his time. The *Pax Romana* had given rise to widespread travel throughout the empire. Because they were not accepted by the ruling powers, the Christian prophets and evangelists stayed in the homes of Christians as they moved from place to place. But there were deceivers who also traveled but did not preach the truth. Men in that category were not to be welcomed. More will be said about this practice in the third letter. Here it is appropriate to see that, whether the visiting errors are people or ideas, the Christian has responsibility to judge whether or not they are true and valid. If they are not, they are to be rejected.

The fearful possibility is that one might lose all he had gained or looked forward to by allowing himself to be host to that which undercuts or opposes his commitment. The hymn writer warned:

> *My soul, be on thy guard;*
> *Ten thousand foes arise;*
> *The hosts of sin are pressing hard*
> *To draw thee from the skies.*[5]

From the vantage point of his long experience the elder can warn, "Be careful who or what you entertain. The battle isn't over. Keep yourself strong. Don't run ahead of God. Test every suggestion or advice by the clear and unchanging commandments of God." These are some things that the ages say to the hours.

Face-to-face Talk Is the Best

2 John 12-13

> 12 Having many things to write unto you, I would not write with paper and ink: but I trust to come unto you, and speak face to face, that our joy may be full.
> 13 The children of thy elect sister greet thee. Amen.

The brief letter is done. The writer knows better than to use up time and paper with needless words. Experience had evidently taught him that one does not have to write a great deal to make a letter meaningful. In fact, he prefers not to put on paper with ink some things that are in his mind to say. They evidently are things which need the response of the other person to accomplish what he desires. He feels that face-to-face talk is the best.

1. The art of good conversation involves good listening as much as good talking. The test is to be found in the understanding and peace of mind that comes from interchange of ideas and feelings. John felt that face-to-face talk could result in their joy being full. There is so much that can be communicated when one can see another's face. Often the eyes are the best communicators of sincerity and feeling. We say to another, "Look me in the eyes and say that!" because we have found that one's eyes can telegraph what is the hidden motivation behind words.

So much is communicated by a look. Words may not be necessary. The facial expressions we use say to another what we really mean. The Psalmist talked about being guided with God's eyes. When Peter had denied his Lord on the night before the Crucifixion, it was not only the crowing of the cock which broke his heart, but also the look that Jesus gave him at that moment. Peter had not realized how close Jesus was. He was struggling to keep himself free and perhaps to sort out in his mind what the arrest of Jesus meant. Peter may have been more truthful than we think when he swore, "I never knew Him." He had not believed that Jesus was the kind of Savior who would save the world by a cross. Whenever Jesus talked about it, Peter argued with Him. At any rate, as he uttered his denial, Jesus turned and looked at him and he at Jesus. No words were said, but Jesus' look broke his heart. That was face-to-face communication.

Sometimes things can sound so cold and dogmatic. One can read words and place in them one's own interpretation so easily that often what is written can convey the very opposite of the writer's meaning. The elder's years had taught him that it is much better to look people in the eye when talking to them. There have been so many assassinations and assassination attempts in recent days that many people have been led to feel that political leaders should remain aloof from the crowds. There is no other way, they say, to guarantee adequate protection for them. But political leaders know that there is no substitute for face-to-face contact. They know the risks but argue that the importance of such contacts makes the risks worth taking.

2. There is also a hint of the wider fellowship when, while talking about the value of face-to-face talk, the elder extends the greeting of other Christians to his readers. The suggestion is that, while talking face-to-face with people, he himself takes on some of their feelings and thoughts. These he will communicate to them and in so doing bind the wider community of believers in one. In a sense in his contacts he becomes a unifier of the Body of Christ. What he receives he passes on. The whole Body is brought closer together. The best strengthener of the unity of faith is the face-to-face talk that illumines and encourages.

In former years the zone rallies which brought together pastor and people of small churches for a day of sharing did as much to build the sense of solidarity and enthusiasm as anything could. The prayer and testimony or class meeting which provided opportunity to look each other in the face as people talked about their experiences in the Christian life did the same thing for those who attended.

The Christians' hope is that the day will come when we shall see Jesus face-to-face. Gospel songs are filled with references to the joy that will be ours who shall see and look upon His face. For face-to-face talk is the best between people and between the disciple and his Lord.

The Third Epistle of
JOHN

Topical Outline of 3 John

Mobile Christianity

Gaius, the Local Christian Host (vv. 1-8)
Diotrephes, a Dog in the Manger (vv. 9-11)
Demetrius, the Missionary (vv. 12-14)

Mobile Christianity

This is a letter to an individual Christian named Gaius. There is no way of knowing for sure who he was or where he lived. It was a fairly common name of the time. Tradition has it that he was the first bishop of Pergamum,[1] but there is no evidence for or against such a suggestion. The elder is taken to be John the Apostle, now in his later years.

1. The letter is particularly interesting for the light it shows on the way the Early Church was advanced. It was written at a time when there was a great deal of travel throughout the Roman Empire. Commerce in material things and ideas was the prime activity of the day. The persecution of the church in Jerusalem plus the commonness of travel both by land and sea around the Mediterranean had resulted in the rapid spread of the gospel. In 300 years Christianity became a world religion and was recognized as the official religion of the Roman state. Those early centuries were years of heroism in the arena and the catacombs. They were also years in which the followers of Jesus, taking His last words seriously, had set out to go to all the world and make disciples of every person. They had experienced His presence in times of danger and discouragement. Not everyone who heard the gospel believed, but always there were some. These new believers banded themselves together for mutual understanding and spiritual development. Churches sprang up everywhere, especially along the well-travelled routes.

Christian evangelists and missionaries were on the move. They stopped in the cities and communities where there were churches. The local Christians took them into their homes. The guests and hosts exchanged ideas and insights and were mutually strengthened. The growth and the unity of the churches were enhanced by this ongoing interchange. But there were problems, too. One difficulty was the "Judaizing Christians" who insisted on obedience to all the law and ritual of Judaism. Paul refers to them as being sent "to spy out our liberty" and suggests they were sent from James and the conservative Jewish Christians in Jerusalem (Gal. 2:4-12).

Another problem was that there were Gnostic brethren who claimed to be "in the know" and separated the spiritual life from the physical in such a way as to encourage immorality. The flesh, they said, could not do anything but evil, so Christians should not try to be pure. They denied that Jesus had a fleshly body, for had He had one, according to their teaching, He could not help but sin. Nevertheless, these Gnostics claimed to be Christians and sought the hospitality of the brothers wherever they went.

2. It was to encourage hospitality to true ministers of the gospel that John wrote all three Epistles. In the first he deals with the error of some teachings and provides tests by which the brothers can discern the truth. In the second he draws upon the experience of the years to reinforce their fidelity to the Christian faith. In the third letter he exhorts the brethren to continue their hospitality to the travelling evangelists for the Kingdom's sake. With all of its problems and risks, John felt mobile Christianity to be the most practical way to fulfill the Lord's command in the Great Commission (Matt. 28:19-20).

3. The letter also demonstrates the very close and personal relationship that such mobility allowed to the greater body of believers. Not only was the bond of Christian love strong between the members of the local church, but it was welded between members everywhere as the travelling emissaries brought word from others. Through the shared

information and love they did become "one great fellowship of love / Throughout the whole wide earth."[2] They shared their needs and concerns. They prayed for and gave to one another as they heard of afflictions and persecution. They all rejoiced in others' victories and awaited with eagerness the news that each traveller brought of the progress of the Kingdom in other places. They were separated by miles but were together in love and faith.

Three illustrations of this process are brought to the reader's attention.

Gaius, the Local Christian Host

3 John 1-8

> 1 The elder unto the well-beloved Gaius, whom I love in the truth.
> 2 Beloved, I wish above all things that thou mayest prosper and be in health, even as thy soul prospereth.
> 3 For I rejoiced greatly, when the brethren came and testified of the truth that is in thee, even as thou walkest in the truth.
> 4 I have no greater joy than to hear that my children walk in truth.
> 5 Beloved, thou doest faithfully whatsoever thou doest to the brethren, and to strangers;
> 6 Which have borne witness of thy charity before the church: whom if thou bring forward on their journey after a godly sort, thou shalt do well:
> 7 Because that for his name's sake they went forth, taking nothing of the Gentiles.
> 8 We therefore ought to receive such, that we might be fellow-helpers to the truth.

1. Gaius, the addressee of the letter, appears to be the layman who had won an enviable reputation among the travellers as an ideal host. Wherever they went, they spoke in high praise of his hospitality. *The elder* greets him with words of good wishes for his prosperity and good health. They are the common words of address but carry this emphasis that the elder knows of his spiritual prosperity and good health. He hopes that his material prosperity and physical well-being may match the spiritual wealth and health he enjoys. The former is nice to have, but the latter is vital. Whether or not one prospers any other way, the well-being of the soul is most important. We sing:

Whatever my lot, Thou hast taught me to say,
"It is well, it is well with my soul."[3]

This is what counts.

Gaius is a joy to the elder because all who meet him and are the guests of his hospitality speak well of him. They say that he has entertained them in truth. The elder lives for the growth of his children in the Lord and so can say that he has no greater joy than to know that the brothers are growing in grace and walking in truth. In a novel about ministering in a local parish, a little girl tells the priest of the parish, "You have a sweet sadness about you that makes me feel when I look at you that I don't want to be wicked anymore." To which the priest replies, "I am sad because people don't love God more than they do!"[4] The elder had the joy of knowing that some do, and their doing is known throughout the fellowship. They become, as Paul describes, living epistles, "known and read of all men" (2 Cor. 3:2).

2. It is a good thing to aid the evangelists and missionaries on their journeys, for that builds the Kingdom. What is done for God should be done generously. Such a way befits doing things for God. Jesus said that what was done for the brethren in His name was done unto Him (cf. Matt. 25:40). They are doing His work. What one would do for Him were He to stop by, one should do for His workman who travels to accomplish His errand at His command. Gaius had the reputation that this was just the way he had assisted the brothers in their travelling ministry.

3. A further reason for this ministry in which Gaius excelled was the commitment of the travellers. The brethren had set out on their mission determined not to take anything from the heathen. They were going in God's name, and they would not be beholden to any man. They were not preaching for money. To receive from the heathen, they felt, would be to compromise their message and integrity. By supporting them, the local Christian became

a partner in the ministry. All cannot go, but all can have a part in the work by supporting in a material way the one who goes. The missionary is not to be seen as seeking to obtain from those to whom he speaks. Instead he speaks for Christ by means of the help that other members of the Body of Christ supply.

4. The concept of *fellowhelpers to the truth* opens the door for all who would to share in advancing the Kingdom. It is not just a responsibility of the clergy. It is the task of the whole Body of Christ to give His message to the world. All can share in the task, and all will share in the reward. Some invest time and talent, while others invest prayer and support; some go to distant places, while others are their hosts on the journey. All are fellow helpers to the truth.

Missionaries are not involved in a partisan operation. They are not out to build an organization or secure their place in one. They are souls that have been brought to the truth. The world lies in sin and error. The truth was made flesh and dwelt among men in Jesus Christ. All who believe on His name are illumined with truth through the Holy Spirit. It is for the truth's sake that they go abroad. It is for the truth's sake that all have opportunity to help them along the way.

As he would want, Gaius, the fellow helper, disappears in the larger picture of the Church on the move. Who he was and what were the specific things he did to speed the missionaries on their journeys is not told. Nor would he wish them to be. He did not do it for recognition, although it did come to him. What he did was for the truth's sake, and that is what mattered most. The work went on; men heard the truth. That was his purpose.

Diotrephes, a Dog in the Manger

3 John 9-11

> 9 I wrote unto the church: but Diotrephes, who loveth to have the preeminence among them, receiveth us not.
> 10 Wherefore, if I come, I will remember his deeds which he doeth,

prating against us with malicious words: and not content therewith, neither doth he himself receive the brethren, and forbiddeth them that would, and casteth them out of the church.

11 Beloved, follow not that which is evil, but that which is good. He that doeth good is of God: but he that doeth evil hath not seen God.

1. Abruptly the elder turns to another figure in the process. By his definition Diotrephes was an evil man. For the elder writes Gaius that *he that doeth good is of God: but he that doeth evil hath not seen God.* For all his pretensions Diotrephes did evil. He was a member of the church, but if he ever had known God, he had long since left off following Him. He appears, however, to have established himself in some place of authority. For although the elder had written to the church, this man blocked any reception by the church of the elder's message. Not only that, but he refused to allow anyone to receive the brethren. If any did, he cast them out of the church. He fits the description of the proverbial dog in the manger. According to the fable, the dog who would not eat hay himself lay in the manger and would not allow an ox to eat it either.

Whatever reason Diotrephes might have had for this behavior, he becomes an illustration of people who will not do right and will not allow others to do so either. The letter suggests that it was because he loved *to have the preeminence.* He had an ego problem. He wanted to be the one who decided who was received and who was not. Amos Wilder suggests that Diotrephes represents an attempted shift in the control of local churches to a more autonomous one.[5] He would not acknowledge the elder's authority. Wilder also suggests that Diotrephes may have taken a different stand in regard to the Gnostic than the elder and so prated against him. Even if this is true, and there were honest ecclesiastical or doctrinal differences between them, Diotrephes stands condemned in his refusal to permit other members to make up their own minds. He stands condemned for wanting to put himself first rather than the cause of Christ. He stands condemned for attacking the elder's authority with *malicious words.*

There is room for differing opinions within the Kingdom, but there is no room for partisan bickering.

2. There are purists who will wonder how such a man ever got into the Church and how he stayed in it. It is very possible that he was at one time a sincere Christian. For there are born-again people who turn back to the world of sin from which they were saved when they accepted the Savior. If this is not true, then much of the exhortation of John is wasted words. He spends a lot of words exhorting Christians to remain true and not to be deceived. The letters he wrote all discuss the strong pressure of erroneous teachers upon the Body of Christ. He warned, "Even now are there many antichrists" (1 John 2:18).

The Church has always suffered more from within than without. In the Revelation of John the presence of members that were not following the truth in several of the churches of Asia is deplored. In numerous parables and teachings Jesus warned that such would be true. In the parable of the wheat and the tares He says they should not be separated until the harvest. "Let both grow together," He advises, "lest while ye gather up the tares, ye root up also the wheat with them" (Matt. 13:29-30). So it should not be surprising to read that such was happening.

3. Whether he will be allowed to stay does not seem to be the purpose of the letter. Incidental, too, is the promise of the elder to face him if and when he comes. Jesus had given the disciples a formula for handling such a problem in the church. He said the obstructionist should be faced on a personal basis first. If that fails, two or three are to confront him. If he still resists reconciliation, then he can be expelled by the church (Matt. 18:15-20). The harvest can be seen as the full judgment of the Body of Christ. He promised that what they decided as a body, heaven would stand by. The process has been used through the centuries, not always successfully, but at least in the attempt to keep the church united if possible.

If anyone objects to Diotrephes' being referred to as a dog, he should read again Rev. 22:15 and remember that the elder said "He that doeth evil has not seen God."

Demetrius, the Missionary

3 John 12-14

> 12 Demetrius hath good report of all men, and of the truth itself:' yea, and we also bear record; and ye know that our record is true.
> 13 I had many things to write, but I will not with ink and pen write unto thee:
> 14 But I trust I shall shortly see thee, and we shall speak face to face. Peace be to thee. Our friends salute thee. Greet the friends by name.

1. The reason for the words of commendation for Demetrius is not apparent. It may be that he is the messenger who brought the letter. It was common to mention and commend the messenger who carried the letter in these times. Or it may be that he is a missionary who brings the letter as he stops on his journey to his assignment. Amos Wilder suggests that he may have been the one whom Diotrephes had assailed and refused hospitality.[6] The abrupt mention of him while he was denouncing Diotrephes could indicate that this is the case. If all three of these possibilities are put together, it would indicate that he had been rebuffed by Diotrephes and perhaps taken in by a member who was later cast out for doing so. Now the elder sends him to Gaius with the letter and promises that he will deal with Diotrephes in a face-to-face encounter.

2. As in 2 John, the elder prefers face-to-face talk to long letters. He had spoken his mind fully. He did not want to put it in writing. He would bring the greeting of the friends when he came, which he hoped would be soon. The phrase *Greet the friends by name* indicates how close were the personal ties among the Christians, though separated by miles. As was previously mentioned, this seems to be one of the benefits of a mobile situation. It was also the strongest weapon against such as Diotrephes. The fellowship of

believers was united in Christ. They also were bound by the ties of Christian love and personal friendship.

3. The credentials of Demetrius which the elder lists could well constitute the characteristics required of a missionary or minister. First, he is commended of everyone who knew him. The messenger of truth must enjoy the full confidence of all who know his life. Second, he is commended of the truth itself. He has the clear inner witness that he is Christ's and that Christ has called him to this ministry. It is not enough to see the need and be moved by it, though this is important in being a fellow helper. But it is vital that the missionary or minister have the inner confirmation of the Spirit.

In Antioch the church leaders were directed to separate Paul and Barnabas to the work whereunto the Spirit had called them (Acts 13:2). The Holy Spirit calls; the Church under His direction recognizes the call. So the third credential Demetrius had was that he was commended of the elder. In modern terms the candidate is officially recommended by the local congregation, testifies to the call of God, and is ordained to the task by church leaders.

4. So in this short letter, by looking at a host, a recalcitrant, a participant, and an elder, the reader is given a picture of mobile Christianity as it began its second century. The years and the centuries have passed since then, but the basic elements of the structure of the Church remain. It is as though our names are among the friends the writer greets, and we acknowledge it and return the greeting in the name of Him who loved us and has washed us from our sins in His own blood, our Savior and Lord, Jesus Christ.

The Epistle of
JUDE

Topical Outline of Jude

The Community of Faith (vv. 1-2)
>   General Greeting (v. 1)
>   General Blessing (v. 2)

The Priority of the Faith (vv. 3-4)
>   The Faith Once Delivered (v. 3)
>   Ungodly Underminers of the Faith (v. 4)

The Despoilers of the Faith (vv. 5-16)
>   Fallen from First Faith (vv. 5-7)
>   Defilers, Despisers, and Degraders (vv. 8-10)
>   Three Frightful Examples (v. 11)
>   Five Pictures of Apostasy (vv. 12-13)
>   The Voice of Enoch (vv. 14-16)

The Holy Faith and Holy Living (vv. 17-23)
>   Mockers of the Faith (vv. 17-19)
>   Building on the Faith (vv. 20-23)

The Author and Finisher of Our Faith (vv. 24-25)
>   Blessed Benediction (vv. 24-25)

A Surprising Book

1. Elmer Homrighausen calls the general Epistle of Jude "a surprising book."[1] It is one of several such books in the Bible. For example, Esther mentions neither God nor prayer. The word we could associate with prayer in the Book of Esther is "fasting." He also points out that Ecclesiastes is the philosophy of a cynic who "finally affirms that the fear of God and moral integrity are the highest obligations of life." The Book of Revelation is filled with imagery and symbolism that is confusing to many who try to understand its message. It is viewed by some as written in cryptic language which would bewilder a pagan while giving comfort to a beleaguered Christian.

Homrighausen quotes Frederic Farrar's evaluation of the document: "The Epistle of Jude certainly presents more surprising phenomena than any other book of the New Testament. In style it is original and picturesque. In tone it is intense, vehement, denunciative. In its point of view, it is Judeo-Christian. In its structure it is Aramaic, abounding in triple arrangement."[2]

It is very close to 2 Peter, chapters 2 and 3. Judge's use of some of Peter's words might indicate that the latter's Epistle had wide circulation in the Early Church. It is far enough removed from the time of the apostles as to contain a deep respect for them as heroes of the past and the foundation upon which the Church had been built and must be maintained.

2. It is surprising in its quotations from two works which the Church refused to accept as a part of the canon of the Scripture: The Book of Enoch and the Assumption of Moses. Jude uses these books as though they had equal

inspiration with the accepted books of the Bible. He refers to events contained in them as facts such as the dispute of Michael with the devil over the body of Moses. While Genesis 6 refers to the mating of The Sons of God with the daughters of men as the explanation for giants, Jude accepts the account in the Book of Enoch which pictures it as the result of the angels' fall. He says they abandoned their assigned estate and became involved in immoral relations with humans.

3. The Epistle of Jude does not spell out either the basic premises of "the faith which was once delivered unto the saints" or the specific heresies of the interlopers who threatened the moral and spiritual purity of the Church. Jude assumes these are known to the reader, and rather than expound them he exhorts for the faith to be kept and the inevitable fate of the heretics to be remembered.

It is surprising in the measure of the inroads into the community of faith by the apostates that it reveals. It reminds one of the surprise Paul expressed that the Galatians had strayed so soon from sound doctrine and from the freedom they had received in Christ Jesus. The intensity of the attack makes clear how deep-seated and dangerous Jude felt the threat to be. Sometimes we are given to fantasizing that the Early Church in its Pentecostal power was a paragon of spiritual life and truth. The Book of Jude probably as much as, if not more than, any other book shows how quickly error can creep in "secretly." It presents one of the strongest refutations of the so-called doctrine of the eternal security of the believer. For it exhorts the reader to remember that the believer's security is not in the antinomian claim that God cannot go back on His word but rather in the responsibility of the believer to live a holy life and keep himself in the love of God.

4. The Epistle leaves no place for the idea that the grace of God will excuse sin in the believer's life. There is no place in the kingdom of God for "sinning Christians." God

is able to keep His children from falling, not by overlooking sin but by presenting them without blemish before the penetrating presence of His glory. The consciousness that one has been made victor is the true basis for exceeding joy. It is the joy that the Christian is what he claims to be through the power of God, "the only wise God our Saviour."

＊

The Community of Faith
Jude 1-2

General Greeting

Jude 1

> 1 Jude, the servant of Jesus Christ, and brother of James, to them that are sanctified by God the Father, and preserved in Jesus Christ, and called.

1. The letter is addressed to the company of believers which is called the community of faith. It is a general letter which includes in its greetings the whole family of Christ's followers. It is written by a person who prefers to describe himself as a *servant of Jesus Christ*. In this he is true to the definition of Christianity given by Jesus himself, who said that He came not to be served but to serve. Jesus often told His disciples that in the Kingdom He had come to set up, greatness consisted of service and ministry to others.

The word Jude uses is really "slave." He belonged to Christ.[3] But it was in no fashion compulsory. He did not follow his Master in chains except in the bonds of love. He served Christ because he wanted to do so. He had no other desire; he wanted no place of authority or fame; he wanted only to be known as a servant of Jesus. He calls himself a brother of James. Presumably he is referring to James, the brother of Jesus, who headed the Early Church in Jerusalem. If that is the one, then Jude also was a brother of Jesus. Yet he does not claim it or hint of it. If he is a brother of the Lord, that is forgotten in his lifelong commitment to be the slave of Jesus.

This is important as his letter is read, for he is strong in his exhortation and denunciations. He does not want his motive misconstrued. What he says is motivated by his love for Christ and Christ's Body, the Church. He wants most to serve his Lord and remembers that Jesus said, "Inasmuch as ye have done it unto one of the least of these my brethren, ye have done it unto me" (Matt. 25:40). By giving himself, he not only serves the community of faith but also identifies himself as an integral part of it. He is not standing aloof and broadcasting advice as an unattached observer. He is involved. For the community of faith is made up of those who have one all-consuming motivation, and that is to serve Jesus, their Lord and Master.

2. Jude expresses this involvement when he says that he had eagerly planned to write them about their "common salvation"; he addresses them as "beloved" (v. 3). For though he was writing to all Christians, he was one with them in the bond of love. They shared a common calling. The people of God are those who respond to what Whittier speaks of as "the gracious calling of the Lord."[4] Jude defines the community of faith as the *called*.

a. They have been *called out*. Paul reminded the Corinthians that they were called out of uncleanness. "Wherefore come out from among them, and be ye separate, saith the Lord, and touch not the unclean thing; and I will receive you" (2 Cor. 6:17). Peter tells the new converts, "Ye should shew forth the praises of him who hath called you out of darkness into his marvellous light" (1 Pet. 2:9). The hymn writer penned,

Called from the world and its idols to flee,
Called from the bondage of sin to be free.[5]

The Christian must live in the world and not be of it. The charter of his salvation is a call to leave sin and evil. He cannot allow himself to compromise at any point with wrongdoing, for he has been called out from all of it. He must have no taint of sin. As God is holy, He calls His people to be holy.

b. They have been *called together.* Paul addresses the Christians in Corinth as those who are "called to be saints, with all that in every place call upon the name of Jesus Christ our Lord, both their's and our's" (1 Cor. 1:2). And again, "Ye were called unto the fellowship of [God's] Son Jesus Christ our Lord" (1 Cor. 1:9). The community of faith is a fellowship of saints called together to be the family of God through Jesus Christ, their Elder Brother. That togetherness is stronger than any other human relationship. Jesus' call seems harsh when He says that His followers must leave father and mother and family. But it is really a call to a higher and eternal relationship. Paul felt very close to those he called "his kinsmen after the flesh," but he tells the saints at Philippi that he gave up everything "for the prize of the high calling of God in Christ Jesus" (Phil. 3:7, 14). This high calling is to the oneness of the community of those who believe. The hymn affirms, "The fellowship of kindred minds is like to that above."[6]

c. They are *called forth.* They are called from what they are to what they should become. Jesus said of the repentant Zacchaeus that he was a child of Abraham. Abraham is the father of the faithful, and to be his son is to be a person of faith. But he is also the father of those who obey the call of God to go forth to a place they do not know. They are pilgrims who look for "a city which hath foundations" (Heb. 11:10). The community of faith is a caravan on its way to a place God has prepared and called them to journey toward. They are a family on the move, blazing new trails, climbing new heights, seeing new vistas, and learning new truths. They walk with God.

3. These to whom Jude writes not only share a common calling; they share a common *love.* Jude identifies the community of faith as the "beloved" of God (vv. 3, 17, 20). The writer of Hebrews says of the "called forth" that God is not ashamed to be called their God (11:16). Frequently the Christians are referred to in the New Testament as those who are loved by God. God so loved the world that He sent His Son. This is His redeeming love. But those who respond to this love come into a new relationship with Him. They are loved as His children. This is His giving love.

In one of his most moving benedictions Paul prays that his readers may experience afresh "the grace of the Lord Jesus Christ, and the love of God, and the communion of the Holy Ghost" (2 Cor. 13:14). This love is full and free. It does not come to us because we love Him. We love God because He first loved us. It is His love for us that draws from us our love for Him. If one wants to love God more, he need only open his heart more to the love of God for him.

The community of faith is a fellowship of love. It is composed of people who love because they are loved. John, the apostle of love, wrote that if God so loved them, they ought to love the brethren. They receive God's love, and in turn they reach out in love for each other. Jesus said this would evidence to the world that they were His disciples. "By this shall all men know that ye are my disciples, if ye have love one to another" (John 13:35). So Jude is in the stream of Christian thought when he addresses the saints as "beloved."

4. The community of faith is also *kept.* Called, beloved, and kept by God.[7] They have their assignment, they are bonded together by love, and they are kept by the power of God. This becomes even more significant when Jude exposes the threats to the faith that he has come to know.

This fact of constant threat has always been the lot of the people of God. Jesus said that His disciples were hated by the world. He warned them that they would face persecution and death for His name's sake. Paul reminded the Ephesians they wrestled against the powers of evil (6:12). The story of the Book of the Revelation is one of conflict against evil and the men who give themselves to it. The hymn advises:

> My soul, be on thy guard;
> Ten thousand foes arise;
> The hosts of sin are pressing hard
> To draw thee from the skies.[8]

In many ways that they know, and in more that they do not know, God keeps and preserves His people. They are in His hand, and no man can pluck them out. He keeps watch upon His own. In His high priestly prayer Jesus prayed, "Holy Father, keep through thine own name those whom thou hast given me, that they may be one, as we are" (John 17:11). Jude says this prayer is being answered. The called and beloved ones are being kept. They are kept for Jesus Christ, for His name's sake.

General Blessing

Jude 2

2   Mercy unto you, and peace, and love, be multiplied.

With these great benefits listed they still have needs. Jude's greetings include the prayer that they may receive *mercy, . . . peace, and love.* In one form or another these qualities are invoked in many benedictions of Paul.

1. Usually Paul uses the word "grace" instead of *mercy.* But it is more a matter of semantics than doctrinal difference. Shakespeare has Portia say:

> *The quality of mercy is not strained,*
> *It droppeth as the gentle rain from heaven*

Upon the place beneath: it is twice blessed;
It blesseth him that gives and him that takes.[9]

It is through the mercy of God that we are saved. It is through the mercy of God that we are kept. It is through the mercy of God that we shall live with Christ forever. We need His mercy each moment of each day.

2. *Peace* is the gracious gift of Christ to His disciples. He said, "Peace I leave with you, my peace I give unto you: not as the world giveth, give I unto you. Let not your heart be troubled, neither let it be afraid" (John 14:27). This peace is an inner serenity so deep that no power can reach it to destroy it. It is the assurance that one is in God's care and approval. It is also a quality of togetherness that exists in the Body of Christ. The writer of Hebrews attached it to holy living and exhorted the community of faith to "follow peace with all men, and holiness, without which no man shall see the Lord" (Heb. 12:14). When Jesus greeted the disciples on the first Easter evening, He twice said, "Peace be unto you" (John 20:19, 21). The context makes it clear that He referred to both their inner heart feeling and their life together. Peace is not a reasoned evaluation of one's state, for Paul calls it "the peace of God, which passeth all understanding" (Phil. 4:7). It is the gift of God through Christ.

3. This peace flows to the community of faith because of God's *love*. The more one accepts of the love of God, the deeper and more lasting is His peace. His love for His children makes His commandments to be a joy to obey. Obedience to His will makes the sense of His presence real and strong. Someone has put it, "I am indestructible as long as I am in the will of God." There is peace in that safety. It exists because the love of God is shed abroad in one's heart by the Holy Ghost (Rom. 5:5).

But realizing the needs of the community of faith, Jude prays these qualities of mercy, love, and peace will be multiplied. He asks that they may come in ever increasing numbers. If one gets the idea that as he matures in the Christian walk he will need them less, he is mistaken. Each day, each month, each year, he will need more and more. But the supply is not limited. God can multiply them to His children with no possibility of exhausting His store. Our needs are the opportunities of our greater blessings.

The Priority of the Faith
Jude 3-4

The Faith Once Delivered

Jude 3

> 3 Beloved, when I gave all diligence to write unto you of the common salvation, it was needful for me to write unto you, and exhort you that ye should earnestly contend for the faith which was once delivered unto the saints.

Before he delivers his soul about the danger threatening the community of faith, Jude tells them he had intended to write on a wholly different subject. Anyone who tries to speak for God knows the weight of the truth he is about to discuss. There is an excitement about voicing His message. So Jude confided that he was eager to write about the things that were believed in common about the salvation they had experienced in Christ. One can imagine he approached the task with thoroughness and zeal. In fact, the message he did deliver is couched in such words of power and vehemence that one could anticipate with what clarity and emotion he would have outlined his theology. Perhaps the Church is the poorer for not having received it. But there were overriding circumstances.

1. He abandoned the project, he says, when he found it more needful to exhort them to *earnestly contend for the faith which was once delivered unto the saints.* Anyone

who has spoken for God knows this as well. One can prepare to deliver a sermon and find excitement and conviction in it, only to come to the moment beset by the deeper conviction that God would have him speak on a different theme for a different purpose. As eager as Jude was to go over with them the essential elements in their common salvation, he found that for the moment at least it was far more important to stand up for it than to explain or expound it. There are times when it is more important to proclaim than to propound.

Sermons should speak to life's situations. There are many things that are true and worthwhile that must await a proper time for their discussion. When one speaks for God, He must speak to situations that are confronting the hearers. Jude had found that the faith was being so strongly challenged that the time had come for its defense rather than its description. The faith, in the sense that it is the body of thought, is susceptible to question and exploration. But it is not to be at the mercy of the unbeliever. It cannot be twisted to the whimsy or lust of those who rationalize. Its reality is in the realm of belief. It is based on the premise that God is true even if "every man [is] a liar" (Rom. 3:4). It is believing what God has said. He is the Author of truth and the Initiator of faith.

2. The truths of God have been revealed by Him. They come to men from Him, and they are called *the faith* because men believe them whether they can prove them true or not. They rest on the basis that one believes God and, therefore, what He has said. This is not to say that they cannot be proved but rather that they are believed because of who said them. Faith always acts in the presence of doubt. Doubt is not a shadow on faith. It only displays the limitation of man's knowledge or insight. What one does not see he believes, because it came from God. If it were irrefutably proven, faith would not be necessary.

The faith was once delivered, not because God is static but because it was true. Man must grow and develop. Faith stands as a dependable guide sent from his Heavenly Father to direct his advance along the right way. It may be hard to explain because now one sees through a glass darkly, but his faith keeps him pointed toward the right though every circumstance seems to deny its validity. Thus God gets him home safely and on time.

3. So Jude abandons his treatise for an exhortation. The emergency of the intrusion by false brethren required it. Sometimes the finest things we say and do are those demanded by the moments and not really planned. Then when we find the situation so altered that all we were going to say and do is out of place, we have to quickly shift gears and confront the needs glaring at us. We wish we had known what we were getting into. Had we known, we would have been so much more prepared. Or would we?

Jesus advises that we need not rehearse what we are to speak, for it will be given us in that moment what we should say. That certainly happened to Jude in this incident. Jesus did not mean that it is wrong to plan. Rather, He was explaining that it is wrong not to shift gears when circumstances change or greater priorities confront us. When men hold to the faith, it is good to explore it. But when they deny the faith, it must be defended.

F. W. Boreham has a delightful series of messages entitled *A Gust of Afterthought*.[10] They are based on the fact that often the most memorable thing someone says is not in the body of his discourse but in the afterthought. The party to the conversation has turned away to leave when one says, "Oh, by the way." And then it happens that the best word is spoken. Jesus tells a story of a man robbed and beaten who was left for dead along the roadside. It just happened that a Samaritan, who turned out to be a true neighbor, came by, and a man who would have died lived and recovered. The Samaritan had not planned to help someone that day. He was on his way to other business. But he became the hero of Jesus' story and the messenger of life to a dying man because he had priorities.

He was willing to set aside his planned activity for the immediate need he confronted. He stands out in great contrast to both a priest and a Levite who evidently had no such priorities. They were slaves to what they had set out to do, and were it not for the Samaritan who came later, the robbed man would have died.

4. Moses might not have been a part of the history of God's deliverance of His people had he not been willing to turn aside from his business of the day to investigate a bush that burned but was not consumed. More important to him that day on Horeb was the way of God than the keeping of sheep. He felt that the burning bush was a call from God, and that had priority. How much better off we all would be if we would count the interruptions of life in this category. If one listens to the testimony of Christians, frequently he hears the sentence, "I had no idea when I started it would turn out like this." Or, "It was totally unexpected. I had something altogether different in mind for the day when . . ."

Of course, one can chase after fantasies. One can turn down byways and be lost. The important thing is to have priorities as obviously Jude had. To him the faith once delivered unto the saints was vital. No matter what else might be planned, this was most important to him. So that whenever or wherever it was threatened, he would drop everything else and contend for it. The gift which God had given to the saints carried for him a high responsibility and worth. Its challenge could not be left unanswered. Like a volunteer fireman in a small community when the alarm sounds, it does not matter what he is doing; he drops it and rushes to battle the flames.

Ungodly Underminers of the Faith

Jude 4

> 4 For there are certain men crept in unawares, who were before of old ordained to this condemnation, ungodly men, turning the grace of our God into lasciviousness, and denying the only Lord God, and our Lord Jesus Christ.

Under the guise of accepting the faith, certain men had crept into the community of faith only to undermine it. They were under the condemnation of God but acted as though they had His approval. They divorced morality from belief. They denied the Lordship of Christ. It would be foolish to waste time explaining doctrine to such men. They had closed minds and lived for pleasure only. They had lifted to the highest priority the lust of the flesh and denied discipline. The gospel for them was that they could be God's and live as they pleased. They argued that the body was evil and could not be changed. They opted for a "faith" which made them acceptable in God's sight apart from what they did in the body. Their hearts were right with God, they said, and what their bodies did could not matter to Him.

Such a challenge to the true faith could not go unanswered. The community of saints have had the faith delivered to them once and for all. They are to keep it in the highest priority. It matters what a person believes and how he lives. His life must exemplify his doctrine. The God who delivered the faith to His people holds them responsible, The apostle Peter uses the phrase "stewards of the manifold grace of God" (1 Pet. 4:10). The faith is not the work of men; it was given by God. Everything else must be put aside, for if the faith is distorted, all is gone.

The Despoilers of the Faith
Jude 5-16

Jude now turns to identify the ungodly men who have been marked for condemnation. Their judgment is more than predestination. It is the fundamental attitude of God against those who knowingly defy His authority. God is a

God of love and mercy, but He is also a God of wrath against those who prove themselves incorrigible. A part of the faith once delivered to the saints is the revelation of God's punishment of sinful persons. While there is "a kindness in His justice / Which is more than liberty," it does not cloud His fidelity nor open the door for licentiousness. God has not only determined that despoilers of the faith will be punished but has also demonstrated this in His relations with them. For all who will it is clear to see.

Fallen from First Faith

Jude 5-7

> 5 I will therefore put you in remembrance, though ye once knew this, how that the Lord, having saved the people out of the land of Egypt, afterward destroyed them that believed not.
> 6 And the angels which kept not their first estate, but left their own habitation, he hath reserved in everlasting chains under darkness unto the judgment of the great day.
> 7 Even as Sodom and Gomorrha, and the cities about them in like manner, giving themselves over to fornication, and going after strange flesh, are set forth for an example, suffering the vengeance of eternal fire.

1. The story of the deliverance of the people from slavery in Egypt under the leadership of Moses contains the record of death and destruction of those who refused to believe and obey God's word. He brought them out of slavery but allowed them to die in the wilderness when they would not go into the land at Kadesh-barnea. To be the recipient of the grace of God is not to be kept from punishment if one refuses to obey the Word or follow the guidance of God. It is easy to think that because one has been forgiven and accepted into the family of God, he is free from the danger of falling. But the record is against such an illusion. God by a miraculous hand and powerful acts brought His people out of the bonds of slavery. They were trophies of His love and care. He fed them and guided them. But disobedience and immorality meant destruction for all of them who participated. This is His way. He did it before; He will do it again.

2. From other sources Jude fills in the suggestions of Genesis 6 and declares that, because the angels left their heavenly abode and became immoral with the women of earth, they were not to marry. Jesus alludes to this when asked about the continuance of the married relationship in the after life. Their estate was to be the high heavens. Their assignment was to be "watchers and holy ones" (cf. Dan. 4:13). Even with this high and holy responsibility they were not immune from temptation, nor from punishment when they succumbed to it. If God would not allow this excursion into lust and sin on the part of the angels but doomed them to *everlasting chains under darkness,* should anyone imagine that He will overlook similar behavior in men?

3. A third illustration that God will not overlook disobedience and immorality is the record of Sodom and Gomorrah. They had become open and brazen in their homosexuality. God destroyed the cities with burning sulfur and the people with everlasting fire. In the memory of man as long as the world lasts, the names of Sodom and Gomorrah will be the symbols of behavior that God will not countenance. When Jesus wanted to emphasize the depth of woe He felt for some cities in His times, He said that if the mighty works that had been done in them had been done in Sodom, it would have repented (cf. Matt. 11:23-24). It is probably an exaggeration to portray how hardened the inhabitants of the cities had become in Jesus' day that they had even gone beyond the point at which Sodom and Gomorrah would have stopped. The point he makes is that God has a rendevous with immoral people under whatever guise they may operate. The rather bold attempt made in current times to make immorality acceptable under the banner of freedom cannot expect any better fate. When man's surrender to lust becomes too complete, God will act. Jude says such a destiny awaited the men who had crept into the community of faith in his time and for all men of all time.

Defilers, Despisers, and Degraders

Jude 8-10

> 8 Likewise also these filthy dreamers defile the flesh, despise dominion, and speak evil of dignities.
> 9 Yet Michael the archangel, when contending with the devil he disputed about the body of Moses, durst not bring against him a railing accusation, but said, The Lord rebuke thee.
> 10 But these speak evil of those things which they know not: but what they know naturally, as brute beasts, in those things they corrupt themselves.

The despoilers of the faith *defile the flesh*, reject authority, and revile the glorious ones. They make the most sacred gathering of the people of God an occasion of boldly carousing together, and thus like the men of Sodom they make mockery of those who seek to follow Christ. Jude seeks to be factual in his accusations but refrains from usurping the prerogatives of God by condemning them. He refers to a story told in the Assumption of Moses. It seems that at Moses' death the devil claimed that in killing the Egyptian, Moses was guilty of murder, and so he had a right to Moses' body. The devil further claimed that he was the lord of the material order, and since Moses' body was material, it belonged to him. This claim the archangel Michael denied by insisting that God who created the material world is Lord of it. Yet in the argument Jude says Michael did not disrespect the devil's existence as a supernatural being and left him to God. *The Lord rebuke thee* is the word Michael used to assert the Lordship of God. He is the Judge, and vengeance belongs to Him.

The despoilers of the faith are not that understanding. They speak of things they do not know. They are given more to speaking from instinct like a brute rather than from reason like a man. Their very lack of reasoning leads them to be destroyed by their own actions which spring from instinct. Their actions which they claim to be right bring them to the very destruction they seek to avoid. They are in Jesus' word "blind leaders of the blind" (Matt. 15:14).

Three Frightful Examples

Jude 11

> 11 Woe unto them! for they have gone in the way of Cain, and ran greedily after the error of Balaam for reward, and perished in the gainsaying of Core.

In order to prove the validity of the accusation and illustrate the scope of it, Jude draws upon three names and events with which they are associated. The three seem to spell out an anatomy of rebellion. There is the way of Cain, the error of Balaam, and the rebellion of Korah.

1. Cain killed his brother Abel. John tells us it was because his works were evil. God told Cain that it was because sin had trapped him. Throughout the Bible Cain has been a symbol of lust and self-indulgence. He hated his brother because he was a righteous man. Cain's way was to follow his desires no matter what stood in the way. His descendants were people of great ability but godless. To live undisciplined lives seemed to pay off in achievement but resulted in arrogance and self-sufficiency. The way of Cain is one which will admit no guilt and seeks only satisfaction of its desires. Cain would not let a good man live, but he populated the world with his children who wandered freely and prostituted their God-given abilities to the satisfaction of base appetite.

2. The error of Balaam was a more sophisticated one. For the sake of money he taught Israel to sin. He had been hired to curse Israel but was unable to do so. Every time he tried, the curse became a blessing. But in the end the blessing became a curse when Israel turned to sin with the daughters of Moab (Num. 25:1). How Balaam did it is not told. Moses says of the women of Moab, "These caused the children of Israel, through the counsel of Balaam, to commit trespass against the Lord in the matter of Peor, and there was a plague among the congregation of the Lord" (Num. 31:16). Jude sees Balaam's error as being headstrong. What God would not permit him to do one

way he sought to do another. The despoilers of the faith, like Balaam, ran greedily after reward. They propagated a way to get around the restrictions. In the Book of Revelation the error of Balaam is described as a gross evil, along with the doctrine of the Nicolaitans (2:14-15). It is putting a stumbling block before people which will lead them to sin. It is making them believe that what is wrong is permissible. When one travels the way of Cain, of self-indulgence, he soon runs greedily after the error of Balaam for reward.

3. The third figure Jude draws on for illustration is Korah. He led a group of people to challenge the leadership of Moses and Aaron, charging them with taking too much to themselves in claiming to speak for God. Korah and his crew of 250 contended that all of God's people should have an equal voice in the direction of the congregation. Their argument has much to commend itself, but it was rebellion masked in the plea for democracy. What they used for their premise is the basic principle of the priesthood of all believers. This was not wrong. What was wrong was to use this argument to push their selfish aims. They really were wanting the rulership. They campaigned for equal rights in order to advance their own lust for power!

Korah and his followers fell into the trap of their own making. Moses had all the 250 leaders bring censers with fire in them and incense to appear before the Lord. Moses then ordered the people to separate themselves from Korah and his followers, and when they did, the earth opened and swallowed the rebels (cf. Numbers 16). So it will be with these men, said Jude. They have followed Korah's pattern of rebellion, and they follow him in death. Rebellion begins in self-interest. It moves to error for reward and perishes in the pitfall of its own making.

Five Pictures of Apostasy

Jude 12-13

12 These are spots in your feasts of charity, when they feast with you,

> feeding themselves without fear: clouds they are without water, car-
> ried about of winds; trees whose fruit withereth, without fruit, twice
> dead, plucked up by the roots;
> 13 Raging waves of the sea, foaming out their own shame; wander-
> ing stars, to whom is reserved the blackness of darkness for ever.

The writer then turns to give five metaphors to picture the tragedy of allowing oneself to become involved in this kind of rebellion.

1. The first is *blemishes on the love feast.* The fellowship of Christians has long been celebrated in love feasts. Eating together in joy was a characteristic of the New Testament Church (Acts 2:46). It was especially noted for singleness and gladness of heart. Jesus had laid down as a universally recognized trait of Christians that they love one another. The point of the love feast is not what is eaten, however, but that Christ's followers eat together in love and joy. Selfishness and self-indulgence are glaring spots on any picture of oneness the love feast purports to show. Paul wrote to the Corinthians deploring the gluttony, greed, and drunkenness which took place when sinful self-centeredness crept into the love feast (1 Cor. 11:20-22). Immoral perversions and overindulgence are the outcome of wrong motives in hearts that are unsurrendered to Christ. What should proclaim the love of Christ—the way in which His followers treat each other—these despoilers of the faith had blemished with a display of their brazen disregard for anyone but themselves.

2. The second metaphor Jude uses is *waterless clouds.* They sweep along propelled by the winds. They promise rain to the parched earth but have no water. The drought-stricken watch them in hope only to be left drier than before. They raise hopes but dash them to the ground as they sweep by, one by one, driven by the wind. Peter refers to them as mist that is driven and does not fall, prefacing this allusion with the picture of wells without water (2 Pet. 2:17). When the clouds carry no rain and are driven by the wind, the reservoirs are soon empty. So

these despoilers of the faith promise but do not fulfill, and the wells are soon dry where they are.

3. The third metaphor is *fruitless trees at harvesttime.* Autumn is the time for fruit. The trees bud in the spring, the fruit develops in the warmth of summer, and it matures in the fall. These despoilers are people whose fruit withers in the bud and is dead. Their roots do not hold. They lie awkwardly in the orchard. The caretaker will remove them for, in Jesus' word, they cumber the ground. The fig tree which grew by the way from Bethany to Jerusalem fell victim of Jesus' curse when He approached it for fruit and found none. The next day the disciples saw that it had withered from His denunciation. Jude seems to have this in mind when he calls them *twice dead,* which is the figure of spiritual death. In the illustration of the Vine and the branches Jesus says that the branches which bear no fruit are cut off and burned (John 15). Frequently in the Bible the people of God are likened to trees that bring forth their fruit in their season. Those who do not are false members of the community of faith. They despoil it; they must be removed.

4. The fourth metaphor is the *raging waves of the sea.* Driven by evil winds, they bring only destruction. They tear the beaches apart, spewing mud and corruption upon the torn shore. Isaiah uses the figure when he writes, "The wicked are like the troubled sea, when it cannot rest, whose waters cast up mire and dirt. There is no peace, saith my God, to the wicked" (Isa. 57:20-21). One who lacks faith is a person who "like a wave of the sea (is) driven with the wind and tossed" (Jas. 1:6). Such a double-minded person will not receive anything from the Lord. These errorists are not men of faith. They fill the house of God with their trash and keep the community of faith in turmoil, leaving only the disgusting memory of their own shame. To use a modern phrase, they leave a bad taste in one's mouth. They always are at their worst in a storm. They leave debris to be cleaned up when they have gone.

5. The fifth metaphor is *wandering stars, to whom is reserved the blackness of darkness for ever.* Jude uses imagery common to apocalyptic thought. In the Book of Revelation stars are the ministers of God. They guide and direct the affairs of men. The devil in his prefallen state was a star of light. Paul urges Christians to "shine as lights in the world" (Phil. 2:15). Jesus told the disciples, "Ye are the light of the world" (Matt. 5:14).

Seamen guide their ships in the night by the stars because their positions in the heavens are fixed. A pilot can safely establish his position and set his course by them. The worst thing that can happen to a wayfarer is to fix his course on a wandering star. It belies its worth to him. It is better to be extinguished than to mislead people by roaming an erratic course. The apocalyptic writers saw a place of utter darkness where irresponsible stars were confined. Modern astronomers talk about a "black hole" in space, a gigantic whirlpool of darkness which gathers up stars and other objects in space and feeds on the energy of their destruction. John the revelator tells of a "bottomless pit" into which will be cast the former "star of the morning" and all who have been deceived by him.

These metaphors say something to us about the worth of the true member of the community of faith. He is to be a pure part of the love feast. The Church is to be a fellowship of the Spirit from which we draw strength, but to which we also must contribute. To be loved is also to accept the responsibility of loving. The Christian must bring water to the parched earth. He must have more than the form of godliness. He must have the power as well. If he abides in Christ, he will bear fruit. Fruitless Christians are an anomaly. The Christian is promised the peace of God which will guard his heart. The serenity of a calm sea is his because he lives in faith and does not doubt. And the Christian shines in the darkness. His light guides because it comes from "the Father of lights, with whom is no variableness" (Jas. 1:17). He can say with the Psalmist, "My heart is fixed, O God" (Ps. 57:7).

The Voice of Enoch

Jude 14-16

> 14 And Enoch also, the seventh from Adam, prophesied of these, saying, Behold, the Lord cometh with ten thousands of his saints,
> 15 To execute judgment upon all, and to convince all that are ungodly among them of all their ungodly deeds which they have ungodly committed, and of all their hard speeches which ungodly sinners have spoken against him.
> 16 These are murmurers, complainers, walking after their own lusts; and their mouth speaketh great swelling words, having men's persons in admiration because of advantage.

From the non-canonical Book of Enoch Jude draws the prediction that the Lord will come *with ten thousands of his saints, to execute judgment* on the ungodly. This is not only for punishment but to demonstrate to all, including the ungodly themselves, the ungodliness of their deeds. While the Book of Enoch was never accepted in the canon of the Scripture, and some of the early fathers questioned the canonicity of Jude because he quoted it, the prediction is within the clear teaching of the Bible concerning both the certainty of judgment and its purpose. The Scriptures are clear that sin and all ungodliness will be punished. It also teaches that punishment is not just to assuage the wrath of God but to show to all the universe the folly of such ungodliness. When the books are opened at the end time, all the world will know the truth and will see their deeds and others' in the light of it. The community of believers have heard harsh words from those who distort the truth. They have heard the very Word of God maligned. God will punish those who uttered the evil statements and will show how wrong were their words and how right were His.

When this unveiling takes place, men will see that the despoilers of the faith were grumblers who sought to undercut the truth of God. They were malcontents who wanted only their own way. They did not care what havoc they would cause getting it. They were great talkers who used boastful words about themselves. They were flatterers who buttered up people for their own advantage. So Jude exhorts the Christian community to reject the despoilers for what they are and to take heart that God knows what they are doing and saying and will expose them in His time.

We, too, should learn to sense this prerogative of faith. As Lowell wrote, it may be:

> *Truth forever on the scaffold,*
> *Wrong forever on the throne.*
> *Yet that scaffold sways the future,*
> *And, behind the dim unknown,*
> *Standeth God within the shadow*
> *Keeping watch above His own.*[11]

Some Christians act as if worldwide conspiracies against God will destroy the community of faith and thwart God's ultimate plans. How wrong they are! God will never be defeated. He will bring in the day of truth. We must trust Him to do it.

The Holy Faith and Holy Living
Jude 17-23

Mockers of the Faith
Jude 17-19

17 But, beloved, remember ye the words which were spoken before of the apostles of our Lord Jesus Christ;
18 How that they told you there should be mockers in the last time, who should walk after their own ungodly lusts.
19 These be they who separate themselves, sensual, having not the Spirit.

When times get the roughest, Christians should remember that those who preceded them knew such times would come. Tempting and tumultous times are not an unexpected development. Jude counsels his readers that the apostles of the Lord Jesus Christ had warned that enemies of the faith would come. Jesus himself had said such experiences were unavoidable (Matt. 18:7). He wanted His followers to know that offenses are inescapable. But He also uttered a woe on those by whom they would come.

The holy faith once delivered to the saints contains the truth of all of this. If one adopts its precepts, he is ready to face opposition and deceit in the knowledge that God understands the threat and plans the vindication of His Word. The life in the Spirit makes clear the error of those who seek to prostitute it. While the possibility of error is always present, the Spirit-filled man has the promise of clear insight. The anointing of the Holy Spirit who abides with the Christian teaches him all things (1 John 2:27). Those who separate themselves from this Spirit separate themselves from truth. They are reduced to sensual living without the Spirit. They become scoffers because the truth of the Spirit no longer makes sense to them. They are given over to reprobate minds which see things on a material and animal level only. Thus when one attacks the holy faith, it is evident he has separated himself from the Spirit. He no longer should be listened to because he no longer has access to truth as it is in Jesus Christ.

Building on the Faith

Jude 20-23

> 20 But ye, beloved, building up yourselves on your most holy faith, praying in the Holy Ghost,
> 21 Keep yourselves in the love of God, looking for the mercy of our Lord Jesus Christ unto eternal life.
> 22 And of some have compassion, making a difference:
> 23 And others save with fear, pulling them out of the fire; hating even the garment spotted by the flesh.

The holy faith is the foundation upon which the Christian can build. This faith is the body of Christian belief.

It is holy because it was given to the apostles as the direct revelation of God through Jesus Christ. It is not something they put together on their own but the truth they received from the Lord. It is holy also because, when it is lived by, it produces holiness of life. As one obeys the truth, the fruit of holiness is produced in both his doing and his being. Paul says, "Being made free from sin, and become servants to God, ye have your fruit unto holiness, and the end everlasting life" (Rom. 6:22).

This is the purpose of faith. It is not just a collection of the things to be remembered that Christians believe. It is the foundation of truth upon which the believer, in obedience to the Holy Spirit, can build a holy character. The superstructure will stand when erected on this foundation. The elements of holiness which make up the faith will be seen in the life that is lived. After all, the best way to contend for the faith is to live it. Just eradicating error is not enough. Truth that does not become flesh winds up in a museum.

The doctrine of entire sanctification and the truth of holiness must be guarded by clear thinking and careful exposition of Scripture. But its best defense is to be found in the lives of those who experience it by the power and presence of the Holy Spirit. People who attack holiness of life are a threat to the Christian community. Their error must be exposed. But the greater danger lies in those who believe in it as a doctrine but never receive it into their lives. The best contenders for the faith are those who live the faith.

1. One of the ways to build oneself up in the holy faith is to pray in the Holy Spirit. "We do not know how to pray as we ought," says Paul, "but the Spirit himself intercedes for us . . . according to the will of God" (Rom. 8: 26-27, RSV). The Holy Spirit prompts the Christian to pray. He is the Teacher who helps the Christian to know what to pray for. He enables the soul to sense the deep things of God. He reveals the areas of life that need to

come under the Lordship of Christ. He guides the Christian in the activities of the Kingdom: "As they ministered to the Lord, and fasted, the Holy Spirit said, Separate me Barnabas and Saul for the work whereunto I have called them" (Acts 13:2, ASV).

Praying in the Holy Spirit is not mindless surrender to something beyond oneself. It is rather mindful obedience to Christ. For the Holy Spirit does not speak of himself but rather brings the things of Christ to the person's attention. The Holy Spirit is not a power that takes one over but the Teacher and Guide who shows one the way to go and enables him to follow it. Praying in the Holy Spirit is having communion with God. It is walking and talking with Him as the first man did in the cool of the day in Eden.

2. A second way to build oneself up is to *keep . . . in the love of God.* This is an exhortation. The love is available for all. It flows rich and free, available to all. Therefore, its power to strengthen and its assurance of worth are only known as one keeps himself in it. It is not our love for God which keeps us but His love for us. It was not his own love that constrained Paul but God's love through Jesus Christ (2 Cor. 5:14). It was when John realized how much he was loved that he could be assured that he would not betray Jesus (John 13:23-25). Nothing outward can separate the Christian from this love (Rom. 8:35-39). The danger lies within. One can turn to other loves. The choice is his. So Jude exhorts, *Keep yourselves in the love of God.*

There is no stronger motivation than love. We love God because He first loved us. Our love is in response to His love. It will only be strong as we allow ourselves to appropriate the full sense of God's love to us. He loved us while we were yet sinners. He loved us for what we are. He loved us for what His love would enable us to be. His love is a perfect love. Our love can only be made perfect as it is centered in Him.

3. A third way to be built up in the faith is to give oneself

to the Christian hope. In His mercy and grace Jesus has promised eternal life to all who believe on Him. It is "not of works, lest any man should boast" (Eph. 2:8-9). When men deserved eternal death for their sins, Jesus died for them. He was Victor over the grave and has, according to His own word, all power. He said in His high priestly prayer that He willed for all who believed on Him to be eternally with Him and share His glory. This is the Christian hope. It is not something we have earned. It is a promise from His mercy who died to redeem us and lives forever to keep His promise. He also said He would come again and receive us unto himself.

The very warmth of His love can make the Christian impatient as he waits the final full mercy of Jesus Christ unto eternal life. The world grows worse and life more tedious. If he dares to say that his Lord delays His coming, he is already on the way to doubt and finally despair. If he tries to read the signs of the times so that he can find assurance in the reality of the promise, that, too, can be a trap, for it leads to the folly of trying to make predictions. True Christian expectancy says, "I do not know when, or how soon, but I know He will come. I shall therefore live every day of my life, whether long or short, expecting Him that day." If Christ gives one this hope, the least one can do is live every moment looking for Him.

4. The fourth way to build oneself up in the holy faith is have compassion on the lost. Jude directs that this compassion be turned to those whose faith has been despoiled. Some are in doubt. They have been overwhelmed by the seeming intellectuality of the despoilers. They are confused by what seems to be the logic of their arguments. In Christian love these are to be convinced of the truth of the faith, and the error of those who attack it. The Christian apologist can help many who have honest doubts and want to be enlightened. As Peter said, the Christian should always be ready to give a reason for the hope that is in him (1 Pet. 3:15). It doesn't do much good to argue about

religion, for usually it is a waste of time. But often a fellow traveller can be helped by reaffirming the faith and discussing the questions or doubts that trouble him. It not only helps the questioner but clarifies and strengthens one's own faith to share it and the reason for it with another.

There are some who are already caught in the fire. These are to be snatched from it. The fire Jude is talking about is probably the flame of immorality and lust. Talking does no good. Only deep compassion and redeeming love can save them. Often the Christian is tempted to look in disgust on those caught in the fires of lust and sin. But the compassion of Christ will not allow this. Of course one must not allow himself to be tainted; he will hate *even the garment spotted by the flesh.*

It may seem trite to talk about loving the sinner and hating his sin, but this is exactly what Jude pleads for. No one is so far gone but what the man of faith will do what he can to snatch him from the fire. He will, however, be just as concerned not to condone the sin. If it seems like a thin line to walk, it is! Yet it is one the Christian will not hesitate to take in order to reach a soul on fire.

It is a moving scene presented in this short book. With strong words and condemnation those who attack the faith once delivered to the saints are denounced. The writer, Jude, a servant of Jesus Christ, has pushed other interests aside to call the faithful to contend for the faith. But it ends with a plea for compassion and the assurance of redeeming love. Error is always a threat to the community of faith. However, the love of God through Jesus Christ is stronger than all that threatens it. The last word is that all is not lost. Men can be saved. Even though there is obvious risk in the saving, it is worthwhile. Perhaps the final and best way to contend for the faith is to be part of the redeeming force that saves those who have been caught in the illusion of error and are already burning in fires their misconceptions have set ablaze. It can and must be done.

The Author and Finisher of Our Faith
Jude 24-25

Blessed Benediction

Jude 24-25

24 Now unto him that is able to keep you from falling, and to present you faultless before the presence of his glory with exceeding joy,
25 To the only wise God our Saviour, be glory and majesty, dominion and power, both now and ever. Amen.

The final benediction is exactly what the Latin term from which it is taken, *benedictum,* means, "a good word." God is an eternal person. He exists in the now. Whatever else He is, He is personal and can be known on a personal basis. He is the ever-present and omnipotent Person. He is able. There is no other like Him. He is the only God. The despoilers of the faith, the Gnostics whom Jude denounced, had built a complicated structure of heavenly beings and persons. Their God was so small they needed to postulate several beings to try to bring any congruity to their system.[12] The faith once delivered to the saints begins with the affirmation that God is a person, eternal and all-powerful. There is no other like or equal to Him; all are under His sovereignty.

1. This one and only God can be known in a personal relationship through Jesus Christ. He said, "He that hath seen me hath seen the Father" (John 14:9). Such a personal relationship was made possible by Jesus on the Cross. He erased the handwriting against men. He provides the way by which all who will believe on Him can come to God. He promised that "if a man love me, he will keep my words: and my Father will love him, and we will come unto him, and make our abode with him" (v. 23). He has

removed the enmity between man and God caused by sin. When there was no other way, Jesus redeemed men to God the Father by His blood which was shed.

Since Christ reconciled men to God, He is able also to keep them from falling. The Cross not only provided forgiveness but also the understanding love and keeping power to bring His followers from earth to heaven. This is the double cure. He was able to save men from wrath so that they could be "accepted in the beloved" (Eph. 1:6). He is able to cleanse and perfect them through the ministry of the Holy Spirit and to present them without blemish before the presence of God. Having suffered for sins, He stands in man's stead before the judgment of God. It is not worthiness but having one's name in His book of life that assures eternal salvation. Men are accepted of God only because they are in Christ who died as the Propitiation for their sins. That is being saved from wrath.

2. There is a second and even better benefit from the Cross. He sanctifies His people through His blood. They are saved by faith in Him and His sacrifice. But He also gives His people the Holy Spirit who applies Christ's blood to their hearts, cleansing them from sin. Thus when they receive the Holy Spirit in His fullness, they are entirely sanctified. This is not to say that they are now all they will be. It is to say that, having taken possession and cleansed the heart of the believer, the Holy Spirit can begin the process of making the Christian conform to Christ's image. In short, the Holy Spirit makes one to be what he is accepted of God to be in Christ. The entrance into these relationships are works of grace. In the first, sin is forgiven and one is given an acceptance before God. In the second and subsequent work, one is cleansed by the Holy Spirit and enabled to live a holy life, being brought into conformity with Christ day by day.

The Christian is kept from falling, not because no matter what he does God will receive him, but because Christ sent the Holy Spirit to make him like himself. John assures us, "Beloved, now are we the sons of God, and it doth not yet appear what we shall be: but we know that, when he shall appear, we shall be like him; for we shall see him as he is" (1 John 3:2). Christ came and made himself like men. He who knew no sin died as a sinner. He made himself like men that men might be made like Him.

Christ then is "the author and finisher of our faith" (Heb. 12:2). He is Author in that He opened the way to God. He made possible our salvation.

> *There was no other good enough*
> *To pay the price of sin.*

He is the Finisher because what He made possible through the Cross He completes through the gift of the Holy Spirit in His fullness.

This is the source of the Christian's exceeding joy. To be saved from wrath brings a deep and abiding sense of relief and gratitude. To be made into the image of Christ brings waves of joy and praise. When one proclaims that "glory and majesty, dominion and power, both now and forever" belong to Him, the Christian joyously responds in a grand amen! When one thinks of all the wonder of redemption, joy is inescapable. On that first Easter evening the disciples, gathered behind closed doors for fear, suddenly saw the Lord. He showed them His hands and side, the symbol of their redemption. Their fear was changed to joy. It is always that way. Whenever Christians sense the presence of the Author and the Finisher of their faith, they exult in joy and blessing.

This is a world of dreadful potentialities. One might listen to the denunciation of Jude on those who would destroy the faith and tremble at the darkness and fire of their immorality and error. But when one turns his eyes on Jesus,

> *The things of earth will grow strangely dim*
> *In the light of His glory and grace.*

This, too, is surprising. As C. S. Lewis put it, the Christian is frequently "surprised by joy."[13] Christ is our Peace; He is our Joy; He is our Savior. To Him *be glory and majesty, dominion and power, both now and ever. Amen.*

The
REVELATION
of John

Topical Outline of Revelation

In the Spirit on the Lord's Day

Revelation 1:1-20

REVELATION 1

Introduction

Rev. 1:1-8

> 1 The Revelation of Jesus Christ, which God gave unto him, to shew unto his servants things which must shortly come to pass; and he sent and signified it by his angel unto his servant John:
> 2 Who bare record of the word of God, and of the testimony of Jesus Christ, and of all things that he saw.
> 3 Blessed is he that readeth, and they that hear the words of this prophecy, and keep those things which are written therein: for the time is at hand.
> 4 JOHN to the seven churches which are in Asia: Grace be unto you, and peace, from him which is, and which was, and which is to come; and from the seven Spirits which are before his throne;
> 5 And from Jesus Christ, who is the faithful witness, and the first begotten of the dead, and the prince of the kings of the earth. Unto him that loved us, and washed us from our sins in his own blood.
> 6 And hath made us kings and priests unto God and his Father; to him be glory and dominion for ever and ever. Amen.
> 7 Behold, he cometh with clouds; and every eye shall see him, and they also which pierced him: and all kindreds of the earth shall wail because of him. Even so, Amen.
> 8 I am Alpha and Omega, the beginning and the ending, saith the Lord, which is, and which was, and which is to come, the Almighty.

1. This book is called "the Revelation of Saint John the Divine," but it is really the revelation of Jesus Christ to John. It is a series of visions given to him about things which must soon take place. Dr. Ralph Earle in the *Beacon Bible Commentary* gives a very thorough description of the most common ways of understanding these visions.[1] In the *preterist* view the visions are for the first readers about things that were happening in their times. In the

historicist view these visions describe events throughout the whole Church age from Pentecost to the second coming of Christ. In the *futurist* view, from chapter 4 on they depict things yet to happen.

There is something to be said for each of these views; yet each seems to have its limitations. This exposition treats the Book of Revelation as a series of highly symbolic visions which speak to Christians of every age. Some events described bear some similarity to happenings in history, at times relating so obviously to known historical events as to make the reader feel the book had prophesied them. Nearly always, however, there is enough difference to suggest they may be yet to occur. While the historicist view thus may have its merits, it is not the perspective of this exposition.

Predictive or futuristic prophecy has its place in the presentation of the gospel. It also has its limits. Jesus told the disciples that it was not for them to know "the times or the seasons, which the Father hath put in His own power" (Acts 1:7). John was among these disciples, and it is reasonable to suppose that He meant him as well as the others. Jesus said no man knew the day or the hour of His second coming, not even He himself while on earth (Mark 13:32). By these statements He seems to be implying that no prophecy gives anyone a certain clue as to when the end time will come. He does admonish His followers to live in constant readiness so that the day will not overtake them unaware. He explained that His prophecies were given so that when they happened, the disciples would remember what He had told them (John 16:4).

2. Prophecy is intended as much for confirmation as prediction. If we can understand the purposes of God and the direction of history, then the events which have happened, and are happening, and will happen, all become confirmations which strengthen our Christian hope and resolve. These expositions are not intended to debate particular interpretations of figures and events that make up these

visions. The very likelihood that the visions did not all occur in chronological order can leave certain areas difficult to resolve and debate concerning them useless. Those who find profit in the study of the prophecies in efforts to predict events will have a different approach.

These expositions are attempted for the one who wants to learn what Revelation is saying to his time and its problems. It is too bad that for the most part preachers have stayed out of this book, especially from chapter 4 on, because they felt the material dealt with prediction and might be hard to handle. Regardless of the amount of prediction there is, the whole book is filled with confirmation, so that *blessed is he that readeth, and they that hear the words of this prophecy.* It is not a timetable of tomorrow. It is the assurance that Jesus Christ is Lord. He is the One who was, and is, and is to come. He is *the faithful witness,* the firstborn from among the dead, *and the prince of the kings of the earth.*

3. Kingdoms come and go as history moves on to its climax. All of this is beyond our control or manipulation. God is in control of all and guides the course of events according to His purpose. In Jesus Christ the God of the universe became very personal for each man, woman, and child in His creation. In Christ He loved them. In Christ they are *washed . . . from [their] sins in his own blood.* With Christ they are made *kings and priests unto God.* God was in Christ Jesus who lived in Galilee and died on the Cross. He brought Him from the dead. This same Jesus will come again on the clouds. It is this message the Revelation brings. It is the good news that whatever happens, —and it may be great and frightening—will be added confirmation of these truths.

4. In its narrowest and most limited sense this book is especially directed to people who are threatened with or about to undergo martyrdom. The highest honors and awards are for them. Violence and bloodshed become almost commonplace as the events unfold. Christ by His

death and resurrection has provided for all who will accept it, a life that is untouched by physical death. This new life in Christ can be the possession of all, whether threatened by martyrdom or not. They live best who have surrendered their lives to it.

The Risen Christ as He Is

Rev. 1:9-20

> 9 I John, who also am your brother, and companion in tribulation, and in the kingdom and patience of Jesus Christ, was in the isle that is called Patmos, for the word of God, and for the testimony of Jesus Christ.
> 10 I was in the Spirit on the Lord's day, and heard behind me a great voice, as of a trumpet,
> 11 Saying, I am Alpha and Omega, the first and the last: and, What thou seest, write in a book, and send it unto the seven churches which are in Asia; unto Ephesus, and unto Smyrna, and unto Pergamos, and unto Thyatira, and unto Sardis, and unto Philadelphia, and unto Laodicea.
> 12 And I turned to see the voice that spake with me. And being turned, I saw seven golden candlesticks;
> 13 And in the midst of the seven candlesticks one like unto the Son of man, clothed with a garment down to the foot, and girt about the paps with a golden girdle.
> 14 His head and his hairs were white like wool, as white as snow; and his eyes were as a flame of fire;
> 15 And his feet like unto fine brass, as if they burned in a furnace; and his voice as the sound of many waters.
> 16 And he had in his right hand seven stars: and out of his mouth went a sharp twoedged sword: and his countenance was as the sun shineth in his strength.
> 17 And when I saw him, I fell at his feet as dead. And he laid his right hand upon me, saying unto me. Fear not; I am the first and the last:
> 18 I am he that liveth, and was dead; and, behold, I am alive for evermore, Amen; and have the keys of hell and of death.
> 19 Write the things which thou hast seen, and the things which are, and the things which shall be hereafter;
> 20 The mystery of the seven stars which thou sawest in my right hand, and the seven golden candlesticks. The seven stars are the angels of the seven churches: and the seven candlesticks which thou sawest are the seven churches.

1. John was a lonely man who was deeply concerned, a prisoner on a lonely island. He doesn't say much about himself except that he is a brother to the Christians in Asia in their suffering, in the kingdom of Christ, and in patient endurance. Of this we can be sure: His loneliness

did not come as much from his exile as from his forced absence from his life's mission. What physical suffering he endured, if any, is never mentioned. The pain he felt was evidently something greater. It came from the absence his imprisonment forced upon him. He was a committed proclaimer of the good news of the gospel of Christ. This was his life's mission and his greatest joy. All else was secondary to him. He would have preferred nearly anything to what he was going through. For far worse than death were the restrictions that kept him from fulfilling this mandate.

On the rock-strewn Island of Patmos in the Aegean Sea there were no ears to hear his words. His message burned within him, but he had no one to listen. His faithful witness of Jesus had resulted in this exile. He had been obedient to his calling without hesitancy or drawing back. His reward for being true to his mission was to be put away from everyone and everything. Now the leadership of the churches in the province of Asia was lost to him. He was tempted by the fact that his obedience to Christ had cost him his friends and his mission.

He was lonely because he had no one with whom to share his feelings and insights. He had no one to disciple as he went forward in faith. He seemed to find no way to gather the exigencies of the experience into a meaningful spiritual victory for Christ and His Church.

2. He was concerned because he did not know how the Church fared without him. Like the apostle Paul, he knew the potential hardship and trials they could face and how much they needed leadership. Unlike Paul, he knew no one like Timothy or Titus whom he could send to find out for him. No reports came to him of how the Christians he called his "children" were bearing up. If only some word could reach him, if only there were some way to know what was going on, he could bear the absence more easily. A good report would warm his heart as he learned of their fidelity and courage. Even a bad report could allow him,

in intercessory prayer, to fight by their side in the Spirit.

3. The warm sun's beating down, the soft wind's incessant push, and the rhythm of tireless waves only added to the despair of this lonely and concerned man who could hear the sounds of the sea and sky but no voice. And then one day everything changed. Suddenly the sense of loneliness was displaced by the sense of the Presence. It was an unforgettable day that changed darkness to light, and despair to hope. He remembered the circumstances clearly; it was during worship on the Lord's Day.

The Lord's Day was the Christians' name for the first day of the week. For them it replaced the Sabbath as the day of worship. It was John's practice to worship on this day just as all the Christians from the beginning of the Church had done. They had made it their Sabbath. Jesus himself had said that the Son of Man was Lord of the Sabbath (Luke 6:5).

a. His first appearance to the disciples following the Resurrection was on the evening of the first day of the week. They had gathered behind closed doors for fear. Jesus was suddenly in their midst, and when they saw His hands and side, their fear turned to joy.

b. The same thing happened on the following Sunday. Thomas, who had not been there on the Resurrection day and said he would not believe unless he saw His hands and side, had come on the second Sunday. Suddenly Jesus was there, and Thomas' doubt was turned to faith as he cried, "My Lord and my God" (John 20:19-29).

c. The Day of Pentecost, seven weeks after Jesus' resurrection was on a Sunday. Again the disciples were gathered, prayerfully seeking to know what to do and where to go. Suddenly the room in which they were sitting was filled with the presence of the Holy Ghost, the Comforter that Jesus had promised to send them to vouchsafe His presence. Their inhibitions were turned to boldness.

All of these events seemed to have set the pattern for the Early Church. From then on they always are recorded as worshipping on the first day of the week. It is indeed, even today, the day that makes a difference. Two millennia have passed, but still when Christians gather in Christ's name, there is joy. The shadows flee and peace comes anew. E. Stanley Jones wrote a hymn which expresses this. The first verse reads:

> We gather here mid templed walls,
> A peaceful presence on us falls.
> Though we are set by many a fear,
> A greater than our fears is here.

Other verses describe the One who is greater than all the needs people bring to worship.[2]

4. John was *in the Spirit on the Lord's day.* He heard a voice which instructed him to write what he was about to see and send it to the churches of Asia. The Voice identified himself as the Eternal One, the First and the Last. The Voice even named the churches to which the letter should be addressed. The sense of loneliness was dispelled by the Presence. What follows then is a letter which John had earlier promised would bless the reader. It is the communication of divine truth by an inspired author toward a specific audience within a well-defined historical setting. The blessing to the reader comes as the Holy Spirit lifts the truth from the setting and applies it to his life and time. Thus, written for a particular time long ago and far away, it speaks to any and every time as the Spirit directs. The letter was to be sent to seven churches, all of which lay in an approximate circle, between 25 and 50 miles from each other. Interestingly, not all the churches within close proximity are included by name. The seven represent them all—or the Church Universal.

5. John turned to see who was speaking to him. When he did, he saw seven lampstands, perhaps in a circle, for he is told later they represent the seven churches to whom the letter is to be addressed. In the middle he sees a heavenly figure. His description represents the *Son of man,* also

described by Daniel (e.g., 7:13). The Person is clothed in a long robe with *a golden girdle* round his breast; His head and hair are white; His eyes are like *a flame of fire;* His feet are like polished bronze; His voice, like the roar of the sea. In His hand the Son of Man held seven stars which John is told represent the pastors of the seven churches. From His mouth came *a sharp two-edged sword,* while His face shone like the sun.

The wonder of the vision and the realization that he was in the presence of the Son of Man caused John to faint. There probably was also the release he felt in the knowledge that the churches were not deserted. The tension was gone. He could not be there, but the Son of Man was. It is significant, too, that the Son of Man is the risen Lord. John had often heard Jesus refer to himself as the Son of Man. It was the name He seemed to prefer to being called the Messiah, although He never rejected the latter appellation.

6. John had been concerned for the welfare of the churches he could not reach. Now he knew that, though he could not be there, Jesus was. There used to be a humorous story about a bishop who wired a conference he was delayed in attending, concluding the telegram with, "God be with you until I get there!" Well, John could rest assured that Jesus was there. Perhaps he saw Him as tending the wicks and replenishing the oil in the lamps.[3] The words indicate that He knew each church, and in several cases He threatened the removal of the lampstand. Unless it changed, it would no longer be able to serve its purpose. He shows special attention to the pastors in the light of their intensified responsibility. He holds them in His hands. The well-known spiritual goes, "He's got the whole world in His hands." Perhaps so. At least John saw that He had the pastors of the churches in His hands.

Thus a lonely and concerned man, on the Lord's Day, finds comfort in his imprisonment and deprivation. He is about to see things that must soon happen. These things quickly make a difference in the life of the church. He need not worry about them, for not only will they be informed, but the risen Lord himself walks among them and holds their messengers in His hands. The story is told of a ship in a storm. The passengers were deeply worried and frightened. One went to the captain's cabin and returned with the reassuring word, "I saw the face of the pilot, and I am well assured."

The Spirit Speaks to the Churches
Revelation 2:1—3:22

REVELATION 2

The second and third chapters of the letter contain messages directed to each of the specific churches. Each message begins with the words *Unto [or, to] the angel of the church of [or, in]* . . . Each message ends with the words *He that hath an ear, let him hear what the Spirit saith unto the churches.* This is followed by a specific promise to the church.

It is reassuring and challenging to be reminded that the Spirit does speak to churches even today. In Acts 13:1-3 it is reported that, while the leaders of the church of Antioch prayed and fasted, the Spirit spoke to them. One wonders if, should the Church pray and fast more often, it might hear the Spirit speaking more precisely and frequently. However, there does seem to be a pattern of the Spirit's message in these two chapters. There is a word of commendation, a word of condemnation, and a word of challenge. The Spirit reminds churches that He knows all about them, and whatever their condition, the possibility of overcoming is always there.

The Church in Ephesus

Rev. 2:1-7

1 Unto the angel of the church of Ephesus write; These things saith he that holdeth the seven stars in his right hand, who walketh in the midst of the seven golden candlesticks;
2 I know thy works, and thy labour, and thy patience, and how thou canst not bear them which are evil: and thou hast tried them which say they are apostles, and are not, and hast found them liars:
3 And hast borne, and hast patience, and for my name's sake hast laboured, and hast not fainted.
4 Nevertheless I have somewhat against thee, because thou hast left thy first love.
5 Remember therefore from whence thou art fallen, and repent, and do the first works; or else I will come unto thee quickly, and will remove thy candlestick out of his place, except thou repent.
6 But this thou hast, that thou hatest the deeds of the Nicolaitanes, which I also hate.
7 He that hath an ear, let him hear what the Spirit saith unto the churches; To him that overcometh will I give to eat of the tree of life, which is in the midst of the paradise of God.

Ephesus was the chief city of Asia Minor. It was situated on the coast nearest to the Island of Patmos. Geographically it was the logical beginning for messages from John. But it had become the Christian center of the late, first-century Church, having been founded by the apostle Paul. It was there Paul had confronted the worshippers of the goddess Diana and, but for the intervention of his friends, might have been destroyed. Paul said that in Ephesus there was an open door and "many adversaries" (1 Cor. 16:8-9). Under the preaching of the first missionary, this church had experienced an outpouring of the Holy Spirit very similar to the initial outpouring on the Day of Pentecost.

1. The pastor of this church is told that their intense devotion is known. They have made clear distinctions between right and wrong, between loyalty and disloyalty, between truth and error. They held people, especially leaders, under the judgment of these clear distinctions. They did not take people for what they said they were but what they had found them to be.

There is much that can and ought to be said for a

strict holding to fundamentals. Loose and careless thinking that allows the lines to blur takes a tragic toll of the spirit. Failure to discern opens the door for the erosion of conviction. Tolerance at its best has limits, or it results in permissiveness. A little chink in the wall allows the flood to sweep in at the last. It is a long and tiring battle to stand firm against compromise. Jesus reminds this church that He knows of their determination to be true and that they have not grown weary. They were tireless defenders of the faith.

2. But this commendation is followed by the warning for which this church at Ephesus will always be remembered. They had left their *first love.* Firm but loveless—what a tragedy! The harbor on which the city was located was continually changing because of its situation. Water became land, and land became water. Like the city harbor, the church's love had moved. The glow and excitement that had equaled Pentecost, in warmth if not in numbers, had been lost. Doctrinally correct, the church was yet lacking in the love which had accompanied its birth.

This is not an unusual happening. Maintaining the glow is not an automatic experience for the Christian. One must be constantly aware of trends which allow the loss of love. There is, of course, a natural rhythm to life that cannot be ignored. No one remains on a constant level. It is but human to experience an ebb and flow of emotions. Then there is the fluctuation of physical strength and well-being which affect, more than we wish to admit, the intensity of our devotion. At any given time one could perhaps look back at his spiritual beginnings and feel that much of its flash is gone. One cannot expect to maintain a fever pitch every moment. There are bound to be times of greater or less fervor. But these waves need not affect the constancy of one's commitment. The initial ecstacy of our conversion, said Wesley, eventually "subsides into a calm and peaceful love," even as Christ *remains* our *first love.*

3. The remedy the Lord suggests, *Remember therefore*

from whence thou art fallen, indicates that it is not the natural rise and fall of feelings that is condemned. It is rather the loss of one's highest love. The first in time and in priority coincide. One may well move from the first without giving up the latter. That they had settled for less than their highest priority seems to be what was charged. Consistent discernment without steadfast commitment is a peril all must avoid. The reference to the *deeds* of the Nicolaitans indicated that they were better at hating than loving. If one loves as Jesus loves, then he can hate what Jesus hates (evil deeds). Hatred of sin, so important for the Christian, must not be had at the cost of love. This church was against sin with such vigor that it had left its first love.

Two actions are advised: *Remember* and *repent.* These will be followed by the third: *Do the first works.* In the midst of the struggle one must find time to remember. It is not that one advances by always looking back, but the reflection of viewing again one's first commitment will reveal, if there is any, a loss of the highest love. Such loss when discovered must either be defended or disavowed. The call to repentance is the Lord's solution. Identifying and turning away from compromise of commitment means returning to *the first works.*

4. The message concludes with a promise and a challenge. The loss of their first love can be regained. The church can overcome the problem and deficiency. The speaking Spirit may point out failures or inadequacies, but He also calls to victorious outcomes. In every situation the people of God can and should overcome. The promise for those who follow Jesus awaits the successful conquest.

The church of Ephesus is promised the opportunity of eating of *the tree of life, which is in the midst of the paradise of God.* Genesis, chapter 2, tells that in the Garden of Eden God made trees to grow pleasant to the sight and good for food. Among these trees were the tree of life and the tree of the knowledge of good and evil. The latter gets all of the attention from then on. No more is said of the tree of life, but the privilege of eating of the fruit of all the trees except the tree of the knowledge of good and evil was given to man. No doubt Adam and Eve had eaten often of the tree of life. In fact, Adam lived longer than any other man except Methuselah. With the destruction of man by the Flood and the subsequent death of Noah, people lived much shorter lives. So the promise to the church of Ephesus that a return to the fruit of the tree of life signals a restoration of a long-lost privilege. It seems to say that lost things can be recovered, and also that return has far-reaching and long-lasting possibilities.

The Church in Smyrna

Rev. 2:8-11

> 8 And unto the angel of the church in Smyrna write; These things saith the first and the last, which was dead, and is alive;
> 9 I know thy works, and tribulation, and poverty, (but thou art rich) and I know the blasphemy of them which say they are Jews, and are not, but are the synagogue of Satan.
> 10 Fear none of those things which thou shalt suffer: behold, the devil shall cast some of you into prison, that ye may be tried; and ye shall have tribulation ten days: be thou faithful unto death, and I will give thee a crown of life.
> 11 He that hath an ear, let him hear what the Spirit saith unto the churches; He that overcometh shall not be hurt of the second death.

The city of Smyrna lies north of Ephesus. It is famed for its claim to be the birthplace of Homer. In the struggles for mastery between Rome and Carthage it had remained faithful to Rome. Both earthquake and hostile armies had wasted and sacked the city. Its name contains the sounds of the word *myrrh,* a spice which is fragrant when crushed and so is associated with suffering. Jesus identifies himself as one acquainted with suffering as He addresses this church. He is the One who was dead and lives again.

1. The church is one of two in the group of seven for which Jesus has no condemnation. He commends the congregation for their works in the midst of tribulation and poverty. He quickly reminds them of their spiritual wealth. He is

aware of the strong opposition there of the people who call themselves Jews (cf. Rom. 2:29). He does not accept their claim of genuine obedience to God. He rather accuses them of being of the synagogue of Satan. Through the years the Church has suffered much from the hands of religious people who have not kept pace with the leadership of the Spirit and have opposed those who have. Perhaps no persecution is as violent as this. The record of Saul of Tarsus before his conversion on the Damascus road is evidence of this misdirected fervor of people who "kick against the pricks" (Acts 9:5; 26:14). Jesus outlines the specifics of such attacks which include trial, imprisonment, and even death.

The message to people and churches who suffer for His name is that the Lord himself is with them. Stephen saw Him standing by the right hand of God as he succumbed to the stones cast upon him. The risen Lord promised His disciples, "Lo, I am with you alway, even unto the end . . ." (Matt. 28:20). He has walked the road ahead of any who obey and take His way. He has been dead and is alive forever. No one who is obedient walks an untried way. There are footprints ahead of him.

2. The message reminds us that to keep step with the Spirit draws the fire of the "establishment" even in the life of the Church. Christ's way seems to take those who follow Him to the very brink of what their companions deem unorthodox. The man who had so violently defended the accepted faith of his fathers, after he turned to follow Jesus, told his former companions, "This I confess unto thee, that after the way which they call heresy, so worship I the God of my fathers, believing all things which are written in the law and in the prophets" (Acts 24:14). One of Satan's most effective weapons is to enshrine the accepted forms until they block the onward march of truth.

3. For such embattled walkers in the light, the Lord has a word of challenge. These obstacles can be overcome, even the synagogue of Satan. The force of evil may be powerful

and threatening, but the Christian can always overcome in the power of the One who has bound "the strong man" (Mark 3:27). The overcomer cannot be hurt of the second death. The allusion is to the spiritual death that overtakes all who do not walk in the light. Smyrna has been called the fearful church. This was in the light of Jesus' warning that His followers should not fear any who can kill them, but rather fear the One (God) who can destroy both body and soul and cast them into hell. This is the second death. Any who die for Jesus' sake will share in the resurrection. Those, too, who embrace the commitment without reservation, even including death, know no more of dying. They have eternal life. They cannot and will not be hurt of the second death. They live and reign with Christ forever.

The Church in Pergamos

Rev. 2:12-17

> 12 And to the angel of the church in Pergamos write; These things saith he which hath the sharp sword with two edges;
> 13 I know thy works, and where thou dwellest, even where Satan's seat is: and thou holdest fast my name, and hast not denied my faith, even in those days wherein Antipas was my faithful martyr, who was slain among you, where Satan dwelleth.
> 14 But I have a few things against thee, because thou hast there them that hold the doctrine of Balaam, who taught Balac to cast a stumblingblock before the children of Israel, to eat things sacrificed unto idols, and to commit fornication.
> 15 So hast thou also them that hold the doctrine of the Nicolaitanes, which thing I hate.
> 16 Repent; or else I will come unto thee quickly, and will fight against them with the sword of my mouth.
> 17 He that hath an ear, let him hear what the Spirit saith unto the churches; To him that overcometh will I give to eat of the hidden manna, and will give him a white stone, and in the stone a new name written, which no man knoweth saving he that receiveth it.

North along the coast at the top of the circle formed by the seven churches was the city of Pergamos. It was a cosmopolitan city with a famous medical center, a university, and the royal residence. Among the many pagan temples was the temple of Asklepios, the god of medicine, which contained the figure of a wreathed serpent. This is the symbol of medicine even today. Here, too, was the enormous altar of Zeus which dominated the city and could be seen for miles. In 29 B.C. a temple was dedicated to the goddess Roma. The emperor Augustus had promoted the imperial religion so that this provincial center became also a center for the state religion. The city was well known for its statuary and its library. It is no wonder that Jesus calls Pergamos the place where Satan's throne is.

1. The Christians in the midst of this diverse cultural and religious pluralism were attempting to establish the throne of God. The message reminded them that their Master knew the hostility of their environment. He was aware of the intensity of the conflict that resulted in the martyrdom of Antipas. They had held fast in it all. It is not surprising that their witness cost them dearly. Jesus had warned His disciples and all who follow Him that persecution and even death would be encountered. In fact He had made the possibility of it a factor in the acceptance of His call. No man, He said, who would not face such a potentiality and be faithful should undertake it.

While the cost of discipleship has not always been death, there has rarely been a time when somewhere in the world it has not. The tumultuous times through which this generation has been passing has seen its share and more of martyrdom. But the mention of Antipas' name reminds us again that the cause of Christ is worth more than life itself. Sometimes it is said, "We have to live." But really we don't. We do have to be true to the faith whether or not we live.

2. While the record of the fidelity and heroism of the church in Pergamos had been firmly established, there were other forces at work in her. Jesus identifies at least a major one as the holding of the doctrine of Balaam. This Old Testament figure who prophesied for Jehovah in spite of himself was never willing to become a supporter of the people of God against the Moabites. He worked to combine the ways of Moab with the ways of God. He taught

Israel to enter into the ritual immorality of Baal worship.

The subtle temptation to make Christianity compatible with other religions is never far away. It lures one into thinking that common ground can be found and distinctions need not be too clear. The Nicolaitans, who had already been denounced in the message to the Ephesian church, and are mentioned again here, may have been the current practitioners of the doctrine of Balaam. They have never been silenced. In every generation of the Christian Church there have been those who proclaim it anew. Pluralism can be the recognition of other ways of worship or living, but for the Christian it must never be the sanction of watering down the demands of the gospel. Jesus drew the line clearly when He declared, "No man can serve two masters" (Matt. 6:24). There it must always be drawn. Syncretism is fostered as the openness of the broadminded, but it is the end of true Christian witness. The apostle Paul urged the Corinthians, "Be ye not unequally yoked together with unbelievers: for what fellowship hath righteousness with unrighteousness? and what communion hath light with darkness?" (2 Cor. 6:14).

3. This then is the challenge before Pergamos, and for that matter, for us all. We must establish the throne of God in every city. We must bear witness to the Lordship of Christ at any cost. We dare not compromise. There is no way to be a friend of God and indulge in the ways of the world. The help Jesus offers is hidden manna and a white stone with a name that only the recipient knows.

Both of these speak of the importance and value of a personal relationship with the Savior. As meaningful and necessary as the relationships we have in the Body of Christ, there is a deeper and more vital one which is between the soul and the Savior. Hidden manna reminds us of Jesus' own words at the well in Samaria, "I have meat to eat that ye know not of" (John 4:32). He was referring to obedience to the very personal mission He has received from His Father. As members of the Body of

Christ we minister to each other, but our sustenance comes from the secret inner source when we are alone with Him. The white stone is variously used: to mark happy days (black to mark sad ones), to indicate in court a not-guilty verdict, to designate the victor in games, or as an invitation to partake of a sacred feast within the temple precincts. For the challenge Jesus gives the Pergamos church any of the above could apply. The significant thing, however, is the white stone He was giving contained a name that only the one receiving it would know. What a beautiful picture it is of the worth and joy of a personal relationship each believer has with Him. Each relationship is his very own secret.

The periodic call that comes for emphasis on the social demands of the gospel are timely and needed. Never should the Church forget its mission of compassion and forgiveness. But the vital strength and life of the Christian comes from his personal victory through Jesus Christ his Lord. The personal gospel is at the very heart of it all.

The Church in Thyatira

Rev. 2:18-29

> 18 And unto the angel of the church in Thyatira write; These things saith the Son of God, who hath his eyes like unto a flame of fire, and his feet are like fine brass;
> 19 I know thy works, and charity, and service, and faith, and thy patience, and thy works; and the last to be more than the first.
> 20 Notwithstanding I have a few things against thee, because thou sufferest that woman Jezebel, which calleth herself a prophetess, to teach and to seduce my servants to commit fornication, and to eat things sacrificed unto idols.
> 21 And I gave her space to repent of her fornication; and she repented not.
> 22 Behold, I will cast her into a bed, and them that commit adultery with her into great tribulation, except they repent of their deeds.
> 23 And I will kill her children with death; and all the churches shall know that I am he which searcheth the reins and hearts: and I will give unto every one of you according to your works.
> 24 But unto you I say, and unto the rest in Thyatira, as many as have not this doctrine, and which have not known the depths of Satan, as they speak; I will put upon you none other burden.
> 25 But that which ye have already hold fast till I come.
> 26 And he that overcometh, and keepeth my works unto the end, to him will I give power over the nations:

27 And he shall rule them with a rod of iron; as the vessels of a potter shall they be broken to shivers: even as I received of my Father.

28 And I will give him the morning star.

29 He that hath an ear, let him hear what the spirit saith unto the churches.

Turning to the southeast and travelling inland away from the coast, one would come to the city of Thyatira. Established as a military fortress by Seleucus I to guard the pass between Hermus and Caicus, it had become of little significance to the Romans. However, it had flourished as an industrial and commercial center. The worship of the sun-god Apollo had been united with emperor worship. It may have been the prospering brass industry or the claims of the emperor to be Apollo incarnate that led Jesus to describe himself as the Son of God with eyes like a flame of fire and feet like burnished bronze. The city was also famous for its purple dye. It was here that Lydia was converted, who later used her home as a place for Paul to stay as he ministered in Philippi.

1. The church is commended for its forward progress. Jesus says, *I know thy works . . . and thy works; and the last to be more than the first.* As we have learned, there was stress and pressure in the church, but these forces did not stop her from moving forward. When we excuse standing still or retreating by describing the problems, we are suggesting something Jesus did not intend. Problems or obstacles are not to stop our march, for He said, "I will build my church; and the gates of hell shall not prevail against it" (Matt. 16:18).

2. But for all of the church's forward movement, strong counterforces were also present. The temptation to permit compromise was there as it was in Pergamos. While not mentioned by name, it is possible the doctrine of the Nicolaitans found some support in Thyatira, too. The figure used here to describe the heresy was another Old Testament name, Jezebel. Ahab had brought her to Israel as his queen, and she had brought her pagan idols. At first it

seemed only permission for her to worship her gods. But what was first tolerated was soon embraced by many in the nation. She taught and seduced God's people to *commit fornication*. This may have meant sexual immorality. However, the Bible generally uses such language to describe worship of any other than God. What Jezebel was allowed to do for herself as a courtesy became a conflicting faith for as many as she could influence. The phrase "food sacrificed to idols" (v. 20, NIV), indicates that a widespread problem in the Early Church was here as well. The phrase *none other burden* (v. 24) is similar to the decision of the council of Jerusalem relative to the Gentile Christians and the Jewish law.

3. The condemnation of Jesus carries the indication of Christian patience. The ironic description of their claim to insight as "knowing the deep things of Satan" (v. 24, RSV) is certainly strong condemnation. But it follows the statement that they have been given time to repent. Since this did not occur, there will be swift and thorough punishment. The punishment is not retribution as much as it is a testimony to the truth that Christ is the Searcher of the mind and heart. Such language serves to remind us that serious, spiritual compromise begins in the inner life. For all that was to be welcomed in the emphasis on personal relationship in the previous letter to Pergamos, there must be a caution against the kind of individuality in religion which makes a man a law unto himself. We are always open in the depth of our mind and heart to Him with whom we have to do. He knows what is in us and what are our real motives no matter how well we may deceive ourselves with clever rationalizations.

4. The challenge to this church is that there is power in submission. When we bring all our lives, thoughts, and motives under the Lordship of Christ, we are entrusted with power we could never have otherwise. The long story of the Christian Church is one of conquest against the most

formidable odds, by meek men made strong through the divine power that is given to them.

It is true that the prediction in this promise over against the actual situation often is contradictory. It requires both the long look and inner look to understand the power that has been given to the Church. When one hears testimonies from those who have undergone severe persecution and have come through triumphant, then one sees this promise in clearer light.

Perhaps the best understanding comes from the added promise that the overcomer will receive the *morning star.* At first glance it seems to be a reference to astrology and the belief that the stars control man's destiny. But when in the 22nd chapter of the Revelation we hear Jesus call himself "the bright and morning star" (v. 16), we understand the magnitude of the gift. He will be with the Christian in all his stand for right and truth both within and without.

REVELATION 3

The Church in Sardis

Rev. 3:1-6

> 1 And unto the angel of the church in Sardis write; These things saith he that hath the seven Spirits of God, and the seven stars; I know thy works, and thou hast a name that thou livest, and art dead.
> 2 Be watchful, and strengthen the things which remain, that are ready to die: for I have not found thy works perfect before God.
> 3 Remember therefore how thou hast received and heard, and hold fast, and repent. If therefore thou shalt not watch, I will come on thee as a thief, and thou shalt not know what hour I will come upon thee.
> 4 Thou hast a few names even in Sardis which have not defiled their garments; and they shall walk with me in white: for they are worthy.
> 5 He that overcometh, the same shall be clothed in white raiment; and I will not blot out his name out of the book of life, but I will confess his name before my Father, and before his angels.
> 6 He that hath an ear, let him hear what the Spirit saith unto the churches.

Continuing on the road from Thyatira in a south-easterly direction, one comes to the site of the city of Sardis. It had a great history. Once it was the capital of Lydia, the home of the fabulously rich Croesus. It had every appearance of being unconquerable. It was destroyed by an earthquake in A.D. 17 and was quickly rebuilt by the emperor Tiberius. Though it sought to be a place of significance through its loyalty to the imperial cult, in John's day it was a city whose glory was its yesterdays. It was a city that had a name to which it did not live up. Who can miss the impact of the Lord's charge?—*Thou hast a name that thou livest, and art dead.*

1. There is a child's poem which goes, "Sticks and stones will break my bones, / But names will never hurt me." Names in themselves cannot hurt if they are justified by what we are. At the same time, to have a name and not live up to it is a cover-up. It is living under false pretenses.

Take the name of one's denomination for instance. It is made glorious by many a story of courage and devotion to truth. It may seem to be an unimportant matter to call oneself by the name. But to do so is to claim connection with all the name has come to mean. It is a libel on one's spiritual predecessors to go by the name and deny the faith it was chosen to designate. To bear a name suggests that one is what the name portrays.

The legend is that Francis of Assisi was once met by a peasant. In the course of the conversation the peasant learned to whom he was talking and was enthralled. At last he asked, "Art thou really Francis of Assisi?" When Francis admitted that he was, the peasant replied, "Then be sure to be all that men say thou art, for many men think well of thee." Names are important. When they are designates of Christian grace, we must be sure to be what our name claims.

2. While the church at Sardis had a name it did not live up to as a whole, there were some in its midst who did. They had not allowed the spiritual disease of most of the

church to soil their garments. Their presence in it seems to offer the best hope for the church.

Sardis was a sleeping church in the sense that it rested on its laurels. It had a name, and that was all that mattered. Its spiritual inactivity had brought death. Its only hope was to remember what it had received and repent. It must hold fast the truth it has been given and observe its moral and spiritual agenda. The saving remnant of those who were awake was there. A few wide-awake, live Christians who refuse to soil their garments can turn the tide of deadly indifference. God was willing to save Sodom and Gomorrah if 10 righteous folk could have been found. Jesus said that if the mighty works which had been done in Capernaum were done in Sodom, it would have repented. There is hope for the worst.

3. The call to repentance and renewal is based not only on the presence of a minority who are alive but also on the fact that Christ might come at any time. The suddenness, like a thief in the night, seems to be the major thrust of Jesus' warning. He does not even hint when. He stresses that every church in every time must live in the reality that He may come suddenly. When He does appear, it will be too late to catch up. Without warning He may be there like the bridegroom in the story of the wise and foolish maidens (Matt. 25:1-13). Both groups were sure the bridegroom would come. Neither had any idea when. The wise kept themselves constantly ready. The foolish, like most of the people in the church in Sardis, were lured to sleep by the delay and were caught unprepared.

4. It is the very lack of clue or sign that makes integrity in one's spiritual life so important. "You do not know," the Lord warns. This fact, He says, should impel them to keep step with those who march with the Victor in white. They are enrolled in the list of the victorious as long as they walk with Him. The book of life is the passport to eternal life with Jesus. He warns the church in Sardis, and us, that no one's name stays there automatically. To be

enrolled in the book requires more than the image or name that one is alive. It requires that he be living and walking with Christ.

While it is sobering and even frightening to realize that one may be dead while he lives or has the name that he does, and it is shocking to know that one can suddenly be removed from the book of life, it is reassuring to see those wonderful few who move about the church in strong and living fidelity which keeps them from being soiled by all that is destructive about them. The glorious few who walk in white give hope to us all that grace to us may be given to follow them as they follow Christ.

The Church in Philadelphia

Rev. 3:7-13

> 7 And to the angel of the church in Philadelphia write; These things saith he that is holy, he that is true, he that hath the key of David, he that openeth, and no man shutteth; and shutteth, and no man openeth;
> 8 I know thy works: behold, I have set before thee an open door, and no man can shut it: for thou hast a little strength, and hast kept my word, and hast not denied my name.
> 9 Behold, I will make them of the synagogue of Satan, which say they are Jews, and are not, but do lie; behold, I will make them to come and worship before thy feet, and to know that I have loved thee.
> 10 Because thou hast kept the word of my patience, I also will keep thee from the hour of temptation, which shall come upon all the world, to try them that dwell upon the earth.
> 11 Behold, I come quickly: hold that fast which thou hast, that no man take thy crown.
> 12 Him that overcometh will I make a pillar in the temple of my God, and he shall go no more out: and I will write upon him the name of my God, and the name of the city of my God, which is new Jerusalem, which cometh down out of heaven from my God: and I will write upon him my new name.
> 13 He that hath an ear, let him hear what the Spirit saith unto the churches.

This is the second of the churches to receive no condemnation of the Lord in their letter. Philadelphia was a newer and lesser city founded by Attalus II (Philadelphus) of Pergamum. It, like Sardis, had been destroyed by an earthquake in A.D. 17 and rebuilt by Tiberius. It was on the main communication line between Rome and the central plateau of Asia Minor.

1. The church in this city was truly a Christian church. It was the church of *an open door*. This open door had been given to the church by her Lord who had *the key of David*. This meant that He would open doors that no man could shut and shut doors that no man could open. Jesus gave them the open doors because they proved their faithfulness. When people complain that they have no open doors, they are really saying something about their trustworthiness. Jesus has the key of David and can open doors whenever there are people who will use them.

Their worthiness consisted not so much in power as in faithfulness. They had little power, in fact, but they had kept His word. In spite of the accusation of people claiming to be the people of God (Jews), they had not denied His name. The door would stay open, and they would be kept in the midst of the temptation which Jesus warned would engulf the world.

The open door reminds us of the missionary task of the Christian Church. Jesus had told the disciples that they must go to all the world. He connected this task with the end time by declaring that when the gospel had been preached to every nation, then would the end come (Matt. 24:14). It was probably less a prophecy than a promise. The whole world is the harvest field. The door is open. There will be persecution. Christians, however, will be kept in the midst of the ordeal which will fall on the world. Of that testing much more will be said later.

2. While there is no word of condemnation to the "open door" church, Jesus does tell them He knows of the presence of *the synagogue of Satan*. He promises that the people in it who claim to be Jews and are not, but lie, will come at last to bow down at their feet.

This verse (9) concurs with numerous words of the apostle Paul identifying Christians as the new Israel. The Early Church had a long struggle with those who contended that Christianity was an extension of Judaism and so must be built on the foundation of strict observance of the law as revealed in the Old Testament and expounded by the rabbis. Paul, especially, in the letter to the Galatians argues the promise to Abraham was to his seed (singular—not many). This seed, he says, is Christ. All who are in Christ then are Abraham's seed and heirs to the promise. In the letter to the Roman Christians he points out that not every child of Abraham was a child of promise (e.g., Ishmael). Then he argues that only the spiritual descendants are the true Israel. In his second letter to the Corinthians Paul proclaims that if a man is in Christ, he is a new creation.

Thus in the letter to Philadelphia, Jesus implies that people who claim to be the children of Abraham because of their race or ritual are not. His heirs are determined by spiritual rather than physical birth. Children of God are born of the Spirit and not the flesh. This fact will finally be recognized by all.

3. This concept is further developed in the promise given for their overcoming. Jesus says they will be pillars in the temple of God. Later John tells that when he saw the New Jerusalem, the city of God, there was no temple in it. But this is not a contradiction. For he heard the voice of God say the tabernacle of God is with men and God would be in their midst. The temple in which the Philadelphians were to be pillars is the community of faith. Their obedience against odds and opposition would make them to be foundations for the whole household of faith. God's church is not a building of brick and stone but of flesh and blood. It is held together (from a human point of view) by those who walk through the open doors to proclaim the gospel to all men.

These are the people concerning whom God is not ashamed to be called their God. They bear the name of God, the name of His city, and the name of Christ. In promising this reward, Jesus says that His name will be a new name. Whatever else He may mean, this is probably a reference to His new position. They have known Him as the Man of Galilee and the risen Lord. In the end time they will know Him in His new position of King of Kings and Lord of Lords.

The Church in Laodicea

Rev. 3:14-22

> 14 And unto the angel of the church of the Laodiceans write; These things saith the Amen, the faithful and true witness, the beginning of the creation of God;
> 15 I know thy works, that thou art neither cold nor hot: I would thou wert cold or hot.
> 16 So then because thou art lukewarm, and neither cold nor hot, I will spue thee out of my mouth.
> 17 Because thou sayest, I am rich, and increased with goods, and have need of nothing; and knowest not that thou art wretched, and miserable, and poor, and blind, and naked:
> 18 I counsel thee to buy of me gold tried in the fire, that thou mayest be rich; and white raiment, that thou mayest be clothed, and that the shame of thy nakedness do not appear; and anoint thine eyes with eye-salve, that thou mayest see.
> 19 As many as I love, I rebuke and chasten: be zealous therefore, and repent.
> 20 Behold, I stand at the door, and knock: if any man hear my voice, and open the door, I will come in to him, and will sup with him, and he with me.
> 21 To him that overcometh will I grant to sit with me in my throne, even as I also overcame, and am set down with my Father in his throne.
> 22 He that hath an ear, let him hear what the Spirit saith unto the churches.

The final city in the circle formed by these seven letters lay in a valley almost 100 miles east of Ephesus. Here there was a cluster of cities: Laodicea, Colossae, and Hierapolis. There were Christian churches in at least two of them. In Paul's letter to Colossae there is the instruction that it be read to the church in Laodicea. The address of this letter seems to pick up the theme in Paul's letter as Jesus identifies himself as the prime Source of all creation, the beginning. Paul's words were "the first-born of all creation" (Col. 1:15, NASB, RSV).

1. Jesus also refers to himself as *the Amen*. Christians know this word as the word of affirmation. In Isa. 65:16 God is called "the God of Amen" (NEB). This Hebrew

phrase is translated "the God of truth." So Jesus, *the faithful and true witness,* now addresses a congregation with the painful words of truth. He hastens to explain that He does so because He loves them. Hebrews 12 contains a longer passage which expounds the chastening of the Lord. It is done that they may be better sons. "Whom the Lord loveth he chasteneth, and scourgeth every son whom he receiveth" (Heb. 12:6). In that passage the writer reminds his readers that human fathers who are faithful in discipline, even though the motives may not always be the best, are revered. So he exhorts them to respect the God who disciplines His children in love and for their good.

2. The church in Laodicea had taken on the characteristics of the city. It was famed for its pure gold, its scarlet wool, and its healing ointment. These resources had brought the city wealth. The church seemed to have made peace with the mood of the city and the emperor cult. It was neither cold to the religion of its environment nor hot toward God. The figure used by our Lord is a very apt one. Water from the nearby hot springs was useful and pleasant for bathing and the like. Cool water from other springs assuaged the thirst. But lukewarm water was good only to make one vomit. Jesus laments, "How I wish you were either hot or cold!" (v. 15, NEB).

This church had lost its power to distinguish or react. It could neither be cold toward evil, nor hot for God. It was sickeningly neutral. In a world of half-truths and indistinct standards this church had become like it. It boasted not of its hot heart but its wealth, its clothes, and its health. The truthful One pronounced it *wretched, and miserable, and poor, and blind, and naked.* Real wealth is *gold tried in the fire.* This is a reference to martyrdom and to the need for them to stand up for something. Real raiment is the pure white garment, or being clothed with the purity of Christian obedience like the martyrs wear. Real healing is the salve of the Holy Spirit which brings cleansing and spiritual sight.

Peter Marshall, the unforgettable chaplain of the United States Senate, once prayed at the opening session of that deliberating body for God to help them to stand up for something lest they fall for everything. This is the burden of the message to the seventh church. They had become self-sufficient, and with it had come a blindness to the radical nature of the gospel. They were located in a key area of their world. A clear-cut witness was needed but was not forthcoming. Jesus loved them, but they made Him sick with their lukewarmness. Their condition was not unique. Such ineffectiveness has plagued the Christian Church through the years. How carefully our ears need to hear what the Spirit says.

3. The rebuke is followed by one of the most beautiful pictures in all of Holy Writ. Jesus says, *Behold, I stand at the door, and knock.* There are three ways in which this warm entreaty may be viewed.

a. It can be understood in an eschatological sense. The Bridegroom is about to arrive; already His knock is upon the door. He seeks to come and share the wonder of the marriage supper and sit with His bride on the throne. "Lukewarm church, repent," He exhorts, "Buy of Me gold, white garments, and eye salve, for I am coming quickly, in fact am already at the door."

b. This verse has been most commonly seen as the faithful invitation to every person to open his heart to the Savior who seeks to enter and share with Him. There is the story of a painter who portrayed Christ knocking at the heart's door. Viewers pointed out that there was no latch and asked if this was a mistake. No, said the painter, that is just the point. Christ knocks at a person's door, but the only way He can enter is if the door is opened from within. There is no other way. Jesus will never break down the door to come in.

To have His presence each one must open the door. Everyone hears the knock sometime, for the One who seeks entrance is no respecter of persons. Someway, somehow, sometime He will call on everyone. The tragedy is that so few hear and fewer still open the door. But those who do, know the joy of that new fellowship. He comes into the heart. There is feasting on the truths of eternal worth. There is the intimacy of His presence. There is the new place of power and meaning as the Christian shares the throne of Christ. All this may describe the joys of the coming reign of Christ in the new heaven and earth but also pictures accurately the new life in Christ here and now when He comes in and takes over.

c. We should remember, too, that each of these letters was addressed to the minister or *angel* of the church. The message seems to be through one for all. Perhaps it is the door of the minister or another who, hearing the knock, may open the door and let Christ into the church. When Peter was in prison, the church gathered and prayed. While they prayed, there came a knock on the door. It was Peter, but no one would believe the little girl who ran to see who was knocking. So the very Christ we seek and implore to come into the life of the church and make it what it ought to be, may be knocking at the door to do just that. Who will hear and open the door so the whole body may be blessed?

The church has felt the need for revival frequently. Often its members prayed earnestly for a blessed visitation of the Holy Spirit to make Christ real in a renewed sense of vision and glory. He is knocking if anyone will open the door. In every local congregation there could be one who is the key to revival and revisitation of the Spirit. He or she may not be the elected head, but if that one will open the door, he will in truth be the servant who precipitates the prayed-for revival. For Jesus promised the joy of His presence, the glory of feasting on His Word, and the achievement of sharing His throne for the whole church if one would open the door.

Whichever one of these three points of view one takes, the challenge is compelling, and the promise is overwhelming. Jesus will come to the heart of all who allow Him. He will come to the church who has someone concerned enough to open the door. He will come and set up His kingdom; and it is now upon us, for the Bridegroom is at the door.

The Lion Who Is a Lamb
Revelation 4:1—8:5

REVELATION 4

A Rainbow Around the Throne

Rev. 4:1-3

> 1 After this I looked, and, behold, a door was opened in heaven: and the first voice which I heard was as it were of a trumpet talking with me; which said, Come up hither, and I will shew thee things which must be hereafter.
> 2 And immediately I was in the spirit: and, behold, a throne was set in heaven, and one sat on the throne.
> 3 And he that sat was to look upon like a jasper and a sardine stone: and there was a rainbow round about the throne, in sight like unto an emerald.

1. Beginning with this fourth chapter, John turns to another vision which occurred after the messages to the churches had been given to him. Both had come during a vision of Christ among the churches. This new vision began with the sight of a door opened in heaven. This is not to be confused with the open door put in Philadelphia, or Ephesus, or Troas, or anywhere Christ makes possible the Church's proclamation of the gospel. They were doors to the hearts of men. This was a door into the presence of God. For he had no sooner seen the open door than a voice like a trumpet invited him to come up. The voice promised that he would see things which are yet to occur. This open door, then, was the opportunity to share the overview from heaven's vantage point. It was the invitation to see things as God sees them. It is an exciting prospect!

John hastens to explain that this journey into overview was a spiritual experience. "I was in the Spirit" (v. 2, RSV) are his words, and they are the same as his description of the vision of Christ in the midst of the churches holding the ministers in His hands. In the Spirit he saw God upon the throne. To be sure, in his Epistles he had written, "No man hath seen God at any time" (1 John 4:12; cf. John 1:18). But then he was talking about physical vision. Here he is speaking of spiritual sight. He only describes God as being *like a jasper and a sardine stone.* His reaction was similar to Ezekiel's who described the One on the throne as looking like sapphire (Ezek. 1:26-28; 10:1). Perhaps what he saw was brilliant light that shone like precious gems. It has not been uncommon for others, even some in modern times, to describe their vision or sense of God's presence in terms of shining light.

2. Both John and Ezekiel testified that around the throne of God there was a rainbow. Rainbows are caused by the brilliance of the sun's rays through moisture-laden air. But for the reader of the Bible the rainbow speaks primarily of the promise of God following the Flood that He would not again destroy the world with a flood. Whenever the rainbow is seen, He told Noah, it will remind man of His promise (Gen. 8:22) that seedtime and harvest would not fail.

For John and the first people with whom he shared his vision, the rainbow spoke to the anxieties about the ongoing of the world. In time of severe drought a rainbow's appearance meant God would not allow drought to last forever. God always keeps His promise. But in the light of what is to follow, the rainbow around the throne must have spiritual meaning. It is the assurance that "he that goeth forth and weepeth, bearing precious seed, shall doubtless come again with rejoicing, bringing his sheaves with him" (Ps. 126:6). It is a promise that God will prosper the proclamation of the gospel. The work of soul-saving and evangelism have the eternal promise of the rainbow.

Seedtime and harvest will not fail. God's Word will not return to Him void (Isa. 55:11).

The Heavens Rejoice at the Wonder of Creation

Rev. 4:4-11

4 And round about the throne were four and twenty seats: and upon the seats I saw four and twenty elders sitting, clothed in white raiment; and they had on their heads crowns of gold.
5 And out of the throne proceeded lightnings and thunderings and voices: and there were seven lamps of fire burning before the throne, which are the seven Spirits of God.
6 And before the throne there was a sea of glass like unto crystal: and in the midst of the throne, and round about the throne, were four beasts full of eyes before and behind.
7 And the first beast was like a lion, and the second beast like a calf, and the third beast had a face as a man, and the fourth beast was like a flying eagle.
8 And the four beasts had each of them six wings about him; and they were full of eyes within: and they rest not day and night, saying, Holy, holy, holy, Lord God Almighty, which was, and is, and is to come.
9 And when those beasts give glory and honour and thanks to him that sat on the throne, who liveth for ever and ever,
10 The four and twenty elders fall down before him that sat on the throne, and worship him that liveth for ever and ever, and cast their crowns before the throne, saying,
11 Thou art worthy, O Lord, to receive glory and honour and power: for thou hast created all things, and for thy pleasure they are and were created.

1. The God who keeps His promises sits on the throne in the center of His universe. Seated around Him are 24 elders. Each has a crown of gold and wears white robes. They present a picture of God's orderly reign. The pattern is not dissimilar to the structure Jethro suggested to Moses (Exod. 18:18-23). Whatever the meaning of the number, these elders portray the rule of God through men. In the garden at the dawn of creation God gave dominion to man (Gen. 1:28). In the Old Testament the line of authority was represented through the 12 tribes, in the New Testament through the 12 apostles. The 24 could be the total of both groups.

2. Out of the throne of God come flashes of lightning and thunder and voices. Before the throne are the spirits of God like lamps burning. Around the throne are the living

creatures with the likeness of: a lion, a calf, a creature with the face of a man, and an eagle. These living creatures are full of eyes, seeing everything. Together with the sea of glass they seem to represent the created order. They join in constant praise; indeed, the whole universe sings praise to the Creator. The language of heaven is praise. The highest words of praise created beings can use are "Holy, holy, holy." The most expressive medium of this praise is song. The Psalmist wrote, "The heavens declare the glory of God" (Ps. 19:1). This vision of John graphically bears out this statement. The living creatures and the elders sing, "Worthy art thou, our Lord and God, to receive glory and honor and power, for thou didst create all things, and by thy will they existed and were created" (v. 11, RSV).

It must be said about praise that it is the response of the soul to the wonder of God's glory. One might watch the heavens rejoicing and giving praise to God and think that God demands it. But praise strengthens the soul. It is not as much required as desired. Abraham grew strong in his faith as he gave glory to God (Rom. 4:20).

God desires man's praise because it will be the soul's greatest joy when it is given. The song of praise that is the symphony of heaven comes from grateful hearts who find joy in praising their Creator. This praise is a timeless activity. The heavens are forever telling the wonder of the work of God's hand.

REVELATION 5

The Heavens Rejoice at the Wonder of Salvation

Rev. 5:1-14

1 And I saw in the right hand of him that sat on the throne a book written within and on the backside, sealed with seven seals.
2 And I saw a strong angel proclaiming with a loud voice, Who is worthy to open the book, and to loose the seals thereof?
3 And no man in heaven, nor in earth, neither under the earth, was able to open the book, neither to look thereon.

4 And I wept much, because no man was found worthy to open and to read the book, neither to look thereon.

5 And one of the elders saith unto me, Weep not: behold, the Lion of the tribe of Juda, the Root of David, hath prevailed to open the book, and to loose the seven seals thereof.

6 And I beheld, and, lo, in the midst of the throne and of the four beasts, and in the midst of the elders, stood a Lamb as it had been slain, having seven horns and seven eyes, which are the seven Spirits of God sent forth into all the earth.

7 And he came and took the book out of the right hand of him that sat upon the throne.

8 And when he had taken the book, the four beasts and four and twenty elders fell down before the Lamb, having every one of them harps, and golden vials full of odours, which are the prayers of saints.

9 And they sung a new song, saying, Thou art worthy to take the book, and to open the seals thereof: for thou wast slain, and hast redeemed us to God by thy blood out of every kindred, and tongue, and people, and nation;

10 And hast made us unto our God kings and priests: and we shall reign on the earth.

11 And I beheld, and I heard the voice of many angels round about the throne and the beasts and the elders: and the number of them was ten thousand times ten thousand, and thousands of thousands;

12 Saying with a loud voice, Worthy is the Lamb that was slain to receive power, and riches, and wisdom, and strength, and honour, and glory, and blessing.

13 And every creature which is in heaven, and on the earth, and under the earth, and such as are in the sea, and all that are in them, heard I saying, Blessing, and honour, and glory, and power, be unto him that sitteth upon the throne, and unto the Lamb for ever and ever.

14 And the four beasts said, Amen. And the four and twenty elders fell down and worshipped him that liveth for ever and ever.

1. In the midst of all this rejoicing a shadow crosses John's heart. He sees a scroll in the right hand of God. It has been written on both sides and sealed with seven seals. The scroll, he seems to sense, is the story of redemption. The blight on creation is man's sin. The beauty and the harmony of creation have been disrupted by man's rebellion. The apostle Paul described it as the groaning of creation for redemption (Rom. 8:22). John seems to know that the scroll contains the plan of redemption, the way in which God will bring back to himself lost man. But when the call for someone worthy to loose the seals and unfold the story was given, no man was found worthy to do it. John says he wept much that no one was found worthy. This is the shadow that falls across the beautiful universe. It is marred by sin, and no one is found to reveal the remedy.

There is a remedy, of course, for He who made man knew what might happen and had a solution. It is all written out and sealed.

2. John's sorrow is assuaged to some degree by the assurance of one of the elders that *the Lion of the tribe of Judah, the Root of David,* has triumphed. He is able to open the scroll and the seven seals (v. 5). This was not news, for it has been the long promise of the prophets. Throughout the history of God's people the growing concept took root that God had an answer for the world's trouble and sin. Hope would come through the Seed of David. The Lion of Judah would prevail. John is reminded of the hope that had sustained Israel, and his tears are dried.

3. But when he sees the Lion, John is surprised by the figure in the midst of the assembled host. It is a Lamb; and even more surprising, it is a Lamb that had been slain. Now the message is clear. The way of salvation is the way of the Cross. In this world men accomplish deeds by strength and power. Christ conquers in the meekness of a lamb that is slaughtered. The wounded Lamb that John saw had horns, the symbol of power, and eyes, the symbol of knowledge. The One who is slain in weakness rules in power and knowledge. There is omnipotence— *seven horns;* omniscience—*seven eyes;* and omnipresence —*the seven Spirits of God sent forth into all the earth.*

The vision brings added support to the Christian claim that God will save the world "not with swords' loud clashing" but "with deeds of love and mercy."[4] The Lion who was promised is the Lamb who was slain. God has raised Him up to be Lord of all. In confidence the Lamb takes the scroll. The four living creatures and the 24 elders, having the censers filled with prayers of the saints, rise to sing a new song. They have sung a song of praise to the Creator. Now they sing a song of praise for redemption.

4. The censers with the prayers of the saints seem to suggest that redeemed men and women have an integral part

in the salvation of the world through prayer. In the seventh chapter this idea is given further support. This is also descriptive of the nature of salvation, for those who are redeemed become prayerfully involved in the winning of others. The people who are saved do not just rejoice in their own salvation; they long for the salvation of those they love and others. The gospel chorus goes, "We're saved, saved to tell others."

5. The elders and the living creatures sing of the worthiness of the Lamb, lauding Him because He had redeemed them to God with His blood from every tribe and language and people and nation and had made them to be kings and priests to serve God and reign on the earth. They are joined by all the hosts of heaven. The numbers of angels John gives are more the symbol of numberless thousands than a particular mathematical figure.[5] They sing of the worthiness of the Lamb. In turn the hosts of heaven are joined by every creature in heaven and earth and under the earth and in the sea, singing praise to God and to the Lamb. Where John first saw only God on the throne as the Object of creation's praise, now he sees the Lamb standing with God, and together they are the Objects of all the hosts of heaven and earth singing their praise for salvation, to which the living creatures reply, "Amen," and the elders fall down and worship. Heaven sings praise to the Creator and a new song of praise to the Redeemer.

REVELATION 6

Salvation Is Accomplished Amid Life's Woes

Rev. 6:1-17

> 1   And I saw when the Lamb opened one of the seals, and I heard, as it were the noise of thunder, one of the four beasts saying, Come and see.
> 2   And I saw, and behold a white horse: and he that sat on him had a bow; and a crown was given unto him: and he went forth conquering, and to conquer.

3 And when he had opened the second seal, I heard the second beast say, Come and see.

4 And there went out another horse that was red: and power was given to him that sat thereon to take peace from the earth, and that they should kill one another: and there was given unto him a great sword.

5 And when he had opened the third seal, I heard the third beast say, Come and see. And I beheld, and lo a black horse; and he that sat on him had a pair of balances in his hand.

6 And I heard a voice in the midst of the four beasts say, A measure of wheat for a penny, and three measures of barley for a penny; and see thou hurt not the oil and the wine.

7 And when he had opened the fourth seal, I heard the voice of the fourth beast say, Come and see.

8 And I looked, and behold a pale horse: and his name that sat on him was Death, and Hell followed with him. And Power was given unto them over the fourth part of the earth, to kill with sword, and with hunger, and with death, and with the beasts of the earth.

9 And when he had opened the fifth seal, I saw under the altar the souls of them that were slain for the word of God, and for the testimony which they held:

10 And they cried with a loud voice, saying, How long, O Lord, holy and true, dost thou not judge and avenge our blood on them that dwell on the earth?

11 And white robes were given unto every one of them; and it was said unto them, that they should rest yet for a little season, until their fellowservants also and their brethren, that should be killed as they were, should be fulfilled.

12 And I beheld when he had opened the sixth seal, and, lo, there was a great earthquake; and the sun became black as sackcloth of hair, and the moon became as blood;

13 And the stars of heaven fell unto the earth, even as a fig tree casteth her untimely figs, when she is shaken of a mighty wind.

14 And the heaven departed as a scroll when it is rolled together; and every mountain and island were moved out of their places.

15 And the kings of the earth, and the great men, and the rich men, and the chief captains, and the mighty men, and every bondman, and every free man, hid themselves in the dens and in the rocks of the mountains;

16 And said to the mountains and rocks, Fall on us, and hide us from the face of him that sitteth on the throne, and from the wrath of the Lamb:

17 For the great day of his wrath is come; and who shall be able to stand?

1. The Lamb breaks the first seal. John discovers that salvation is carried on in the midst of trouble and catastrophe. These common woes of life have been called the judgments of God. Such they were in Egypt. The difference here is that they fall on all. No living creature has avoided the woes that are now presented. The white horse and its rider depict the conquerors who have ridden roughshod

over innocent men, women, and children. The red horse and its rider represent the war and conflict which has bathed the world in blood, and no nation has avoided it. The black horse and its rider who has scales in his hands speak of famine, inflation, and scarcity. The pale horse and its rider are death. These four woes have always been present in greater or lesser degree throughout history. To be sure, they are judgments of God because they are the fruit of man's inhumanity to man and his rejection of God's way. But they are also the common lot of every man.

The fifth seal reveals the souls of the martyrs under the altar. They have been slain for their testimony to the Word of God. They cry with a loud voice for justice to be done, but their cries do not bring cessation of the killing of people who follow the Lamb. They are given white robes and told to rest yet for a season until the list is completed of those who are to die for their testimony. Men have been forced to die for their faith in every generation. It is still sadly a part of the common woes that occur. No one who follows the Savior is sure when he will be asked to join their martyrdom.

The sixth seal, when opened, precipitates a series of cosmic upheavals. So great is it that the kings and great men as well as the common lot hide themselves. They cry out that the great day of wrath has come. Two things compound their fear. One is that cosmic events have always terrified men. The second is the inner conviction that the events are related to their conduct. They have made God angry. Their consciences speak forth to accuse them.

2. While they are pictured in frightening intensity, one cannot escape the fact that all of the above-described woes are common to life. Conquest, conflict, famine, death, martyrdom, and cosmic upheaval are no respecters of persons. They mar and ruin the beauty of life for all they touch. The people of God are not immune. The gospel must be preached and lived in the midst of them all. This

is not to say that providential circumstances do not often protect the servants of Christ, for they do. But such interventions are miracles and so happen only in special cases for specific reasons. One of the servants of Christ may be supernaturally spared while another falls victim. Some people are tempted to think that being spared is God's greatest and best protection. Jesus taught that God's best was to bear witness to His presence in the midst of them. When He foretold of the woes that come to mankind, He said, "In your patience possess ye your souls" (Luke 21:19).

Those who fulfill the Great Commission must understand that these kinds of woes will come in some measure. They must be faithful to their task in spite of and in the midst of them. Christ does not call His followers to an easy life. He calls them to be faithful. One may fear that these woes are too many and come too often. One may earnestly pray to avoid them for the gospel's sake, and still not have his prayer answered. Yet it should be some comfort that God knows all about it, and He has a purpose greater than all that may happen. This watchcare of the Heavenly Father is dramatically testified to in the seventh and part of the eighth chapters.

REVELATION 7

Who Shall Be Able to Stand?

Rev. 7:1—8:5

1 And after these things I saw four angels standing on the four corners of the earth, holding the four winds of the earth, that the wind should not blow on the earth, nor on the sea, nor on any tree.
2 And I saw another angel ascending from the east, having the seal of the living God: and he cried with a loud voice to the four angels, to whom it was given to hurt the earth and the sea,
3 Saying Hurt not the earth, neither the sea, nor the trees, till we have sealed the servants of our God in their foreheads.
4 And I heard the number of them which were sealed: and there were sealed an hundred and forty and four thousand of all the tribes of the children of Israel.
5 Of the tribe of Juda were sealed twelve thousand. Of the tribe of

Reuben were sealed twelve thousand. Of the tribe of Gad were sealed twelve thousand.
6 Of the tribe of Aser were sealed twelve thousand. Of the tribe of Nephthalim were sealed twelve thousand. Of the tribe of Manasses were sealed twelve thousand.
7 Of the tribe of Simeon were sealed twelve thousand. Of the tribe of Levi were sealed twelve thousand. Of the tribe of Issachar were sealed twelve thousand.
8 Of the tribe of Zabulon were sealed twelve thousand. Of the tribe of Joseph were sealed twelve thousand. Of the tribe of Benjamin were sealed twelve thousand.
9 After this I beheld, and, lo, a great multitude, which no man could number, of all nations, and kindreds, and people, and tongues, stood before the throne, and before the Lamb, clothed with white robes, and palms in their hands;
10 And cried with a loud voice, saying, Salvation to our God which sitteth upon the throne, and unto the Lamb.
11 And all the angels stood round about the throne, and about the elders and the four beasts, and fell before the throne on their faces, and worshipped God,
12 Saying, Amen: Blessing, and glory, and wisdom, and thanksgiving, and honour, and power, and might, be unto our God for ever and ever. Amen.
13 And one of the elders answered, saying unto me, What are these which are arrayed in white robes? and whence came they?
14 And I said unto him, Sir, thou knowest. And he said to me. These are they which came out of great tribulation, and have washed their robes, and made them white in the blood of the Lamb.
15 Therefore are they before the throne of God, and serve him day and night in his temple: and he that sitteth on the throne shall dwell among them.
16 They shall hunger no more, neither thirst any more; neither shall the sun light on them, nor any heat.
17 For the Lamb which is in the midst of the throne shall feed them, and shall lead them unto living fountains of waters: and God shall wipe away all tears from their eyes.
1 And when he had opened the seventh seal, there was silence in heaven about the space of half an hour.
2 And I saw the seven angels which stood before God; and to them were given seven trumpets.
3 And another angel came and stood at the altar, having a golden censer; and there was given unto him much incense, that he should offer it with the prayers of all saints upon the golden altar which was before the throne.
4 And the smoke of the incense, which came with the prayers of the saints, ascended up before God out of the angel's hand.
5 And the angel took the censer, and filled it with fire of the altar, and cast it into the earth: and there were voices, and thunderings, and lightnings, and an earthquake.

1. Between the opening of the sixth and seventh seals there are two events recorded that may appear to be unrelated. However, the sixth chapter closes with the question, "Who shall be able to stand?" The first verse of the

seventh chapter suggests the answer. No one could stand were it not for the restraining hand on the destructive forces poised for ultimate devastation. John saw four angels at the four corners of the earth. They were holding four winds to keep them from blowing. Then another angel cried to them that the earth was not to be destroyed until the work of redemption (sealing) is finished.

History is filled with moments when God has intervened to keep His world from being obliterated. He has promised, and given a rainbow in proof, that seedtime and harvest will not fail. The winds are held back until the work of bringing home the family of God is complete. So certain is the completion of the task that John even hears the number of the redeemed. To be sure this is not a precise figure for the number is a multiple of a thousand which indicates it represents an infinite number. Those who are yet to be saved, John learns, together with those who already have been make a multitude so great that no man can number them.

Sometimes the work of evangelism seems painfully slow. It is easy to feel that it is a hopeless or at least fruitless endeavor. But when the work is done at last, the great, new family of God from every nation and kindred and people and tongue will stand before the throne, wearing white robes and with palms in their hands. They will sing redemption's story. They have come out of *great tribulation,* which could refer to the woes that have been described in the preceding chapter. They were born in a world which knows anguish and pain. In the world to come these woes are gone forever for those who have accepted the redemption Christ offers.

2. The woes of life, wearisome and frightening though they may be, will one day be past. Verses 15 to 17 contain some of the most comforting and reassuring words in all the Bible. They very pointedly include the whole family of the redeemed. While they do not promise relief from life's storms, they do promise the presence, care, and com-

fort of the Lamb of God. He has suffered more than any of His servants. He did so to save them from eternal punishment and share with them the glory of the kingdom of God. He suffered because He loved them. He comforts them because He knows what they have suffered.

So John's vision becomes an exhortation. The work of proclaiming the gospel and bringing men to the Savior is not done in a secluded haven. It will be carried on in the midst of life's woes. Their cruel blows will be felt by those who witness for the Lord. But they have the promise of God's restraining hand until their work is done. And in addition they will have the eternal joys of living forever with the whole family of the redeemed in the presence of the Redeemer.

REVELATION 8

3. There is another factor in the work of evangelism pictured briefly at the beginning of the eighth chapter. The seventh seal is opened. For a half hour there is silence in heaven. Perhaps this means in part that what will follow is so terrible that the hush of awful apprehension had fallen on the rejoicing hosts. And well it might, for no man who has experienced the love of Jesus can ever contemplate the judgment of the wicked with anything but deep sorrow and awe. It may be the hush of surprise, for with the opening of the seventh seal seven angels stand before the throne of God and are given seven trumpets. The last woe involves seven severe judgments. God's restraint so that the gospel can be proclaimed does not lesson but, in fact, intensifies the impact of His judgment.

Before the trumpets are blown, however, and this series of terrible judgments falls, there appears another angel with a golden censer. In this censer there is incense mixed with prayers of all saints. These are offered before the throne. One cannot help but feel that this event is equally, if not more so, responsible for the half hour silence. It seems to say that heaven listens when the saints pray. This, like God's restraining hand, is another major factor in the work of evangelism. God hears prayer. Prayer can bring the solution of problems and the salvation of the lost. In 2 Chron. 7:14 God promised that, if His people would humble themselves and pray, healing and forgiveness would come to them. This promise has been claimed throughout the years as Christians have prayed for revival.

When the prayers of all saints had been offered and had risen with the incense before the throne of God, the angel took the censer and filled it with the fire from the altar. He *cast it into the earth: and there were voices, and thunderings, and lightnings, and an earthquake.* The prayers had gone up, and the fire came down. In Acts 4 it is recorded that, in the midst of threats of death upon the apostles for preaching Christ, they prayed, and the place was shaken. Prayers are heard, and they bring shaking and the fire of God.

Whatever the woes of life that may encounter the Christian's obedience to the Great Commission, John's vision reminds him that God will restrain the fiercest winds and bring success at last. The Christian's part is to be faithful and to pray. For heaven is still while God hears his prayer. The very vessel that carries his prayer to God brings back to earth the fire from the altar which shakes and changes things.

The Consequences of Sin Call for Repentance
Revelation 8:6—11:19

The Beginning of Sorrows
Rev. 8:6—9:21

6 And the seven angels which had the seven trumpets prepared themselves to sound.

7 The first angel sounded, and there followed hail and fire mingled with blood, and they were cast upon the earth: and the third part of trees was burnt up, and all green grass was burnt up.

8 And the second angel sounded, and as it were a great mountain burning with fire was cast into the sea: and the third part of the sea became blood;

9 And the third part of the creatures which were in the sea, and had life, died; and the third part of the ships were destroyed.

10 And the third angel sounded, and there fell a great star from heaven, burning as it were a lamp, and it fell upon the third part of the rivers, and upon the fountains of waters;

11 And the name of the star is called Wormwood: and the third part of the waters became wormwood; and many men died of the waters, because they were made bitter.

12 And the fourth angel sounded, and the third part of the sun was smitten, and the third part of the moon, and the third part of the stars; so as the third part of them was darkened, and the day shone not for a third part of it, and the night likewise.

13 And I beheld, and heard an angel flying through the midst of heaven, saying with a loud voice, Woe, woe, woe, to the inhabiters of the earth by reason of the other voices of the trumpet of the three angels, which are yet to sound!

1 And the fifth angel sounded, and I saw a star fall from heaven unto the earth: and to him was given the key of the bottomless pit.

2 And he opened the bottomless pit; and there arose a smoke out of the pit, as the smoke of a great furnace; and the sun and the air were darkened by reason of the smoke of the pit.

3 And there came out of the smoke locusts upon the earth: and unto them was given power, as the scorpions of the earth have power.

4 And it was commanded them that they should not hurt the grass of the earth, neither any green thing, neither any tree; but only those men which have not the seal of God in their foreheads.

5 And to them it was given that they should not kill them, but that

they should be tormented five months: and their torment was as the torment of a scorpion, when he striketh a man.

6 And in those days shall men seek death, and shall not find it; and shall desire to die, and death shall flee from them.

7 And the shapes of the locusts were like unto horses prepared unto battle; and on their heads were as it were crowns like gold, and their faces were as the faces of men.

8 And they had hair as the hair of women, and their teeth were as the teeth of lions.

9 And they had breastplates, as it were breastplates of iron; and the sound of their wings was as the sound of chariots of many horses running to battle.

10 And they had tails like unto scorpions, and there were stings in their tails: and their power was to hurt men five months.

11 And they had a king over them, which is the angel of the bottomless pit, whose name in the Hebrew tongue is Abaddon, but in the Greek tongue hath his name Apollyon.

12 One woe is past; and, behold, there come two woes more hereafter.

13 And the sixth angel sounded, and I heard a voice from the four horns of the golden altar which is before God,

14 Saying to the sixth angel which had the trumpet, Loose the four angels which are bound in the great river Euphrates.

15 And the four angels were loosed, which were prepared for an hour, and a day, and a month, and a year, for to slay the third part of men.

16 And the number of the army of the horsemen were two hundred thousand thousand: and I heard the number of them.

17 And thus I saw the horses in the vision, and them that sat on them, having breastplates of fire, and of Jacinth, and brimstone: and the heads of the horses were as the heads of lions; and out of their mouths issued fire and smoke and brimstone.

18 By these three was the third part of men killed, by the fire, and by the smoke, and by the brimstone, which issued out of their mouths.

19 For their power is in their mouth, and in their tails: for their tails were like unto serpents, and had heads, and with them they do hurt.

20 And the rest of the men which were not killed by these plagues yet repented not of the works of their hands, that they should not worship devils, and idols of gold, and silver, and brass, and stone, and of wood: which neither can see, nor hear, nor walk:

21 Neither repented they of their murders, nor of their sorceries, nor of their fornication, nor of their thefts.

The opening of the seventh seal revealed the imminence of seven judgments of God upon the wicked world. They are, in fact, a seventh of life's common woes. They are judgments which are intended as warnings. Like the plagues on Egypt, which were sent not so much to punish Pharaoh (although they were deserved) as to bring him to the point of letting the people of Israel leave, these trumpets announce catastrophes designed to bring repentance. They could be called God's interim judgments. Some of them are quite similar to the plagues visited on Egypt, such as hail, blood, and darkness. A fourth, elements of fire like hot lava from a volcano, is added. The last three are preceded by further warnings of an angel who cries, *Woe, woe, woe.*

The purpose of these judgments is to call the world to repentance. The destruction and suffering is great in this series of judgments, but never worldwide. In the first four, a third part of the world is smitten.

REVELATION 9

In the fifth and sixth judgments the scope or time of the suffering to be inflicted is limited. But always the restraining hand of God is seen. He allows terrible catastrophes to happen but limited them in order that the remainder of the people might repent. Partway through the series the added warnings are given which suggests that the desired repentance did not result. At the end of the ninth chapter are the sad words: *And the rest of the men which were not killed by these plagues yet repented not of the works of their hands, that they should not worship devils, and idols of gold, and silver, and brass, and stone, and of wood: which neither can see, nor hear, nor walk: neither repented they of their murders, nor of their sorceries, nor of their fornication, nor of their thefts.*

In this case, at least, the death penalty was not a deterrent. Two-thirds of the world saw men die for their sins but did not repent. It may very well be that the death penalty is a proper and appropriate retribution for crimes which deprive people of life, but the hard heart of sinful man is such that even when he knows and sees the consequences of sins, he still does not repent. The surgeon general of the United States has warned that smoking, especially cigarettes, leads to lung cancer. But millions continue to smoke, even many physicians themselves.

1. One cannot read the story of the severe judgment that John records in the eighth and ninth chapters of the Revelation without realizing the extent to which God has gone and will go to bring men to repentance. The apostle declared that He was "not willing that any should perish, but that all should come to repentance" (2 Pet. 3:9). Here is shown the foolhardiness of the sinner who knows and sees one warning after another and yet will not turn from his sin.

2. As terrible as these pictures are, they are not exaggerated or untrue to life. They have happened and they will happen to many generations. In some ways they are happening in much less measure all the time. Many a pastor has sought to help people in times of distress which are clearly judgments upon them and has been left with the question, "What more has to happen before they change?" God's judgments are fair but restrained. There's a wideness in His mercy and a kindness in His justice which is more than liberty, the much-loved hymn extols.[6] Samson had disobeyed God and shared the secret of his strength with a woman who traded him physical pleasure for the chance to enslave him, and his God-given strength was gone. For some time blinded by the loss of his eyes, he was hitched to a mill and ground corn like an ox. But the Bible says that one day he realized his hair was beginning to grow. This meant he could have another chance, and he did. His punishment was severe but not without an opportunity to repent (Judg. 16:22, 28).

3. What should be the Christian's response to this? Like those who remain, he sees the judgment of God and knows what it means about sins and final destiny. There are four answers given in the 10th and 11th chapters that will be examined in the next section. At least the Christian should see this both as warning and prediction. God's judgment is now restrained, but it will one day be full measured. Jesus told the disciples that, when they see these kinds of things, they should understand that these are but the

beginnings of sorrow. If men repent, a new day can come; but if they do not, all that has happened is but a prelude to the final day. Judgments will not be less but greater. The plight of the sinner grows progressively worse.

Christian Witness to a World in Judgment
Revelation 10:1—11:19

REVELATION 10

The Angel and the Thunders

Rev. 10:1-7

> 1 And I saw another mighty angel come down from heaven, clothed with a cloud: and a rainbow was upon his head, and his face was as it were the sun, and his feet as pillars of fire:
> 2 And he had in his hand a little book open: and he set his right foot upon the sea, and his left foot on the earth,
> 3 And cried with a loud voice, as when a lion roareth: and when he had cried, seven thunders uttered their voices.
> 4 And when the seven thunders had uttered their voices, I was about to write: and I heard a voice from heaven saying unto me, Seal up those things which the seven thunders uttered, and write them not.
> 5 And the angel which I saw stand upon the sea and upon the earth lifted up his hand to heaven,
> 6 And sware by him that liveth for ever and ever, who created heaven, and the things that therein are, and the earth, and the things which are therein, that there should be time no longer:
> 7 But in the days of the voice of the seventh angel, when he shall begin to sound, the mystery of God should be finished, as he hath declared to his servants the prophets.

1. When judgment comes, the proclivity of men to ignore its call makes the Christian's witness both needed and risky. Two woes have passed, and there is no repentance. Then John sees another angel. He does not come with warning, however; he comes with promise—there is a rainbow around his head. The storms have been fierce among

men. In the pause that comes before the seventh and final judgment, the angel appears with words of encouragement. He has with him the light of the throne and the sign of God's faithfulness to this promise. The angel brings a little scroll that is open in his hand. With a loud voice he cries out that there will be no more delay; God's patience is at an end. He promises that when the seventh trumpet sounds, the mystery of God will be finished, as He has declared through His prophets. The day of salvation is not unlimited; there will be an end.

2. It is a dramatic moment for John. The light and rainbow are themselves reminiscent of his vision of the throne. When the angel speaks, John describes it as the roar of a lion. The voice of the angel is accompanied by seven thunders. They were not just echoes, however; for John starts to write down what the message of the thunders is, and he is stopped by a voice from heaven telling him not to write it down. When Paul was caught up into heaven, as he describes it in 2 Corinthians 12, he heard "unspeakable words, which it is not lawful for a man to utter" (v. 4). Mankind is told all they need to know but not all there is. Jesus once said to the disciples that He had many things to say, but they were not able to bear them then (John 16:12). One is whimsically tempted to wonder what the message of the thunders would have revealed. Perhaps the mysteries of the Book of Revelation would be solved. At least John heard them and understood, even though he was not allowed to speak them. There are times when the things God has revealed to us are better kept as "God's secrets."

3. To say the least, it is moving to see this picture. Here is a heavenly messenger with all the brilliance and promise of the throne of God, standing with one foot on the land and one on the sea. His voice is as commanding as that of the jungle lion which makes all the rest of the animals tremble in silence. With an open scroll in his hand which he raises to heaven, he announces that God has set a time

for the end. Then there will be no more long-suffering or patience. The judgments of God which were to bring men to repentance have fallen on them, and they are steadfast in their refusal to repent. The long story of the efforts to win the love and loyalty of His highest creation will be ended. The long list of those who have obediently witnessed, many at the cost of their lives, is about complete. There remains only the sounding of the seventh trumpet, and the end comes.

But before it does, the world is to see four vignettes of Christian witness to the world in judgment.

Eating the Little Book

Rev. 10:8-11

> 8 And the voice which I heard from heaven spake unto me again, and said, Go and take the little book which is open in the hand of the angel which standeth upon the sea and upon the earth.
> 9 And I went unto the angel, and said unto him, Give me the little book. And he said unto me, Take it, and eat it up; and it shall make thy belly bitter, but it shall be in thy mouth sweet as honey.
> 10 And I took the little book out of the angel's hand, and ate it up; and it was in my mouth sweet as honey: and as soon as I had eaten it, my belly was bitter.
> 11 And he said unto me, Thou must prophesy again before many peoples, and nations, and tongues, and kings.

The first picture is one very similar to the call of the prophet Ezekiel. John is told to ask for the scroll. When he does so, the angel tells him to eat it. It is sweet to eat but becomes bitter in his stomach. In both situations the prophets are told to preach to people who have proven themselves to be stubborn and hardhearted. The Word of God is pleasant to all who receive it. It is the food that delights the eater. But for John it turned bitter within, for it must be shared. In spite of all that terrifies one in the world around him when the judgments of God are released, there is another deeper concern which is the urgency of the message of God. "The days are hastening on," as the carol puts it. The Word of God, which is so sweet and meaningful to those who will accept it, must be proclaimed.

The Measuring Rod

Rev. 11:1-2

> 1 And there was given me a reed like unto a rod: and the angel stood, saying, Rise, and measure the temple of God, and the altar, and them that worship therein.
>
> 2 But the court which is without the temple leave out, and measure it not; for it is given unto the Gentiles: and the holy city shall they tread under foot forty and two months.

The second vignette portrays the Church, the people of God. The angel, presumably the same one who held the book, now gives John a measuring rod and tells him to measure the temple of God. For the Christian, the temple of God is the body of believers. God is in their midst, and together they form the living temple. They are held together by love and the fellowship of the Spirit. They are one in Christ. At all times, but especially in the hour of judgment on the world, the Church itself must be subject to self-discipline. Discipline is a part of the obligation and strength of the people of God.

The outer court of the Temple in Jerusalem was one where both Jew and Gentile could mingle. Gentiles could not come into the Temple proper. Because of this the outer court became the symbol of the accommodation the people of God made with the worldly powers. Judaism had survived because of this accommodation the outer court symbolized. The Church cannot and must not allow itself this accommodation. Its strength is maintained as it keeps itself separated from the world. Times of judgment require renewed commitment. The angel seems to suggest that the outer court fraternization had led to the trampling of the holy city. This may be a reference to the destruction of Jerusalem. It certainly should be a warning to the Church to put itself under the measuring rod. Christ's purpose is to gather unto himself a unique people unstained by the world. There must be enough difference between the Church and the world to be noticeable; especially is this true when the world reels under the judgments from its sins.

The Two Witnesses

Rev. 11:3-18

3 And I will give power unto my two witnesses, and they shall prophesy a thousand two hundred and threescore days, clothed in sackcloth.
4 These are the two olive trees, and the two candlesticks standing before the God of the earth.
5 And if any man will hurt them, fire proceedeth out of their mouth, and devoureth their enemies: and if any man will hurt them, he must in this manner be killed.
6 These have power to shut heaven, that it rain not in the days of their prophecy: and have power over waters to turn them to blood, and to smite the earth with all plagues, as often as they will.
7 And when they shall have finished their testimony, the beast that ascendeth out of the bottomless pit shall make war against them, and shall overcome them, and kill them.
8 And their dead bodies shall lie in the street of the great city, which spiritually is called Sodom and Egypt, where also our Lord was crucified.
9 And they of the people and kindreds and tongues and nations shall see their dead bodies three days and an half, and shall not suffer their dead bodies to be put in graves.
10 And they that dwell upon the earth shall rejoice over them, and make merry, and shall send gifts one to another; because these two prophets tormented them that dwelt on the earth.
11 And after three days and an half the Spirit of life from God entered into them, and they stood upon their feet; and great fear fell upon them which saw them.
12 And they heard a great voice from heaven saying unto them, Come up hither. And they ascended up to heaven in a cloud; and their enemies beheld them.
13 And the same hour was there a great earthquake, and the tenth part of the city fell, and in the earthquake were slain of men seven thousand: and the remnant were affrighted, and gave glory to the God of heaven.
14 The second woe is past; and, behold, the third woe cometh quickly.
15 And the seventh angel sounded; and there were great voices in heaven, saying, The kingdoms of this world are become the kingdoms of our Lord, and of his Christ; and he shall reign for ever and ever.
16 And the four and twenty elders, which sat before God on their seats, fell upon their faces, and worshipped God,
17 Saying, We give thee thanks, O Lord God Almighty, which art, and wast, and art to come; because thou hast taken to thee thy great power, and hast reigned.
18 And the nations were angry, and thy wrath is come, and the time of the death, that they should be judged, and that thou shouldest

give reward unto thy servants the prophets, and to the saints, and them
that fear thy name, small and great; and shouldest destroy them which
destroy the earth.

The third picture is of the two witnesses who, when
they have completed their mission, are killed by the beast
from the bottomless pit. Their bodies lie in the streets
three days and a half while the men of the world rejoice
over their destruction. Then the spirit of life enters into
them. They are called up into heaven, and their enemies
behold them in the cloud.

1. There are many nominations for the identities of these
witnesses. Since there are other visions which include
Moses and Elijah, they are suggested. Both were with
Jesus in the Transfiguration. Both have mystery and supernatural circumstances surrounding their departure
from this life. They personify the law and the prophets.
They relate to the power given the witnesses to shut heav-
en so it would not rain, to turn the waters to blood, and to
plague the earth. However, the candlesticks and olive
trees are the figures used of Zerubbabel and the high priest
Joshua, who loomed large in the return of Israel from the
Exile (Zechariah 3—4). It could be that traits of both are
in part intended.

2. The number two symbolizes the authenticity of a witness. When Jesus sent out the disciples on their first
preaching assignments, it was by twos. In His formula for
the discipline of erring members, Jesus instructs the
Church to send two and promises that where two or three
are gathered in His name He is in the midst (Matt. 18:15-
20). All of these references seem to indicate that the two
witnesses are the Church bearing her testimony and proclaiming the gospel in the world under the judgment of
God. They prophesy in humility, clothed in sackcloth. The
strength of Christian testimony is its recognition of its own
weakness and confession of its dependence upon God.

3. There is no human "triumphalism" in this picture.

The witnesses do whatever they can in the power of God. They have His protection while they complete their assignment. But they have been sent to witness to a Christ-rejecting world, and that world under the leadership of the beast from the bottomless pit accomplishes their death and rejoices sadistically over it. They are vulnerable and suffer death for their witness.

What this must have said to the Christians of John's day and soon thereafter who died for their faith! What it says to us upon whom the ends of the world have come! Our authenticity lies not in our protection or success from a human point of view. We must be faithful and, as far as we are able, complete our tasks in the confidence that if it kills us, our Master died before us. The God who raised Him from death shall make us alive as well. The authenticity of the witnesses was that they were faithful unto death, and after three days and a half God raised them to life. Peter told the disciples in the Upper Room that when they chose one to be a disciple in place of Judas they should, among other qualifications, take one who was a witness to Christ's resurrection. Well, these witnesses qualify for discipleship. They experience in their bodies the resurrection power of their Lord.

4. They are called up into the heavens. This is the only event in the Revelation which in any remote sense could correspond to Paul's teaching of a rapture of the saints. It certainly is not a secret event as is sometimes postulated by those who seek to put events together, for the witnesses ascend to heaven in a cloud and their enemies behold them. All the world knew at last that their rejoicing over the death of the witnesses was premature. It only revealed their own stubborn disposition to reject the message of God. Their rejoicing had hardly gotten under way when the men stood before them alive as testimony to the power of the resurrection and then were honored of the Lord to be with Him in heaven. All of this was done in the sight of men and to the glory of God.

5. The Church does suffer reversal. There are times when she seems to be defeated. There are tragedies which bring the enemies of God to rejoice. The world often delights in the stricken messengers of God. But the last word is the power of God. He raises men from the dead; He honors His servants. His Word does not return to Him void but accomplishes the purpose whereunto He has sent it. The contrast between the short-lived rejoicing of the nations over the slain witnesses and the rejoicing to which the resurrected witnesses are called is that the latter lasts forever. Even the people who had the brief days of triumph were shaken by an earthquake that killed 7,000 of them, and the rest acknowledged the God of heaven.

The seventh angel sounded the trumpet as the picture of the witnesses faded from John's view. There were great voices in heaven which announced that *the kingdoms of this world are become the kingdoms of our Lord, and of his Christ.* The elders declared that what is to happen is fair and just. The nations, they say, are angry, but the time has come for vindication of truth and reward to the servants of God.

The Ark

Rev. 11:19

> 19 And the temple of God was opened in heaven, and there was seen in his temple the ark of his testament: and there were lightnings, and voices, and thunderings, and an earthquake, and great hail.

Before the sound of the trumpet has ceased and the climactic events of the end time come into view, we catch a fourth fleeting glimpse which relates to the Christian witness in a world under judgment. The temple of God was opened in heaven, and there was seen the ark of His testament.

1. Since there is no temple as such in heaven, the meaning is that the ark of his testament is in the midst of the Church (God's newer temple). In all of the conflict and

suffering resulting from its faithful witness to a world under judgment, the body of the redeemed have the eternal promise of the Divine Presence which comes to her through the Holy Spirit. At the birthday of the Church the Holy Spirit came with the sound of a rushing, mighty wind. At the close of the gospel age He is seen in the midst of the Church.

2. Historically the ark was the embodiment of God's presence. It was a simple box chest that would mean very little in itself. It was because it symbolized His presence that it was honored and powerful. It was portable and could be carried wherever the people of God went. They never need be without Him. In battle its presence meant victory. In travel its presence meant protection and achievement. Wherever God asked His people to go, His presence was assured if the ark was with them.

3. There were three things in the ark: the tablets of stone, the manna, and Aaron's rod that budded.

a. The law reminds us that God's presence does make demands upon His children. He is a holy God and requires that those who serve Him do so in holiness. Whatever may be said of grace and forgiveness has no real value unless the validity of the law of holiness is assumed. Paul, the great apostle of salvation by faith, exhorts that the Christian must be holy: *God hath not called us unto uncleanness, but unto holiness* (1 Thess. 4:7).

b. The manna reminds us of God's provision. He will supply all the needs of His people according to His riches in glory (Phil. 4:19). This is important as the demands of the journey or the battle are faced. There is strength and nourishment, wisdom and help at every point. The presence of the ark says to the Church: Do not fear, for the One who supplies all your needs is with you. It is significant, too, as one contemplates the demands of holiness. Faithful is He that calls the Christian to holiness, for He can and will accomplish it. It is common in some circles, while emphasizing grace, to say that no man can live up to the Ten Commandments. This may be true if one is talking about human ability apart from God. But the ark with its omer of manna reminds us that, what God has required in the tablets of stone, He enables by the manna He did and will supply.

c. Then, too, there was in the ark the rod that budded. It was in an hour of challenge to the call of God upon Aaron that the leaders of the 12 tribes of Israel were to bring, each one, a rod and lay it before the Lord. The one that budded would indicate the authentic leader. It was Aaron's rod that did bud and testified to the people that he was God's man for the time (cf. Numbers 17).

The presence of this rod in the ark reminds the Church that she has the protection of God. He will stand by them that stand by Him. Jesus uses these words when promising the disciples that those who acknowledge Him before men will be acknowledged by Him before His Father in heaven (Matt. 10:32). Paul's advice to Timothy was to avoid those who challenged the truth of the Bible, and he assured the young preacher, "Nevertheless the foundation of God standeth sure" (2 Tim. 2:19).

4. In spite of what men say, the final authentication comes from God. It does not matter what the world thinks or says about the Church. The ark is the promise that God will keep watch and acknowledge His own. God told Ezekiel, when He called him to prophesy, that Israel was stubborn and might not hear him. But He affirmed that whether they heard him or did not, they would know that a prophet of God had been among them (Ezek. 2:5). This is the comfort of seeing the ark in the midst of the temple of God.

Over the ark was to be a mercy seat, or cover, of pure gold. Two figures of cherubim were to be over it, facing each other. Their wings were spread, symbolizing the overshadowing of God's mercy. There God promised He would meet with His people and speak to them of His will. The law, the provision, and the protecting authentication are all overshadowed by God's mercy. As the hymn describes it,

> *Heaven comes down our souls to greet,*
> *While glory crowns the mercy seat.*[7]

5. To bear witness in a world in upheaval is a frightening responsibility. The very cruciality itself could overwhelm the Christian and cause him to mar the word he gives. In such a moment the Christian should look again at the ark of God's testament in the midst of God's people. By it He promises

> *For I will be with thee thy trials to bless,*
> *And sanctify to thee thy deepest distress.*[8]

All of this is in our minds, if not in theirs, who hear the angel with the seventh trumpet sound the end. God has kept His promise; He has been with His people through the presence of the Holy Spirit unto the end of the world. The vision of the ark and all it represents gives eloquent fulfillment to the promise of Jesus when He gave the Great Commission (Matt. 28:18-20). The little scroll that was open, the measuring rod, the two witnesses, and the ark all tell how He is with the Church "alway, even unto the end," as He promised.

We have reached the end. How long or short it will be, no one can say with authority. This much is certain: Whether long or short, John was given the privilege through the vision on the Isle of Patmos to say authoritatively that he saw the consummation of all things. God kept His promise all the way until the trumpet sounded and the end came.

War in Heaven and on Earth

Revelation 12:1—14:20

REVELATION 12

Chapter 12 begins the second major division of Revelation. The final end of the world as it now exists has been announced. When the seventh trumpet sounds, John is told the end has come. The end time involves struggle and victory and judgment. All of this John sees in a series of visions.

Perhaps it is important to understand that these visions are not necessarily chronological. It may well be that they are recorded in the order that they were seen, but this is not specifically stated. The phrase "After this I beheld" (cf. 7:9) seems to indicate that a vision followed a previous one. Yet neither the space between nor the causal connection is given. At times it appears that several visions of the same event are reported. Each perhaps has its particular vantage point, as will be noted. To try to place the events of these visions in order is difficult if not impossible because of this. Their purpose is not to reveal a timetable of history as much as to reaffirm the Christian hope. The purpose of this exposition is to try to grasp the spiritual truths these visions were meant to convey to the first readers, and see how they apply to those who followed —even to us.

The second half of the book begins with a flashback or replay. In our television-oriented culture we understand this technique. Both in the development of dramatic themes and in the understanding of events, such as sports, we often see what has previously happened thrown into the presentation to explain or enhance the viewing. This kind of thing is done by the vision John has of a battle in heaven which is continued on earth.

The Struggle in Heaven

Rev. 12:1-12

> 1 And there appeared a great wonder in heaven; a woman clothed with the sun, and the moon under her feet, and upon her head a crown of twelve stars:
> 2 And she being with child cried, travailing in birth, and pained to be delivered.
> 3 And there appeared another wonder in heaven; and behold a great red dragon, having seven heads and ten horns, and seven crowns upon his heads.
> 4 And his tail drew the third part of the stars of heaven, and did cast them to the earth: and the dragon stood before the woman which was ready to be delivered, for to devour her child as soon as it was born.
> 5 And she brought forth a man child, who was to rule all nations with a rod of iron: and her child was caught up unto God, and to his throne.
> 6 And the woman fled into the wilderness, where she hath a place prepared of God, that they should feed her there a thousand two hundred and threescore days.
> 7 And there was war in heaven: Michael and his angels fought against the dragon; and the dragon fought and his angels,
> 8 And prevailed not; neither was their place found any more in heaven.
> 9 And the great dragon was cast out, that old serpent called the Devil, and Satan, which deceiveth the whole world: he was cast out into the earth, and his angels were cast out with him.
> 10 And I heard a loud voice saying in heaven, Now is come salvation, and strength, and the kingdom of our God, and the power of his Christ: for the accuser of our brethren is cast down, which accused them before our God day and night.
> 11 And they overcame him by the blood of the Lamb, and by the word of their testimony; and they loved not their lives unto the death.
> 12 Therefore rejoice, ye heavens, and ye that dwell in them. Woe to the inhabitants of the earth and of the sea! for the devil is come down unto you, having great wrath, because he knoweth that he hath but a short time.

1. A great wonder appeared in heaven. In a vision John sees *a woman clothed with the sun, and the moon under her feet.* She wears a tiara of 12 stars. The very language helps one understand that she represents something significant to the story of redemption.

Since she is related to events that happened in the past, maybe even before creation, she does not represent a historical person. The Christian view of Christ the Redeemer is that He is the Lamb slain before the foundation of the world. The woman pictures for us the truth that God brings salvation through His people. The promise to the first woman, Eve, was that her seed would bruise the head of the serpent. Moses promised that One would rise up from his brethren like unto him. Isaiah promised that a young maid would bear the Child who would save the people from their sins. These promises were fulfilled when the Virgin Mary brought Jesus into the world.

So the woman depicts the truth that God will bring salvation through the child of a woman. Most interpreters see the woman as the Church, which is given feminine appellations frequently in the Bible. Paul refers to the Church as the Jerusalem which is above, the mother of us all. The wise man asks, "Who is she that looketh forth as the morning, fair as the moon, clear as the sun, and terrible as an army with banners?" (Song of Sol. 6:10). Her crown of 12 stars could represent Israel. However, the Church had its 12 apostles. It is probably better to think of the woman as representing the people of God. She would then be the mother of all who are born of the Spirit from the very beginning of time.

2. She is with child. Her place in the cosmic plan is to be fruitful and multiply. Later we are told that she has children throughout the earth (v. 12). The ongoing of human life itself is often described as having begun in heaven. Christians use this figure for the salvation experience. They call it being born from above into the family of God. The baby is not Christ. For he will not rule the nations

with the rod of iron (cf. Rev. 19:15). Rather she brings into the world offspring which have their destiny in the ongoing of history. Men are ruled by men with the rod of iron. The dragon, who is the leader of all that is evil, the devil, awaits the birth of the child to devour him. He is a supernatural predator who seeks to destroy all who can be instruments of good. He has great power, for in John's vision he drew a third part of heaven with his tail and cast it upon the earth.

The woman gives birth to her child, which is caught up into God's care, and the woman flees to the wilderness. The refuge has been prepared by God. She is there for three and a half years, a number which in itself is symbolic of martyrdom and resurrection.

3. The message is the same as the warning of Paul, "We wrestle not against flesh and blood, but against principalities, against powers, against the rulers of the darkness of this world" (Eph. 6:12). The warfare began long ago before the world began, the vision tells us. Michael and his angels fought against the dragon and defeated him. The devil and his angels were cast out of heaven. Nowhere in biblical literature are we told when this occurred, but always it is described as before the world began. In the very beginning of human history the devil appears as a serpent and deceives the first couple. This is the characteristic of his strategy—deception. The battle is a struggle for truth. It began long ago and will continue to the end.

4. John hears a hymn of praise in the midst of the vision which proclaims the kingdom of Christ as the victor in the battle for truth. Whenever and wherever the power of falsehood and deception is defeated, the kingdom of truth is established. The hymn includes the people of God, especially the martyrs who loved not their lives to the death. The struggle, it seems, is a fierce and costly one. Like the Lamb whose blood was shed, the saints who follow share in the wounds of the battle. But their wounds are the marks of their victory in the blood of the Lamb.

The far-reaching scope of the battle for truth against evil is seen in the rejoicing of the heavenly hosts. They have been deeply involved and now sing the praise of God who has given to them the victory in the struggle. You see, *victory* is not just a warm, joyous word the Christian uses in praise. It means there has been a struggle, and the Christian has risked life itself but has won. But praise is not blind. It has its warning along with its rejoicing. The battle has been won in heaven. The issue has been decided there. The battle, however, continues on earth. Woe, says the hymn, to men on earth because the devil has come down. He will attack all the more fiercely since he knows he has been defeated and will soon be finished. He knows his time is short.

This is a consistent Christian theme. The devil is the Christian's adversary. He will deceive all he can. But he comes to earth from a defeat in heaven. His power is limited, and his time is short. He tries all the harder because of these facts. The Christian is warned to beware of the devil because of his ability to deceive. But he is also encouraged to resist the devil, for in the power of the Holy Spirit he can make the devil flee from him (Jas. 4:7).

The Struggle Continues on Earth

Rev. 12:13-17

13 And when the dragon saw that he was cast unto the earth, he persecuted the woman which brought forth the man child.
14 And to the woman were given two wings of a great eagle, that she might fly into the wilderness, into her place, where she is nourished for a time, and times, and half a time, from the face of the serpent.
15 And the serpent cast out of his mouth water as a flood after the woman, that he might cause her to be carried away of the flood.
16 And the earth helped the woman, and the earth opened her mouth, and swallowed up the flood which the dragon cast out of his mouth.
17 And the dragon was wroth with the woman, and went to make war with the remnant of her seed, which keep the commandments of God, and have the testimony of Jesus Christ.

1. Having lost out in heaven, the devil turns to persecute the woman. The picture is one primarily now of revenge.

It is not stated, but the idea seems to be that, since the devil cannot destroy the child of the woman, he sets out to persecute the mother. The child is safe in the protection of God. We see no more of him. The protection of the woman is her flight to a haven that is inaccessible to the devil. Some writers have seen in the picture of the woman fleeing on the wings of a great eagle a reference to God's words to Israel, "Ye have seen what I did unto the Egyptians, and how I bare you on eagles' wings, and brought you unto myself" (Exod. 19:4).

Frustrated by her safe flight, the devil seeks to destroy her with a flood. The earth helps the woman by swallowing up the flood. The God of creation has put it into nature itself to battle on the side of truth. Deborah sang that "the stars in their courses fought against Sisera" (Judg. 5:20). E. Stanley Jones contended that nature is such that men break themselves on her when they struggle against God's truth.[9] In spite of all the catastrophes that occur, basically this is a friendly universe to men and women of truth. We are reminded of the Old Testament promise that, when the enemy comes in like a flood, God will raise up a standard against him (Isa. 59:19). The figure is a military one. It speaks of drawing a line of defense. For the woman in John's vision the standard was a friendly earth which swallowed up the flood sent by the devil.

2. The devil, angry because of his inability to destroy the woman, goes to make war against her seed. They are the Church who keep the commandments of God and have the testimony of Jesus Christ. It is not really because he hopes to win or has any illusions about the outcome of the struggle, that the devil attacks. It is the striking out of a wounded predator who wants only to hurt because he is hurt. It is a waste of time to ascribe any intelligent purpose or strategy to works of evil. They make no sense and are not intended to do so. They are the thrashings of an angry devil who has lost and will lose the final conflict against truth.

The Christian is to be alert but not fearful. He must be on the lookout for the deceptions of the wicked one, but he must also be confident that one small word, Jesus, will drive him away.[10] The demons in the New Testament story ask Jesus, "Art thou come to destroy us?" (Mark 1:24; Luke 4:34). They knew what the outcome of the struggle would be (Matt. 8:29). Christians should know, too, and by putting on the whole armor of God, stand in the midst of every struggle. The battles will not last for long, and they shall be victorious.

REVELATION 13

The Devil Gets Help from the Sea

Rev. 13:1-10

1 And I stood upon the sand of the sea, and saw a beast rise up out of the sea, having seven heads and ten horns, and upon his horns ten crowns, and upon his heads the name of blasphemy.
2 And the beast which I saw was like unto a leopard, and his feet were as the feet of a bear, and his mouth as the mouth of a lion: and the dragon gave him his power, and his seat, and great authority.
3 And I saw one of his heads as it were wounded to death; and his deadly wound was healed: and all the world wondered after the beast.
4 And they worshipped the dragon which gave power unto the beast: and they worshipped the beast, saying, Who is like unto the beast? who is able to make war with him?
5 And there was given unto him a mouth speaking great things and blasphemies; and power was given unto him to continue forty and two months.
6 And he opened his mouth in blasphemy against God, to blaspheme his name, and his tabernacle, and them that dwell in heaven.
7 And it was given unto him to make war with the saints, and to overcome them: and power was given him over all kindreds, and tongues, and nations.
8 And all that dwell upon the earth shall worship him, whose names are not written in the book of life of the Lamb slain from the foundation of the world.
9 If any man have an ear, let him hear.
10 He that leadeth into captivity shall go into captivity: he that killeth with the sword must be killed with the sword. Here is the patience and the faith of the saints.

1. The devil, we may assume, stands on the seashore and calls for help from the sea. We are to see how the evil one plans to make war on the children of the woman. From out of the sea there comes a beast with 7 heads, 10 horns, and on his horns 10 crowns. He is blasphemous in his claim of divinity. When Daniel saw a like vision, it was of four beasts: a lion, a bear, a leopard, and then the fourth (similar to this one) was a fierce beast with 10 horns; the beast John saw had characteristics which for his first readers were closely parallel to Rome. For today it may well depict the power of secular humanism.

2. The beast did miraculous things and inspired the worship of all whose names were not written in the book of life of the Lamb. People exalted him, asking, "Who is like unto the beast? who is able to make war with him?" And make war he did. He won battles that seemed to threaten the success of the Church, at least for a time. His power is in part the awesomeness of his words and deeds. He had momentum. That is, his victory comes because his reputation overpowers even the saints. The cult of success deceives many. They decide that however it contradicts the truth of God, if it succeeds, it must be right and align themselves with it.

3. John takes a moment after describing the forward sweep of blasphemy, to warn that success may be the pattern of its own downfall. He who leads into captivity shall be taken captive. He who kills by the sword shall die by the sword. John reminds his readers that this is the patience and faith of the saints. They are not taken in by the impressive power and claims of entrenched evil. They know that evil will fall by the same power it has used for success. Likewise, when one tries to do God's work by human means, he is bound to suffer the consequences of the very techniques which will result in ultimate failure. Just because the sword is used for God's kingdom does not exempt the user from failure.

It is a timely warning. Christians often watch the success of human enterprises and feel that is the pattern for spiritual victory. If the Church succumbs to the temptation of using earthly means to do heavenly tasks, she will suffer the same defeat as the source of those means. It is a warfare, and the devil uses a most effective strategy in the beast from the sea who inspires worship by his high claims and his impressive record.

The Devil Gets Help from the Earth

Rev. 13:11-18

11 And I beheld another beast coming up out of the earth; and he had two horns like a lamb, and he spake as a dragon.

12 And he exerciseth all the power of the first beast before him, and causeth the earth and them which dwell therein to worship the first beast, whose deadly wound was healed.

13 And he doeth great wonders, so that he maketh fire come down from heaven on the earth in the sight of men,

14 And deceiveth them that dwell on the earth by the means of those miracles which he had power to do in the sight of the beast; saying to them that dwell on the earth, that they should make an image to the beast, which had the wound by a sword, and did live.

15 And he had power to give life unto the image of the beast, that the image of the beast should both speak, and cause that as many as would not worship the image of the beast should be killed.

16 And he causeth all, both small and great, rich and poor, free and bond, to receive a mark in their right hand, or in their foreheads:

17 And that no man might buy or sell, save he that had the mark, or the name of the beast, or the number of his name.

18 Here is wisdom. Let him that hath understanding count the number of the beast: for it is the number of a man; and his number is Six hundred threescore and six.

1. After the warning John sees another beast arise from the earth. This second beast has horns like a lamb but speaks like a dragon. He is Antichrist. He exercises all the powers of the first beast and orders worship of the first beast who was wounded but healed. In addition he calls fire from the skies and deceives people with the miracles he works. He has the ability to give life to the wounded beast. Like his counterpart who taught the people to worship the dragon, this Antichrist causes people to worship the beast by threatening to kill all who will not. He devises a mark which is put on the forehead of all who worship the beast, so that no one can buy or sell if he does

not have this mark. This identification seems like a grim counterpart to the seal of God upon His children. It is counterfeit but effective. The more the work of God is imitated and fitted to man's carnal ambition, the more it is hailed as true.

2. So again the writer feels the need to give a warning. "Let me give you a tip," he says. Here is insight. The number of the beast is 666. It is, he says, the number of a man. The false prophet is a person. He may appear to do supernatural things because of the power of evil he has embraced, but he is not a superhuman character. The number six is the number of humanity. Six repeated three times could be humanity claiming divinity. It is a trinity of humanity. This does not say who he is. But John reminds his readers that however frightening he and his power may seem, they are to remember he is a man and no more. The power exercised may be awesome, but it is evil and has been defeated. When a man claims divinity and even seems to prove it, he is still a man and stands before the eternal God as only a man. To be in Satan's control does not make him more than a man.

3. So from the sea and the land the devil draws these instruments for his struggle and deception. This may be one reason that, when the angel comes to announce the end, he puts one foot on the land and the other on the sea. It symbolizes the power and authority of God whose message he comes to deliver. God's Word and truth will prevail. To see the power and deception of the beasts controlled by the devil is to wonder what hope there is for the victory of truth. Then one remembers that the angel came and stood on the land and the sea and announced that there would be no more delay. The work of God in redemption would now come to its final and full completion.

REVELATION 14

The Army of God

Rev. 14:1-13

1 And I looked, and, lo, a Lamb stood on the mount Sion, and with him an hundred forty and four thousand, having his Father's name written in their foreheads.

2 And I heard a voice from heaven, as the voice of many waters, and as the voice of a great thunder; and I heard the voice of harpers harping with their harps:

3 And they sung as it were a new song before the throne, and before the four beasts, and the elders: and no man could learn that song but the hundred and forty and four thousand, which were redeemed from the earth.

4 These are they which were not defiled with women; for they are virgins. These are they which follow the Lamb whithersoever he goeth. These were redeemed from among men, being the firstfruits unto God and to the Lamb.

5 And in their mouth was found no guile: for they are without fault before the throne of God.

6 And I saw another angel fly in the midst of heaven, having the everlasting gospel to preach unto them that dwell on the earth, and to every nation, and kindred, and tongue, and people,

7 Saying with a loud voice, Fear God, and give glory to him; for the hour of his judgment is come: and worship him that made heaven, and earth, and the sea, and the fountains of waters.

8 And there followed another angel, saying, Babylon is fallen, is fallen, that great city, because she made all nations drink of the wine of the wrath of her fornication.

9 And the third angel followed them, saying with a loud voice, If any man worship the beast and his image, and receive his mark in his forehead, or in his hand,

10 The same shall drink of the wine of the wrath of God, which is poured out without mixture into the cup of his indignation; and he shall be tormented with fire and brimstone in the presence of the holy angels, and in the presence of the Lamb:

11 And the smoke of their torment ascendeth up for ever and ever: and they have no rest day nor night, who worship the beast and his image, and whosoever receiveth the mark of his name.

12 Here is the patience of the saints: here are they that keep the commandments of God, and the faith of Jesus.

13 And I heard a voice from heaven saying unto me, Write, Blessed are the dead which die in the Lord from henceforth: Yea, saith the Spirit, that they may rest from their labours; and their works do follow them.

In contrast to the great host of people who worship the beast and receive his mark so that they can buy and sell, John sees a vision of those who follow Christ. This vision counterbalances the former vision of the dragon's temporary success. The army of God is dramatically symbolized by the martyrs. They are numbered, standing with the Lamb on Mount Zion. All through the Book of Revelation special honor is given to those who have forsaken every earthly interest to follow Jesus. The martyrs are the special people of this book.

1. The army of God has certain characteristics.

a. The army of God is made up of redeemed men who have committed all to Christ. They have but one desire, and that is to be with Him. In obedience they follow where He goes. They have His name written in their foreheads; they have His mark upon them. They do not call attention to themselves but to Him.

b. The army of God is made up of redeemed men who are happy. They sing a song distinctly their own. No one can learn it unless he has been redeemed by the blood of Christ. The joy reverberates throughout heaven like the voice of many waters; it rolls like thunder; it has the depth and resonance of harps. Earlier John had heard the angels and the heavenly beings singing of God's holiness. Now they are silenced as the redeemed sing. As one put it, "They will fold their wings, / For angels never felt the joy that our salvation brings."

c. The army of God moves under the banner of truth. No lie is found in their mouths; they are without blame before the throne of God. These firstfruits of Jesus' resurrection are made holy, as He prayed, by the truth. The Word of God is their weapon. They live by it, and they proclaim it to all. They do not have to rehearse their lines as they bear their witness. The testimony, a means of overcoming, is from their hearts and from their lives. One has well said, "Only people who tell the truth do not have to remember what they said!"

d. The army of God advances under formidable air cover. Three angels are seen who summarize the victory of the army of truth over the dragon, the beast, the false prophet, and the hosts of men deceived by them. Lon

Woodrum spoke at a preachers' meeting from the sixth verse of this 14th chapter. He said the angels portrayed preachers. They must speak from above the things around them. Their viewpoint must be from the "long look." Again, their message is the everlasting gospel. It is the eternal good news that there is salvation in Jesus to all who confess their sins and accept His forgiveness. It is the good news that for every need of man God has the gift of the Holy Spirit. And third, their message is to go to all the world, *to every nation, and kindred, and tongue, and people.*

2. The angels, each with a specific prediction or piece of advice, announce that the final judgment and related events are certain and imminent.

  a. The first angel calls for reverence and praise to God, for He will act in judgment. He who made all things will judge all things. His purpose, obscured by the sin of people, will at last be made clear. It will accomplish the universal worship of the Creator.

  b. The second angel introduces a theme which will be spelled out in graphic detail from the 17th chapter on. It is that the city of man is doomed to final and full destruction. Built upon false and blasphemous worship of the creature rather than the Creator, its destruction will testify to the truth of God by which His army has conquered.

  c. The third angel in a characteristically evangelical fashion calls for all men to understand that, if they accept the mark of the beast, they share in the inevitable destruction which is about to fall on the city of man. You see, character determines destiny. All who live by the sword die by the sword. All who live a lie live forever in its torment. All who turn their love and worship inward on themselves are caught in a "black hole" of eternal unrest. There is no peace, ever, for any who, because they worship the beast, must drink the wine of the wrath of God.

3. The army of God is characterized by the patience and

faith of its soldiers. They keep the commandments of God. Their obedience qualifies them to be instruments of His truth and builders of His kingdom.

> For not with swords' loud clashing,
> Nor roll of stirring drums;
> With deeds of love and mercy,
> The heavenly Kingdom comes.

They have the faith of Jesus, who saw beyond the power of sinful men the greater power and purpose of His Father, and could say, "Fear not, little flock; for it is your Father's good pleasure to give you the kingdom" (Luke 12:32). The patience of the saints comes from the conviction that what God calls them to do He will enable them to accomplish. Paul wrote the Thessalonians that God had not called them to be unclean but to be holy (1 Thess. 4:7). Then he added, "Faithful is he that calleth you, who also will do it" (5:24). Their patience is seen, too, in the knowledge that, however imperfect their performance, God will help them to "grow in grace" (2 Pet. 3:18). They do not give up if they fail to keep the commandment fully. They know God will forgive and judge them more by motive than performance. They have the faith of their Master and look not at the things that are seen but at the things that are not seen (2 Cor. 4:18).

4. With such an army of His followers the Lamb will prevail. Too many look at the power, deception, and success of the beast and the false prophet and are terrified. They fear that even the strongest cannot stand against them. And this might be true if one were to look at human wisdom and strength alone. But the picture of evil's all-out challenge must be seen in the light of the inevitable outcome. They are not pictured to make the reader be in awe of Satan and his cohorts. As Luther's hymn rejoices, "One little word shall fell him." That word is Jesus. The sweep of sin's sway over the world only enhances the sure victory of the Lamb and His followers. The patience and

faith of the saints is that they keep the commandments of God and the faith of Jesus and are victorious. It may appear a costly conflict, but God tells John to write, *Blessed are the dead which die in the Lord from henceforth: Yea, saith the Spirit, that they may rest from their labours; and their works do follow them.* It is a golden text for martyrs and for all Christians.

The Harvest at the End Time

Rev. 14:14-20

> 14 And I looked, and behold a white cloud, and upon the cloud one sat like unto the Son of man, having on his head a golden crown, and in his hand a sharp sickle.
> 15 And another angel came out of the temple, crying with a loud voice to him that sat on the cloud, Thrust in thy sickle, and reap: for the time is come for thee to reap; for the harvest of the earth is ripe.
> 16 And he that sat on the cloud thrust in his sickle on the earth; and the earth was reaped.
> 17 And another angel came out of the temple which is in heaven, he also having a sharp sickle.
> 18 And another angel came out from the altar, which had power over fire; and cried with a loud cry to him that had the sharp sickle, saying, Thrust in thy sharp sickle, and gather the clusters of the vine of the earth; for her grapes are fully ripe.
> 19 And the angel thrust in his sickle into the earth, and gathered the vine of the earth, and cast it into the great winepress of the wrath of God.
> 20 And the winepress was trodden without the city, and blood came out of the winepress, even unto the horse bridles, by the space of a thousand and six hundred furlongs.

1. In this section of seven verses we see the vision of the final harvest. In one of His parables about sowing the seed, Jesus explains to His disciples that "the harvest is the end of the world" (Matt. 13:39). This vision employs a wealth of symbolism from Daniel, Joel, and Ezekiel. John sees the Son of Man on a white cloud. He has a crown on His head and a sickle in His hand. An angel from the temple tells Him to thrust in His sickle since the harvesttime has come. The picture is one of a grain harvest. All the sheaves of grain are gathered, and the tares are burned. This is the way Jesus said it would be. For a time the tares or weeds are allowed to grow along with the grain. They remain un-

til the grain is ripe and harvesttime has come. Then the harvest will be gathered and the weeds destroyed.

God has the patience to await the ripening of the wheat until the mature grain appears; then the great separation is ordered. All that is good is preserved; all that is worthless is burned and destroyed. This is what harvesttime is all about. It is on God's timetable, being carefully monitored. When the moment has come, the harvest will be gathered. Whatever may be the scope and terror of the final judgments which are outlined in this vision and described in the 16th chapter, the important fact is that when harvesttime comes, God gathers the fruit and destroys the residue. And when it comes, it is the eventual end of the world as it has been known and the beginning of the "new heavens and a new earth, wherein dwelleth righteousness" (2 Pet. 3:13).

2. The vision of the harvest is really a dual event—the harvest of the grain gathered by the sickle of the Son of Man and the harvest of grapes gathered by another angel with a sharp sickle. This harvest John sees as ordered by the angel who has charge of the fire that came from the altar. While Jesus refers to the world as a field of various soils, He also refers to it as a vineyard. In one place He used the vineyard as a parable of the disciples' relationship to Jesus. "I am the vine, ye are the branches," He told them (John 15:5). As long as they live in the Vine, they would have life and grow and bear fruit. If they were fruitless, they would be pruned and burned.

In this vision the world is the vineyard, and the grapes, unfortunately, are evil fruit. They are ripe with their blood and are to be gathered and thrown into the winepress of God's wrath. The grapes of wrath are to be trodden outside the city, the place where evildoers are punished. Jesus' crucifixion outside the gate of Jerusalem signified that He was numbered among the transgressors. It may very well be that He is pictured as treading the winepress in Isaiah 63 because, having died there for sin,

He becomes the appropriate One to administer punishment to evil. Who it is that treads the winepress here is not stated, but vast and awful is the crushing. Blood flowed from the press in a stream as deep or high as the bridle on a horse and flowed for 200 miles—about the distance from Jerusalem through the Dead Sea to the Red Sea.

3. The harvest is twofold—the gathering of the good grain by the Son of Man and the gathering and crushing of the evil by the angel with a sharp sickle in the command of the angel in charge of fire. At the end of the world the good are forever with the Lord in joy; the evil are crushed and punished forever. This is everywhere the teaching of the Bible. As John sees the end time in his vision, this motif is clear. The end spells happiness for the redeemed and terror for the unbelieving. So Jesus, in talking about the end, says that the disciples should anticipate it with joy. "Lift up your heads; for your redemption draweth nigh" (Luke 21:28) are His words. He told the parable of the wheat and the tares and later explained it to the disciples that "the harvest is the end of the world" (Matt. 13:39). He then foretold the destruction of the wicked and summarized, "Then shall the righteous shine forth as the sun in the kingdom of their Father. Who hath ears to hear, let him hear" (v. 43).

No one can complain that all this may mean cruel and unusual punishment. The warnings are many. God has faithfully portrayed the picture for men in many places and ways. The symbolisms multiply as He, because He is long-suffering, tells men through His messages that harvest is coming. "Whatsoever a man soweth, that shall he also reap" (Gal. 6:7).

REVELATION 15

The Song of Moses

Rev. 15:1-4

> 1 And I saw another sign in heaven, great and marvelous, seven angels having the seven last plagues; for in them is filled up the wrath of God.
> 2 And I saw as it were a sea of glass mingled with fire: and them that had gotten the victory over the beast, and over his image, and over his mark, and over the number of his name, stand on the sea of glass, having the harps of God.
> 3 And they sing the song of Moses the servant of God, and the song of the Lamb, saying, Great and marvellous are thy works, Lord God Almighty; just and true are thy ways, thou King of saints.
> 4 Who shall not fear thee, O Lord, and glorify thy name? for thou only art holy: for all nations shall come and worship before thee; for thy judgments are made manifest.

1. It may be noted that, while those who follow the beast give worship and blind obedience, there is no music in their lives. In contrast heaven is filled with music, which seemed to remain as a captivating melody in John's mind. He turns from viewing the carnage of the winepress to remember another sign or forecast in heaven. The seventh trumpet had blown, the one which was to signal the end of the mystery of God. Now appeared seven angels having the seven last plagues. The restrained judgment of God is done. Only the certain and final judgment remains. It will be the outpouring of His wrath. While the seven angels

come out of the temple dressed in white, the victorious followers of the Lamb begin the song of Moses.

2. The sea of glass described in chapter 4 takes on the color of fire, much like the Red Sea. On this sea, like the children of Israel who escaped Pharaoh in the Red Sea, stand those who have the victory over the beast, his image, his mark, and his number, with harps in their hands. Their days of struggle are done. Their day of rejoicing and singing has come. In a previous vision they are heard singing a song no man could sing who had not shared in their struggle and victory. Now their song is revealed, or they sing another which came out of a similar struggle and victory. It is called *the song of Moses . . . and the song of the Lamb*. The inclusion of Moses may refer to Exod. 15:1-18 or Deuteronomy 32, hymns of praise to God proclaiming His power and justice. The first is the song that the children of Israel sang after their victory at the Red Sea. The other is the song Moses sang to Joshua and the people as he prepared to turn the leadership to the man God had chosen to take the people across Jordan and into the Promised Land.

3. The Song in Deuteronomy contains the words of the "salvation story":

For the Lord's portion is his people; Jacob is the lot of his inheritance. He found him in a desert land, and in the waste howling wilderness; he led him about, he instructed him, he kept him as the apple of his eye. As an eagle stirreth up her nest, fluttereth over her young, spreadeth abroad her wings, taketh them, beareth them on her wings: so the Lord alone did lead him, and there was no strange god with him. He made him ride on the high places of the earth, that he might eat the increase of the fields; and he made him to suck honey out of the rock, and oil out of the flinty rock (32:9-13).

These words bring comfort to those who trust God with their all. They bring shame to those who hesitate to trust Him. The song of the saints is that God tenderly cares for

His people. If they are to pass with other men through the time of great tribulation, they need not fear. They stand on the sea of glass and sing of God's care and tenderness.

This same theme was the song of those who experienced the Red Sea deliverance. Led by Moses, they sang of the triumph, picturing in detail how the horsemen of Pharaoh followed them into the sea and perished. Then in triumphant praise of God they sang, "Who is like unto thee, O Lord, among the gods? who is like thee, glorious in holiness, fearful in praises, doing wonders? Thou stretchedst out thy right hand, the earth swallowed them. Thou in thy mercy hast led forth the people which thou hast redeemed: thou hast guided them in thy strength unto thy holy habitation" (Exod. 15:11-13).

4. As they wing their way from long ago and far away to our situation where the struggle may be wearing and the spiritual warfare intense, such thoughts are very meaningful and reassuring to Christians today. Think what they meant to the people of Asia Minor who rankled under the persecution of Rome. They remind us that, if worst comes to worst, God has been through all this (and more) with His people before. He will not fail His children now! The redeemed, especially the martyrs, sing the song of Moses both for their own praise to God and for the reassurance of all who follow in His way. For, as we are told elsewhere, "God [has] provided some better thing for us, that they without us should not be made perfect" (Heb. 11:40). Across the centuries still comes the song of triumph when failure seems certain, of a God who stands in the shadows of history "keeping watch upon His own."

The Wrath of God Is Prepared

Rev. 15:5-8

> 5 And after that I looked, and, behold, the temple of the tabernacle of the testimony in heaven was opened:
> 6 And the seven angels came out of the temple, having the seven plagues, clothed in pure and white linen, and heaving their breasts girded with golden girdles.

7 And one of the four beasts gave unto the seven angels seven golden vials full of the wrath of God, who liveth for ever and ever.
8 And the temple was filled with smoke from the glory of God, and from his power; and no man was able to enter into the temple, till the seven plagues of the seven angels were fulfilled.

1. The very word *plagues* carries the thought of more than calamity. It suggests punishment visited on wrongdoers for the benefit of the afflicted. These plagues, aimed at the beast and his followers, are to vindicate those who have prevailed and are now gone from the earthly scene. Since John does not ever mention the Rapture of which Paul writes in his letters to the Thessalonians and the Corinthians, one can assume that it has occurred, and that by the time the final bowls of wrath are outpoured, the saints have already crossed the sea of glass and sing the song of Moses and the Lamb in the heavenly Kingdom.

2. The angels who are to pour out the bowls come from the temple. They are God's messengers, and their tasks belong to the glory of God though it be expressed in wrath. They are robed in white to signify their purity. They are not executors who relish the bloody business of revenge. They are the pure instruments of God's purpose. They are choice servants who are *girded with golden girdles* to signify their importance as messengers of God, doing His will.

3. The wrath they will administer is not of their doing. It belongs to the eternal purpose of God and so is given them by one of the four living creatures who are always at the throne of God. When the bowls are given to the angels, the temple is filled with the smoke of the power and glory of God. No man can enter the temple until the grim and necessary task is finished. There is nothing human about the final expression of the wrath of God. Although God has chosen human vessels to bring the message and reveal His will all through the gospel age, this final act is His and His alone. No man can be a part of its administration.

The day of human activity in the "gospel story" is done. There remains no more sacrifice for sin but only certain looking for and hastening to judgment which will be full and thorough. It is the work of the eternal God, who has decided the day of mercy has ended. The day of wrath has dawned. Whatever else may occur in later visions as they may involve this world, they must precede the final judgment and destruction of the wicked. God has taken over, and the story from the human side of history is complete. Whatever follows belongs to another world and its concerns. God has demonstrated His long-suffering. Every opportunity His love and patience could provide has been extended to men. The day of salvation ends, and the day of judgment comes surely and suddenly.

REVELATION 16

Charge to the Angels

Rev. 16:1

> 1 And I heard a great voice out of the temple saying to the seven angels, Go your ways, and pour out the vials of the wrath of God upon the earth.

1. The writer of Hebrews warns, "It is a fearful thing to fall into the hands of the living God" (10:31). The apostle Peter preached, "But the day of the Lord will come as a thief in the night; in the which the heavens shall pass away with a great noise, and the elements shall melt with fervent heat, the earth also and the works that are therein shall be burned up" (2 Pet. 3:10). John sees these predictions fulfilled in the pouring out of the seven bowls of God's wrath. They follow the pattern of the plagues of Egypt and the restrained judgment announced by trumpets, except in varying order. They also differ in their

intensity and scope. What God has done in the way of restrained judgment, seeking repentance from men, at last falls on the whole world in full measure.

It is a picture of God in an activity which is frightening. If it seems unlike Him, it is because we miss the meaning of grace. The goodness of God is best understood over against the severity of His judgment. For the universe to have structure, there must be immutable moral laws. Men do not break God's laws; they break themselves in violating them. The song of Moses and the Lamb looks forward to the outpouring of God's wrath as evidence of the justice of the King of heaven: "Just and true are thy ways, O King of the ages!" (15:3, RSV).

2. The execution of God's wrath is both thorough and appropriate. Those who have suffered persecution and death from the hands of evil men are safe in heaven. Evil men receive just retribution for what they have done. The Book of Revelation has a special message to those martyred for the cause of Christ. This is true in part because those who first read it faced martyrdom every day. How can God allow such tragedies to occur? The book reminds us that, while God is patient and long-suffering, a time will come when His patience ends. Then in judgment ultimately fair the world of evil men will be punished for their sins.

This also is the conviction of the apostle Paul: "For as many as have sinned without law shall also perish without law: and as many as have sinned in the law shall be judged by the law . . . in the day when God shall judge the secrets of men by Jesus Christ according to my gospel" (Rom. 2:12, 16). On Mars' Hill he had said, "Forasmuch then as we are the offspring of God, we ought not to think that the Godhead is like unto gold, or silver, or stone, graven by art and man's device. And the times of this ignorance God winked at; but now commandeth all men everywhere to repent; because he hath appointed a day, in the which he will judge the world in righteousness by that man whom he hath ordained; whereof he hath given assurance unto all men, in that he hath raised him from the dead" (Acts 17:29-31).

The First Bowl

Rev. 16:2

> 2 And the first went, and poured out his vial upon the earth; and there fell a noisome and grievous sore upon the men which had the mark of the beast, and upon them which worshipped his image.

When the first bowl was emptied, grievous sores came on all who had the mark of the beast and had worshipped his image. In Egypt Moses and Aaron threw ashes into the air which covered the land, causing men and animals to break out with boils and sores. Men had taken evil into their lives and now wore its mark. The sores, whether they came from the sky or their own inner corruption, were a judgment directly related to their sin. So here in Revelation. There is no immunity from the evil infection of sin. Men bear in their bodies the sores of their wicked ways. They had been warned by the angel that whoever took the mark of the beast would drink from the wine of God's wrath. Now it had happened.

The Second Bowl

Rev. 16:3

> 3 And the second angel poured out his vial upon the sea; and it became as the blood of a dead man: and every living soul died in the sea.

The second bowl is similar to the second trumpet, reminiscent of the turning of the river Nile to blood. In the case of the bowl of wrath it is not a river but the sea. When the second trumpet sounded, a burning mountain was thrown in the sea, and only a third part was fouled. But when the second bowl was poured, the whole sea was made like the blood of a dead man. Every living thing in the sea died. It was out of the sea that the beast came who deceived men and controlled them. The angel of God who announced the end time stood with one foot on the sea, symbolizing the higher authority of God. Now the sea pays the price in blood. From out of it came evil, and now it is filled with a dead man's blood. One is reminded of Paul's words, "The wages of sin is death" (Rom. 6:23).

The Third Bowl

Rev. 16:4-7

> 4 And the third angel poured out his vial upon the rivers and fountains of waters; and they became blood.
> 5 And I heard the angel of the waters say, Thou art righteous, O Lord, which art, and wast, and shalt be, because thou hast judged thus.
> 6 For they have shed the blood of saints and prophets, and thou hast given them blood to drink; for they are worthy.
> 7 And I heard another out of the altar say, Even so, Lord God Almighty, true and righteous are thy judgments.

The outpouring of the third bowl completes the plague of blood. The rivers and fountains of waters become blood. In the plague in Egypt the river Nile, the ponds, the pools, and even the water in the kitchen utensils were turned to blood. This picture seems to be that inclusive. The pollution was thorough and complete. The defilment of the waters of the world by blood occurs in two stages. The second bowl visits the sea in punishment for the coming of the beast; the third bowl is related to the shedding of the blood of the martyrs. The angel of the waters says that God is righteous in this act because *they have shed the blood of saints and prophets, and thou hast given them blood to drink; for they are worthy.* And this time another cry is heard from the altar. It is probably the cry of the martyrs themselves who in the fifth chapter are seen under the altar praying for just retribution. Now the cry is, *Even so, Lord God Almighty, true and righteous are thy judgments* (v. 7).

We cannot disagree. The punishment is in kind and severity directly related to the sins. The cry "They are worthy" brings both a shudder as we think of the kind of punishment of which we are worthy and a rush of praise as we remember that the grace of God has appeared to all. All of us may escape the judgment of which we are worthy by accepting the grace of the Lord Jesus Christ who, while we were yet sinners, died for us. On the Cross He drank the gall mixed with wine, for us.

The Fourth Bowl

Rev. 16:8-9

> 8 And the fourth angel poured out his vial upon the sun; and power was given unto him to scorch men with fire.
> 9 And men were scorched with great heat, and blasphemed the name of God, which hath power over these plagues: and they repented not to give him glory.

The fourth bowl was poured out on the sun. It seems to have greatly increased its intensity so that men were scorched by its great heat. This is the opposite to the fourth trumpet, where the sun and moon and stars are darkened. The more scientists get to know about the sun, the more such an event is understandable. The occasional explosions or variations known as sun spots even today cause widespread phenomena on earth. So much of life is the product of the sun's rays. It brings growth and healing. Its warmth is a friend to man who needs help against the winds and storms that sweep the earth. Its light and energy are tapped for the ongoing of human activity. Primitive man worshipped the sun as a god, since it was so much the giver of life to him. But under that warm and friendly sun man has pursued his self-centered and often wicked ways. Its benefits he, too frequently, has turned to his pride or lust. To abuse anything God has placed here for our welfare is to risk the abuse that it can bring when it becomes an instrument of God's wrath.

But man in his sin does not see the justice of God's judgment. He turns in rage and blasphemy to curse God because of his pain and sores. Poor, pitiful, sinful man— he can curse but not repent! He refuses to accept judgment as a call to repentance but rather blasphemes his Creator and holds steadfastly to his sin and his rebellion. The sun and God who made it are the friends of man and seek his good. The friendship he refuses, and so terrible punishment at last must come.

The Fifth Bowl

Rev. 16:10-11

> 10 And the fifth angel poured out his vial upon the seat of the beast; and his kingdom was full of darkness; and they gnawed their tongues for pain,
> 11 And blasphemed the God of heaven because of their pains and their sores, and repented not of their deeds.

The fifth bowl is directed to the throne of the beast. It was poured out on him. A similar plague in Egypt left Pharaoh and the people with darkness for three days. When the fourth trumpet was blown, there was darkness. When the fifth trumpet was sounded, a falling star released swarms of locusts which became like an invading army so thick that sun and earth were darkened. In the time of an eclipse of the sun the darkness is awesome for the brief time the sun is completely covered by the moon. One cannot escape the hush such darkness brings. There was a day in United States history when an especially thick cloud darkened a great part of the Eastern seaboard, and hundreds panicked. But there is a greater darkness. Jesus said, "If . . . the light that is in thee be darkness, how great is that darkness!" (Matt. 6:23).

Darkness without and within is the picture when the wrath of God is outpoured. And it seems the pain and agony of the burning sun remain as men continue in the darkness to curse God and refuse to repent. Their anguish is increased as they gnaw their tongues in pain. All that man uses for his happiness and pleasure has been turned against him. His blasphemy from his pain is all that breaks the silence of the darkness when "the sun refused to shine." There was a moment of such darkness at the Cross. Its shadow should have warned men; but it did not, at least the most of them. And now the light men would not walk in has become darkness.

The Sixth Bowl

Rev. 16:12-16

12 And the sixth angel poured out his vial upon the great river Euphrates; and the water thereof was dried up, that the way of the kings of the east might be prepared.

13 And I saw three unclean spirits like frogs come out of the mouth of the dragon, and out of the mouth of the beast, and out of the mouth of the false prophet.

14 For they are the spirits of devils, working miracles, which go forth unto the kings of the earth and of the whole world, to gather them to the battle of that great day of God Almighty.

15 Behold, I come as a thief. Blessed is he that watcheth, and keepeth his garments, lest he walk naked, and they see his shame.

16 And he gathered them together into a place called in the Hebrew tongue Armageddon.

When the sixth bowl is poured out on the great river Euphrates, it is dried up and a passageway opened for the *kings of the east.* The rivers not only marked boundaries; they often were natural fortifications. The children of Israel could nót enter the Promised Land until a miraculous opening occurred. The river Euphrates was a barrier that held back the enemy from the East. Now the barrier becomes a highway. With waters gone, the dry bed provides excellent transportation facilities. The way is opened for the kings of earth to gather to do battle with the army of God at a place called Armageddon. This climactic battle is referred to several times in the ensuing chapters.

The judgment on rebellious man is the removal of the restraints to his ambitions. To use the words of Paul, God has given him over to his reprobate mind (Rom. 1:28). He is free now to defy the Almighty. It is not that God has surrendered, for man's struggle against God will fail and bring about his utter destruction. Armageddon becomes the name of man's greatest thrust and final defeat. The description of the plans is interrupted by the repeated warning that Jesus will come as a thief, and happy is he who is ready. The reader is not to be overwhelmed by the threat of Armageddon.

The Seventh Bowl

Rev. 16:17-21

17 And the seventh angel poured out his vial into the air; and there came a great voice out of the temple of heaven, from the throne, saying, It is done.

18 And there were voices, and thunders, and lightnings; and there was a great earthquake, such as was not since men were upon the earth, so mighty an earthquake, and so great.

19 And the great city was divided into three parts and the cities of the nations fell: and great Babylon came in remembrance before God, to give unto her the cup of the wine of the fierceness of his wrath.

20 And every island fled away, and the mountains were not found.

21 And there fell upon men a great hail out of heaven, every stone about the weight of a talent: and men blasphemed God because of the plague of the hail; for the plague thereof was exceeding great.

The seventh bowl is poured out into the air. A voice out of the temple in heaven and the throne calls, "It is done!" John had heard Jesus use almost the same words from the Cross, "It is finished" (John 19:30). As it did at the Cross, the earth shook; only now it was the greatest earthquake ever. The great city called Babylon, the Christian's code word for Rome, was divided in three parts by the violent upheaval, and the mountains and islands disappeared. Gigantic hailstones weighing nearly 100 pounds fell upon men, and they repented or continued their blasphemy.

So with a final conclusive battle and an unparalleled upheaval of the earth and sky, the wrath of God is visited upon men. So the day of salvation ends. All have been saved who would. The rest now face the existence and consequence they have chosen in rejecting the grace of God. The further events of this final day will be spelled out in other visions John shares. They give graphic detail and specific significance. The eternal state of men and God will be symbolically portrayed with the comfort and assurance to the righteous and just reward to the wicked. God created, He loved, He tried to redeem all, He gathered to himself those who would, and He judged and punished those who would not. The whole idea was right, and so He will purge and bring into eternal existence a new heaven and new earth wherein dwells righteousness.

The City of Man

Revelation 17:1—18:24

REVELATION 17

All through the Book of Revelation there has loomed the shadow of the enemies of God. They have controlled the kingdoms of the world and persecuted the children of God. They have been pictured in various symbols, all of which were intended to alert the faithful as to who they were and what were their intentions. In the 17th chapter the reader is given the vision which identifies the foe and predicts the final outcome. Among the figures is one which is shared by other New Testament writers, that of a city. The writer of Hebrews, in commenting on the faith of Abraham, describes people whom God loves as being pilgrims and strangers on the earth; they find on earth "no continuing city" (13:14), and so they look for one to come. For this insight, he says, God is not ashamed to be called their God. Then he concludes, "For he hath prepared for them a city" (11:16).

Man is inherently gregarious. Early in human history he gathered in groups, and the city became the symbol of his strength and ability. The cities quickly developed a religious dimension, and divine qualities have been claimed for them. Babel, Nineveh, Babylon, Athens, and Rome all are recorded in sacred literature as cities that drew the condemnation of God. Jesus had His most scathing rebuke for cities like Capernaum and Bethsaida.

He said of them that, if the mighty works which had been done in them had been done in Sodom and Gomorrah, they would have repented.

Modern man is no different. Today great strip cities form rapidly all over the world. Their population is numbered in the millions. They swallow up ever-increasing acres of land. Their gigantic skylines, like Babel, seem to be stretching toward the very throne of God. They boast of man's ingenuity and skill. They also form great ghettos where every crime of greed and lust is bred. They house the palaces of the rich, and their streets are trod by the poor and the homeless. They are an unforgivable blasphemy. They claim to protect and satisfy, but they rape and destroy. God has a controversy with the city. The details of His indictment are the messages of the next two chapters.

The City Is a Harlot

Rev. 17:1-6

> 1 And there came one of the seven angels which had the seven vials, and talked with me, saying unto me, Come hither; I will shew unto thee the judgment of the great whore that sitteth upon many waters:
> 2 With whom the kings of the earth have committed fornication, and the inhabitants of the earth have been made drunk with the wine of her fornication.
> 3 So he carried me away in the spirit into the wilderness: and I saw a woman sit upon a scarlet coloured beast, full of names of blasphemy, having seven heads and ten horns.
> 4 And the woman was arrayed in purple and scarlet colour, and decked with gold and precious stones and pearls, having a golden cup in her hand full of abominations and filthiness of her fornication:
> 5 And upon her forehead was a name written, MYSTERY, BABYLON THE GREAT, THE MOTHER OF HARLOTS AND ABOMINATIONS OF THE EARTH.
> 6 And I saw the woman drunken with the blood of the saints, and with the blood of the martyrs of Jesus: and when I saw her, I wondered with great admiration.

One of the seven angels who had the bowls of God's wrath talked with John and invited him to observe the judgment of God on the city. The city is called Babylon. Every description of it, however, makes plain that Rome is in the mind of John. It is intended to speak especially to the Christians who were already suffering under the heavy hand of that city which worshipped its emperors as gods. *Come hither; I will shew unto thee the judgment of the great [harlot] that sitteth upon many waters,* says the angel.

1. The use of Babylon carries two thoughts for the Christian.

   a. It was a code word for Rome, which usage kept the letter from being used as evidence of treason. At the same time it reminded the Christian that God had dealt with Babylon in her pride and thoroughly destroyed her so that she is no more.

   b. It also said, What God did to Babylon He will do to Rome *or any city* which in her pride tries to usurp the place of God.

2. The use of the language of sex sins has been the common characteristic of both the Old and New Testaments. Blasphemy and idolatry are referred to as fornication or adultery. The love of God and His people, or Christ and His Church, are described as the love of a husband and wife. Thus any other love or worship is put in the language of unfaithfulness to marriage vows or illicit sex. The sex language probably refers primarily to the city's spiritual sin. But its expression is generally in sexual indulgence and perversion (see Rom. 1:18 ff.).

3. John is taken *in the spirit into the wilderness.* It was in the wilderness where he saw the woman who represented the people of God. It is, therefore, not coincidental that in the wilderness John sees the scarlet woman. She is not, of course, the same one who flew there on wings given her of God. The picture rather is of the harlot seeking to identify herself with the previously portrayed beautiful one. The sin of the harlot is intensified because she claims the haven of the woman whose seed the dragon persecuted.

   The harlot sits upon a scarlet beast. The beast is pictured as the same one who came from the sea. He is the human instrument of Satan. The woman is decked with costly precious stones and dressed in purple and scarlet. These are the colors of royalty and undisciplined pleasure. She is the picture of wealth, political power, and lust or pleasure. In her hand is a golden cup full of abominations. She is the epitome of self-indulgence. The city is the work of man's hand and the site of his self-worship and exploitation of others.

On the forehead of the harlot is written the words, "Babylon the great, mother of harlots and of earth's abominations" (RSV). The abominations are many, but for John the greatest was the martyrdom of the saints. He said she was drunk with the blood of the saints and the martyrs of Jesus. What the city does to all who seek in her a supplying of their needs is one thing and terrible, but what the city does to draw the blood of the children of God is the greatest of her abominations. The power to destroy the messengers of God intoxicates her.

When John sees her, he is greatly puzzled. He wants to understand the meaning of the vision. He understood the picture of the woman who fled to safety on wings given her of God. But what of the woman carried by the beast? Who is she? What does she represent?

The Beast and His Harlot
Rev. 17:7-18

7 And the angel said unto me, Wherefore didst thou marvel? I will tell thee the mystery of the woman, and of the beast that carrieth her, which hath the seven heads and ten horns.
8 The beast that thou sawest was, and is not; and shall ascend out of the bottomless pit, and go into perdition: and they that dwell on the earth shall wonder, whose names were not written in the book of life from the foundation of the world, when they behold the beast that was, and is not, and yet is.
9 And here is the mind which hath wisdom. The seven heads are seven mountains, on which the woman sitteth.
10 And there are seven kings: five are fallen, and one is, and the other is not yet come; and when he cometh, he must continue a short space.
11 And the beast that was, and is not, even he is the eighth, and is of the seven, and goeth into perdition.
12 And the ten horns which thou sawest are ten kings, which have re-

ceived no kingdom as yet; but receive power as kings one hour with the beast.
13 These have one mind, and shall give their power and strength unto the beast.
14 These shall make war with the Lamb, and the Lamb shall overcome them: for he is Lord of lords, and King of kings: and they that are with him are called, and chosen, and faithful.
15 And he saith unto me, The waters which thou sawest, where the whore sitteth, are peoples, and multitudes, and nations, and tongues.
16 And the ten horns which thou sawest upon the beast, these shall hate the whore, and shall make her desolate and naked, and shall eat her flesh, and burn her with fire.
17 For God hath put in their hearts to fulfil his will, and to agree, and give their kingdom unto the beast, until the words of God shall be fulfilled.
18 And the woman which thou sawest is that great city, which reigneth over the kings of the earth.

The angel promises John that he will explain the symbolism of the beast with the seven heads and the 10 horns and the woman he carries.

1. There are two very significant characteristics to the explanation the angel gives. One is the comparison/contrast to Christ and the beast. The other is the history and prediction of events that had occurred or were to occur in Rome.

   a. The beast is described as the one who was and is not; Christ is the One who was slain and lives forever. The beast comes out of the netherworld and will return to it; Christ came from the glory and will take His followers there with Him. The beast will for a time seek to emulate Christ, but at last he and all who worship him will go to perdition. His followers think the beast will live again, but they are deceived. And they have no promise of life: Their names are not in the book of life, for this book contains the names of those who refused to worship the beast.

   b. The seven heads are the seven mountains on which the harlot, or the city, sits.

   (1) This is a clear identification of the imagery of the harlot and beast with the city of Rome, famous for its location on seven mountains. Slowly but carefully the symbolism of the book has led up to this moment. Every factor has indicated that the visions were speaking of the

struggle of Rome against the Church. But at last the identification has been positively asserted, and John pauses to emphasize the fact: *Here is the mind which hath wisdom.* So we can add, *The seven hills tell the story.*

(2) It is very difficult to match verses 10 and 11 with Roman history although it is intended to do so. Who are the five that have fallen? Who is the reigning one? And who is the eighth who is also among the seventh? It is impossible to say with any great accuracy. The most likely is Nero come back to life. In late New Testament times the legend persisted that Nero would come back to life. It was probably born of the dread people had of him, just as for years after World War II the rumor persisted that Hitler was alive and in hiding and would reappear to threaten the world again. Nero could be the one who was, and is not, and is to come. He was one of the seven and was predicted to return. John is not saying that he will but that one who appears to be Nero will return.

(3) The inability to fit the prediction perfectly does not take from the validity of the identification with Rome. There is enough for those who read it first to catch the significance and the message. There is enough which does not quite match to feel the message is for other times as well and to be heartened by its message. For its message is that the city of man is in conspiracy against God. The city seeks blasphemously to counterfeit the gospel. It dares to proclaim its leaders as saviors. It demands the worship of its inhabitants, and it makes war on the Lamb. The city will not prevail. The Lamb will be victorious. If the beast pictured is not Rome, it is another great city or league of cities or countries which will become intoxicated with its power and draw together others who must have one mind (for this, too, is a demand of the city). It will make war on the Lamb.

2. The angel explains that the waters on which the harlot sat are the people, and nations, and tongues. They represent the world of humans. The city is not a superimposed

entity. It is the personification of the people. It is the creation of them. The city of man is the sum total of man's abilities and his aspirations. Taking advantage of and rising up from the inner heart of unregenerate man is this product which appears to cover the whole earth—the city. It defiantly says to God, "Man does not need You. He can care for all his needs, heal all his woes. His hand can make a home, safe and secure against the storms of life."

3. The city makes war on the Lamb because of its boast to need no other salvation than the one that science and ingenuity can provide. She does not rule by love. She rules by trapping men into submission by catering to their lust. They seek fulfillment in all the city claims to provide. But they hate her. This is the story of lust. It pours out strength in search of joy. It is intoxicated with the pleasure of the moment, but empty-hearted it turns to hate the very object of its venture. As a man takes the privilege he buys from the harlot and expends his strength in an explosion of pleasure only to hate her when it is done, so the world of men are seduced and deceived by the whorish city sitting on the waters. They are captured by her lures but hate her in their hearts. The poet wrote:

> *The Worldly Hope men set their Hearts upon*
> *Turns Ashes—or it prospers; and anon,*
> *Like Snow upon the Desert's dusty Face*
> *Lighting a little Hour or two—is gone.*

The harlot, said the angel who carried the wrath of God in a bowl, is the great city which has dominion over the kings of the earth.

REVELATION 18

The City Is Doomed

Rev. 18:1-3

> 1 And after these things I saw another angel come down from heaven, having great power; and the earth was lightened with his glory.
>
> 2 And he cried mightily with a strong voice, saying, Babylon the great is fallen, is fallen, and is become the habitation of devils, and the hold of every foul spirit, and a cage of every unclean and hateful bird.
>
> 3 For all nations have drunk of the wine of the wrath of her fornication, and the kings of the earth have committed fornication with her, and the merchants of the earth are waxed rich through the abundance of her delicacies.

Much about the city is attractive. But much about her is threatening. Many a Christian has stood in awe of her and wondered how the cause of Christ could ever succeed in her. Many have given up. There is no hope either in her or because of her. Reluctantly we acknowledge this is true.

John now sees a mighty angel who cries with a strong voice that the city is doomed. She has become the dwelling place of evil. In all of her boasting she is really a captive. She dresses and acts as if she has control of all, but sadly she is in the hold of every evil spirit and every foul bird. The kings have become intoxicated with her power, and the merchants have become rich with the wealth of her wantonness. The kings have been her customers, the merchants her pimps.

Certainty and confidence mark the angel's proclamation of the doom of the city. What he says about it we know already, but the earth is lightened as he announces the city is doomed and her blasphemies are to be punished. There is hope, not in the city's ability to keep her promise, but in God's determination to bring her into judgment. The situation brightens with the glory of the strength and confidence of this mighty angel. He has said the word which spells the end of the enemies of God. No one seemed to be able to explain the fall of Napoleon to British troops when he had every means to be invincible—except the historian who asserted, "He bothered God."[11] The city of man bothers God. It will fall, and that truth lightens the landscape.

Come Out of Her, My People

Rev. 18:4-8

> 4 And I heard another voice from heaven, saying, Come out of her, my people, that ye be not partakers of her sins, and that ye receive not of her plagues.
> 5 For her sins have reached unto heaven, and God hath remembered her iniquities.
> 6 Reward her even as she rewarded you, and double unto her double according to her works: in the cup which she hath filled fill to her double.
> 7 How much she hath glorified herself, and lived deliciously, so much torment and sorrow give her: for she saith in her heart, I sit a queen, and am no widow, and shall see no sorrow.
> 8 Therefore shall her plagues come in one day, death, and mourning, and famine; and she shall be utterly burned with fire: for strong is the Lord God who judgeth her.

1. The rationale for the doom of the city of man is given by *another voice from heaven.* It calls for the people of God to abandon the city while there is time. Of course, people of God have to live in the city. The call is not to literally leave the city for a mountaintop, as some have done. *It is a call to abandon the thinking, the aspirations, and the sin of the city.* They have to be in it, but they need not be of it. They are called out because the doom of the city is sure and will happen in a moment. There will be no time to get out when the judgment falls. Jesus uses the same imagery when He suggests that men pray their flight not be in the winter. He advises the flight to be immediate without taking time to gather things together. The city's pretense has been long and involved. But its destruction is to be sudden.

They are called out because the city is intoxicating. It captures the mind and corrals the emotions. It is a way of thinking that destroys one's spiritual life. It makes the things that are seen appear to be real. It narrows the scope of values to the immediate and sensual. There is no way to be a pilgrim and a stranger on the earth without confessing that the city of man is not for you. One's earthly home may be in the city, but he must come out of its way of life so that he can sing:

> *I am a stranger here within a foreign land,*
> *My home is far away upon a golden strand.*[12]

The apostle Paul describes this being in the city but not of it as being an ambassador for Christ (2 Cor. 5:20). An ambassador lives in a land and a city not his own; his citizenship is elsewhere. He is there on business for his king. The call to the disciple of Christ in a world which lays its tribute at the city of man, is to live a holy life. He must bear witness in the city, but all of the city must be taken out of him. He joins the angel who is calling for the city's destruction.

2. The hymn of this victory asks for the city to be rewarded in the measure that she has sinned. It prays for the punishment to be in kind. She has lived wantonly—let her have her measure of mourning. She has filled the cup for others—let her drink fully from it. In pride she has claimed infallibility and royalty. She says, "A queen I sit, I am no widow, mourning I shall never see" (v. 7, RSV). She boasts she is in control, has no commitments, and can find pleasure whenever and wherever she wishes. Therefore, she must be cut off suddenly.

3. Here is a warning, not only to the city of its coming doom, but also to the Christian—of things he must avoid or disclaim if he is to be a true ambassador for Christ. Pride must be eradicated from his heart. He must not worship at the altar of success. He must not seek to make pleasure his goal. "God resisteth the proud, and giveth grace to the humble" (1 Pet. 5:5). His only hope is in God's abundant grace. What man cannot do or be of himself God gives in the Holy Spirit. We are to come out of the worldly city's pride and rest upon God's grace and power!

The Kings and Merchants Mourn

Rev. 18:9-19

9 And the kings of the earth, who have committed fornication and lived deliciously with her, shall bewail her, and lament for her, when they shall see the smoke of her burning,

10 Standing afar off for the fear of her torment, saying, Alas, alas that great city Babylon, that mighty city! for in one hour is thy judgment come.

11 And the merchants of the earth shall weep and mourn over her; for no man buyeth their merchandise any more:

12 The merchandise of gold, and silver, and precious stones, and of pearls, and fine linen, and purple, and silk, and scarlet, and all thyine wood, and all manner vessels of ivory, and all manner vessels of most precious wood, and of brass, and iron, and marble,

13 And cinnamon, and odours, and ointments, and frankincense, and wine, and oil, and fine flour, and wheat, and beasts, and sheep, and horses, and chariots, and slaves, and souls of men.

14 And the fruits that thy soul lusted after are departed from thee, and thou shalt find them no more at all.

15 The merchants of these things, which were made rich by her, shall stand afar off for the fear of her torment, weeping and wailing,

16 And saying, Alas, alas that great city, that was clothed in fine linen, and purple, and scarlet, and decked with gold, and precious stones, and pearls!

17 For in one hour so great riches is come to nought. And every shipmaster, and all the company in ships, and sailors, and as many as trade by sea, stood afar off,

18 And cried when they saw the smoke of her burning saying, What city is like unto this great city!

19 And they cast dust on their heads, and cried, weeping and wailing, saying, Alas, alas that great city, wherein were made rich all that had ships in the sea by reason of her costliness! for in one hour is she made desolate.

The angel had designated kings and merchants as those who profited by the harlot. The kings had enjoyed the air of divinity given them in the city's religion of secular humanism. The merchants had enjoyed the wealth they gained from the city's exploitation of the natural and human resources it had been able to amass. The angel who brightened the earth noted that these two groups would stand afar to mourn the city's destruction. We must not let the shift in symbolism fool us. It is not that the angel means the kings and the merchants will escape the destruction of the city; only those whose names are written in the book of life will do that. It rather is that in their lament we can see the basic sin of the city.

Both recall the glory they had sought in her. The kings moan, *Alas, alas, that great city Babylon, that mighty city! for in one hour is thy judgment come.* They recall the intoxication of the power they relished—so sweet when they thought they had it, so soon gone. The merchants lament that no man wants their merchandise anymore. It is an impressive list of merchandise the angel details— gold, silver, precious stones, pearls, fine linen, purple, silk, scarlet, thyine wood, vessels of ivory and precious wood, brass, iron, marble, cinnamon, odours, ointments, frankincense, wine, oil, flour, wheat, beasts, sheep, horses, chariots, slaves, and the souls of men. The merchants, like the kings, cry, *Alas, alas that great city.* In one hour all its wealth has been laid waste. One is reminded of Jesus' advice, "Lay not up for yourselves treasures upon earth, where moth and rust doth corrupt, and where thieves break through and steal" (Matt. 6:19).

The kings and merchants are joined by the shipmasters and sailors and all whose trade is on the sea, weeping and asking, "What city was like this great city?" They weep for what they thought they had, and lost so quickly. Missionary Jim Elliot, martyred in the jungles of South America, wrote memorably: "He is no fool who gives what he cannot keep to gain what he cannot lose."[13]

The Final Dirge

Rev. 18:20-24

> 20 Rejoice over her, thou heaven, and ye holy apostles and prophets; for God hath avenged you on her.
> 21 And a mighty angel took up a stone like a great millstone, and cast it into the sea, saying, Thus with violence shall that great city Babylon be thrown down, and shall be found no more at all.
> 22 And the voice of harpers, and musicians, and of pipers, and trumpeters, shall be heard no more at all in thee; and no craftsman, of whatsoever craft he be, shall be found any more in thee; and the sound of a millstone shall be heard no more at all in thee;
> 23 And the light of a candle shall shine no more at all in thee; and the voice of the bridegroom and of the bride shall be heard no more at all in thee: for thy merchants were the great men of the earth; for by thy sorceries were all nations deceived.
> 24 And in her was found the blood of prophets, and of saints, and of all that were slain upon the earth.

The angel seems to have had enough of the mourning of the people who cast their lot with the city of man and experienced its sudden destruction. He calls for the heavens to rejoice. God has finally avenged His elect who, Jesus said, cry to Him day and night. Jesus has said He would avenge them speedily (Luke 18:8), and so He will. The heavens rejoice not only because the city has received her deserts but also because God has kept His promise. He has warned against the folly of man's sin and pride. For too long man has appeared to be successful in his rebellion—for God is long-suffering. He gets no joy in man's destruction; He wishes for all to come to repentance. But He is a God of justice and truth; He balances the books. Truth has been vindicated; righteousness has been exonerated. Why shouldn't the heavens rejoice?

Then another mighty angel takes a great millstone and casts it into the sea. He explains that in like manner the city of man is thrown down and disappears. It will not be seen again. For all the boast of permanence, the city of man has a brief day and a sudden ending. The waters close over the spot, and nothing marks the place—it disappears. No longer will there be heard in her the voice of the harp or any music. The song of pleasure may be upbeat, but it dies. There is no sound of craftsmen at work or the throbbing of construction. No light, no love remain. All the city promised has eluded the pursuers, and the silence of doom is eternal. She did not keep her promise. She left only the blood of the prophets, the saints, and of all that were slain.

The Hallelujah Chorus

Revelation 19:1-21

REVELATION 19

The Heavens Rejoice

Rev. 19:1-6

> 1 And after these things I heard a great voice of much people in heaven, saying, Alleluia; Salvation, and glory, and honour, and power, unto the Lord our God:
> 2 For true and righteous are his judgments: for he hath judged the great whore, which did corrupt the earth with her fornication, and hath avenged the blood of his servants at her hand.
> 3 And again they said, Alleluia. And her smoke rose up for ever and ever.
> 4 And the four and twenty elders and the four beasts fell down and worshipped God that sat on the throne, saying, Amen; Alleluia.
> 5 And a voice came out of the throne, saying, Praise our God, all ye his servants, and ye that fear him, both small and great.
> 6 And I heard as it were the voice of a great multitude, and as the voice of many waters, and as the voice of mighty thunderings, saying, Alleluia: for the Lord God omnipotent reigneth.

1. It is very easy to be captivated with the pictures of violence and destruction in Revelation and forget that it is a book of victory. The darker side is given to make the light shine brighter. The important thing is not that catastrophic times are in store for men; it has been that way throughout history. The scenes portrayed are unusual even though they may be greatly intensified; yet in some ways they are familiar. They are, in fact, so much a macro-

cosm of true life that hardly a generation since the book was written has not seen a few events which make the similarities seem more than coincidental. This has not only kept the glorious hope of the final victory alive but also the message of the book ever relevant.

2. The evil successes are not the point, however. The book was written to say that God is and will always be victorious. So the description of the inevitable end of the city of man fades into another vision, that of the rejoicing multitudes of heaven. Handel incorporated the scene into his oratorio which has become famous with the "Hallelujah Chorus." So moving is it that the king of England, when he heard it, stood in tribute to the majestic sweep of its cadence and truth. It is customary now for audiences to stand when the first chords of the chorus begin. The theme of the chorus is the adoration of the reigning Lord.

3. In the vision John now records, the hosts of heaven are praising God that He is true and righteous and has dealt with the city of man as it deserves. The 24 elders and the four beasts, who always appear when the focus is on the throne of God, join in the praise with *Amen; Alleluia*. This is the theme of the book—not how terrible things will become before the end but how great is God. He rules over all. Nothing that could possibly happen will in any way thwart that glorious truth.

4. John hears the multitude which sounded like *many waters*. The very roar of the seas around his prison island become a symbol of the eternal praise of the hosts of heaven because the Lord God reigns forever. The sound was also like many thunderings. Perhaps what he could not write he cannot forget. He was restrained from telling what the seven thunders said, but he gives a clue as to the content. Like everything else in these graphic visions, they declare the glory and praise of God who is forever victorious. What were the symbols of his imprisonment, the sea and storms, have become instruments of praise to God.

The Wedding Announcement

Rev. 19:7-9

> 7 Let us be glad and rejoice, and give honour to him: for the marriage of the Lamb is come, and his wife hath made herself ready.
> 8 And to her was granted that she should be arrayed in fine linen, clean and white: for the fine linen is the righteousness of saints.
> 9 And he saith unto me, Write, Blessed are they which are called unto the marriage supper of the Lamb. And he saith unto me, These are the true sayings of God.

1. The mighty hallelujah not only acclaims the all-powerful Ruler but also calls for rejoicing the Lamb is to take a wife. The triumph of the Eternal is not only that He rules over all but also that His Son is to receive a bride and an eternal inheritance. The destruction of the city of man portrayed as a scarlet woman is in sharp contrast to the eternal vitality of love and purity. The counterfeit which makes up the ways of men fails, and the heavens are glad. They are also glad that the Lamb who was slain and lives forever victorious will take to himself a bride. She has been made ready, the song declares. She is pure and prepared.

2. The Bride's clothing is fine linen, pure and white. John adds that *the fine linen is the righteousness of saints*. The saints are clothed with a righteousness which is pure and fitting for the Lamb, clothing not of their own making but the gift of grace. Evil men hate them because they are the witness to the cleansing that all men need and evil men refuse. For the first readers of the book the picture had special meaning, for previously they had heard that martyrdom was a way of washing one's garments in the blood of the Lamb, that the martyrs wear white and are worthy to walk with the Lamb. In a strict sense the Bride is made up of all who give their lives for the witness of Jesus. We shall consider the spiritual significance of this martyrdom in the next chapter.

3. *The marriage supper of the Lamb* was not designed to be confined to the Bride, for the announcement is an invi-

tation. All are invited. If the will of God were the only factor involved, all the created world of men would be there, for He wills that all men should be saved and come to the knowledge of the truth (1 Tim. 2:4). Though all are invited, not all will come, is the teaching of Jesus. He also said that some who come would not be allowed to remain because they did not have the proper attire (Matt. 22:11-13). Blessed or happy are all who are called. One might add the implied truth—if they accept and come.

It is an occasion of joy. It is a feast of good things and blessings. The Communion service is intended to anticipate the great and glorious marriage supper of the Lamb. It is made possible by His death, it is true, but it is not to be observed in sorrow, rather in joy. It does not call attention to the Lamb's suffering only, but also to His marriage. Happy are those who will attend the supper. Happy are those who look forward in joy.

The author emphasizes the element of joy by adding that these are the true words of God. Joy is very near to the basic nature of God's relationship with His people. It is His joy to share; it is His joy to give. It is His joy to see all things come to fulfillment. It is His joy to acknowledge the validity of the relationship He has with His people. And this joy is known in some measure by all who are His. The joy of the Lord is their strength. When they are together in His presence, there is the fullness of joy. When the gospel story was first told to the shepherds on the hillsides of Judea, they were told that they were receiving tidings of great joy (Luke 2:8-16). That joy is realized at the marriage supper of the Lamb.

The Discipline of Worship

Rev. 19:10

> 10 And I fell at his feet to worship him. And he said unto me, See thou do it not: I am thy fellowservant, and of thy brethren that have the testimony of Jesus: worship God: for the testimony of Jesus is the spirit of prophecy.

1. Worship is a common activity of humankind. It is as

natural to worship as to breathe. I recall hearing a news reporter tell of a moment he witnessed in Germany just before the outset of the Second World War. He had been assigned to report the rise of the Third Reich. He saw people grow in confidence and pride as they saw Germany becoming strong. He grew accustomed to the cheering and lavish praise that was being heaped upon Adolf Hitler as he forged the Axis and gobbled up the small nations around him. But the reporter recalled one unforgettable moment at Berlin. Hitler was returning from having completed the uniting of Germany and Italy in a defense pact. The crowds, he said, were unusually large around the train depot. The Führer arrived and greeted them, but strangely there was only silence. The reporter turned to a German newsman and asked why there was no cheering. "Because," replied the newsman, "one does not applaud God."

2. How easy it is to worship and, alas, to worship the wrong thing or deity! Paul accused the men on Mars Hill of being too religious. They worshipped all the gods they knew, and in fear that they might have left one out, they erected a monument to "an unknown God" (Acts 17:22). Worshipping was not wrong. It was the objects of their worship which were. John tells us of a mistake he made in worship. An angel had told him of the marriage supper of the Lamb and the joy of being invited to it. Overcome by this word and all that he had been seeing, John falls at the feet of the angel to worship him. "Don't do it," the angel remonstrated; "God alone is to be worshipped." The angel insists that he, too, is a *fellowservant*. He, too, is involved in *the testimony of Jesus*. This, he says, is the heart of all forth-speaking—the testimony of Jesus. Jesus is the heart of all the prophets have to say. The message is not greater than the One of whom it speaks. He is the One who gives the message meaning.

Some worship evil, it is true. But good men can make the mistake of worshipping what is good instead of the God who is the Source of all good. It is the error of substituting the good for the best.

The incident and the advice is repeated in the last chapter of the book (22:8-9). One cannot help but wonder how John made such a serious mistake again so soon. Some suggestions will appear later as to how it might have happened. It is sufficient now to say that this tendency to worship something less than we should is deeply ingrained in the human mystique. Paul had warned the Colossians that they must not worship angels. "Let no man beguile you of your reward in a voluntary humility and worshipping of angels, intruding into those things which he hath not seen, vainly puffed up by his fleshly mind" (Col. 2:18).

3. Worship is to God alone, the angel tells John and us all. There is nothing that can rightfully take His place or stand alongside Him in our adoration. The event is meaningful in this light. Angels are beautiful figures. Their ministry to men, their praise of God, their faithfulness in His service are all traits that make them adorable to men. And in a sense they are a promise to men that they will eventually share existence with them. The angel is high above man but is not beyond the scope of man's attaining. God is. He is above and eternally beyond every creature. Worship which springs so spontaneously from men's hearts must be disciplined and directed to God alone, the only object which is really worthy of it.

The Faithful and True Leader

Rev. 19:11-16

> 11 And I saw heaven opened, and behold a white horse; and he that sat upon him was called Faithful and True., and in righteousness he doth judge and make war.
> 12 His eyes were as a flame of fire, and on his head were many crowns; and he had a name written, that no man knew, but he himself.
> 13 And he was clothed with a vesture dipped in blood: and his name is called The Word of God.
> 14 And the armies which were in heaven followed him upon white horses, clothed in fine linen, white and clean.

15 And out of his mouth goeth a sharp sword, that with it he should smite the nations: and he shall rule them with a rod of iron: and he treadeth the winepress of the fierceness and wrath of Almighty God.

16 And he hath on his vesture and on his thigh a name written, KING OF KINGS, AND LORD OF LORDS.

1. Following the mild rebuke of the angel to John is another vision. This one is of a rider on a white horse. The vision differs from the first woe which followed the breaking of the first seal. That rider went forth conquering and bringing sorrow and suffering with his bow. This Rider is *called Faithful and True*. He judges in righteousness and makes war on evil. His eyes are as a flame of fire, and He wears many crowns on His head. He has a name that is known only to himself. His nature is above and beyond human understanding. By this the reader is clued to the person of Christ. He has "a name which is above every name: that at the name of Jesus every knee should bow . . . and that every tongue should confess that Jesus Christ is Lord to the glory of God the Father" (Phil. 2:9-11). His robe is dipped in blood. While it is not His name which indicates His identity with God, He is called the Word of God. This latter name makes the identification with Jesus complete. In his Gospel John refers to Jesus as the Word. "The Word was made flesh," he writes, "and dwelt among us, (and we beheld his glory, the glory as of the only begotten of the Father,) full of grace and truth" (John 1:14).

2. The Rider has an army of people who are dressed in white, the garments of the martyrs and overcomers. They, too, are astride white horses. He is one with them and they with Him. "For both He that sanctifieth and they who are sanctified are all of one: for which cause he is not ashamed to call them brethren" (Heb. 2:11). He really does not use His army, for out of His mouth is a sharp sword with which to smite the nations. He acts to express God's righteous judgment of the world. The imagery changes long enough for the Rider to be said to tread the winespress of God's wrath. In other words His conquest is the accom-

plishment of the just and fierce anger of God which has been withheld until the day of salvation is done. In the Rider and His army this anger will break forth in terrible and complete punishment of every wrongdoer and every evil thing.

3. The all-inclusiveness of this conquest is to be seen in the name on the garments of the Rider, which is *KING OF KINGS, AND LORD OF LORDS.* He is faithful to the will and righteous judgment of God. He is true to the eternal plan and purpose of God to deal with evil and set up an eternal kingdom. He is the Instrument by which God keeps His promise.

A Feast for the Birds

Rev. 19:17-21

> 17 And I saw an angel standing in the sun; and he cried with a loud voice, saying to all the fowls that fly in the midst of heaven, Come and gather yourselves together unto the supper of the great God;
> 18 That ye may eat the flesh of kings, and the flesh of captains, and the flesh of mighty men, and the flesh of horses, and of them that sit on them, and the flesh of all men, both free and bond, both small and great.
> 19 And I saw the beast, and the kings of the earth, and their armies, gathered together to make war against him that sat on the horse, and against his army.
> 20 And the beast was taken, and with him the false prophet that wrought miracles before him, with which he deceived them that had received the mark of the beast, and them that worshipped his image. These both were cast alive into a lake of fire burning with brimstone.
> 21 And the remnant were slain with the sword of him that sat upon the horse, which sword proceeded out of his mouth: and all the fowls were filled with their flesh.

1. The thoroughness and the terribleness of the destruction of the armies of the beast and the 10 kings is conveyed in the imagery of carnage which draws all the fowls of the heaven for a great feast. In a sense it contrasts with the marriage supper of the Lamb. A voice called for all men to attend the latter. An angel calls the birds before the battle so that his invitation to them is a prediction of the utter destruction of the rebellion. The beast and the false prophet are cast into a lake of fire that burns with brimstone.

2. The feast of the birds is referred to by Jesus in His discourse with the disciples. He was telling them of His impending suffering. He prophesied that the days of the Son of Man would be like the days of Noah. At that time they ate, they drank, they married, until the day Noah entered the ark. Suddenly the Flood came and destroyed them all. It was also like that in the days of Lot. They ate, they drank, they bought, they sold, they planted, they built. Suddenly fire and brimstone rained from heaven and destroyed them all. Then He added, "I tell you, in that night two persons will be on one bed, the one will be taken and the other left; two women will be grinding together, the one will be taken and other left. Two will be in the field; the one will be taken and the other left." The disciples asked, "Where, Lord?" Where will these from the bed, the mill, and the field be taken? Jesus answered, "Where there is a corpse there the vultures will flock" (Luke 17:34-37, NBV).

3. Vultures gather where there is dead flesh. A large number of them in one spot, on the ground or in the air, is a sure sign something is dead nearby. This fact enables John to understand the magnitude of the destruction when Christ deals finally and fully with the forces of evil. The contrast with the wedding feast cannot be missed. After the redeemed have gathered for the marriage supper of the Lamb and have eaten in joy, there is another feast that follows. The birds, especially the vultures, gorge themselves with the flesh of the slain from Armageddon. The division is thorough; it includes all. From the bed, the mill, the field, wherever they are who follow the beast and have received his mark, they are taken for destruction. The beast and false prophet are taken and cast in a lake of fire. All who follow them are slain by the sword which issued from the mouth of the Rider on the white horse. The destruction is complete.

4. If these pictures seem ghastly, one should remember that evil is no light matter. It is a malignancy so deadly

that only a thoroughgoing eradication of it can deal adequately with it. It must be rooted out and burned with unquenchable fire until no vestige remains. Evil cannot be reformed; it must be destroyed. Its destruction is accomplished by the power of truth. The sword which issues out of the mouth of the Rider of the white horse pictures the truth from the mouth of Christ. Truth prevails even though it is placed on a scaffold. So Jesus promised, "Ye shall know the truth, and the truth shall make you free" (John 8:32).

Reigning with Christ
Revelation 20:1-15

REVELATION 20

John shares in this 20th chapter of the book a vision which is difficult to place in a timetable of events. This is not an exception, since the book is a series of visions which reveal truths, not timetables. The period it covers is identified as 1,000 years, which is a symbol of too many years to number. Peter says that 1,000 years are with the Lord as one day (2 Pet. 3:8). The *thousand years* are probably more indicative of the timeless and endless quality of Christ's reign than of its length in years. It appears to follow the final destruction of the armies of the beast and the 10 kings at Armageddon. But it is followed by the description of another battle with the kings of the nations similar enough to argue that it is a flashback and precedes Armageddon. Yet to assert this seems to contradict all the events leading up to the final victory and for that matter the very nature of life itself.

Whatever the solution of the problem of trying to place it in the overall scheme of things, it does give a meaningful answer to the question, How do men reign with Christ? Whenever it actually occurs (and the scholars have debated this question for centuries), it does speak to the spiritual problem of those who follow Jesus and share in His glory. It is as though in the midst of the visions which foretell the final victory of the Lamb and the destruction of evil, John sees a picture which among other things speaks to the inner life. The promise that men will reign with Christ is an enticing one. Two of His disciples took the promise politically and vied for the right and left sides of the throne.

Let us look at this troublesome yet exciting promise. Jesus is Lord. He will reign, and those who follow Him will share in His reign. The four beasts and the 24 elders around the throne sang, at the outset of the visions, that the Lamb had redeemed His people by His blood "out of every kindred, and tongue, and people, and nation; and [had] made [them] unto . . . God kings and priests: and [they] shall reign on the earth" (5:9-10). In the 20th chapter this promise is fulfilled. And in the fulfillment there is a pattern which is equally relevant for spiritual victory. Whatever else 1,000 years of peace and rule of Christ may symbolize, it outlines clearly the path to spiritual victory for the Christian. It shows us how we can have the reign of Christ in our hearts and lives. It defines the peace which Jesus said He would give to His disciples, a peace unlike that which the world gives. The peace the world gives is fleeting at best; the peace Jesus gives, lasts.

The Strong Man Bound

Rev. 20:1-3

> 1 And I saw an angel come down from heaven, having the key of the bottomless pit and a great chain in his hand.
>
> 2 And he laid hold on the dragon, that old serpent, which is the Devil, and Satan, and bound him a thousand years,
>
> 3 And cast him into the bottomless pit, and shut him up, and set a seal upon him, that he should deceive the nations no more, till the thousand years should be fulfilled: and after that he must be loosed a little season.

The vision begins with the descent of an angel from heaven who had the key to the bottomless pit, the great abyss. He also had a great chain in his hand. He took the devil, who is also called the serpent and Satan, and bound him for 1,000 years. He then cast the devil in the bottomless pit for 1,000 years so that he could no longer deceive the world.

1. Early in His ministry Jesus was accused of casting out Satan by the power of Satan. He replied that such a charge was ridiculous, for it would mean that Satan was warring against himself. He then said that no man entered the strong man's house unless he first bound the strong man. He seemed to be referring to His defeat of the devil in the temptation in the wilderness. Jesus could cast out devils, i.e., loot the strong man's house, because He had bound the strong man. Perhaps this is what He meant when He cast the demon out of the boy when the disciples were unable to do so. When they asked Him why they could not and He could, He responded, "This kind goeth not out but by prayer and fasting" (Matt. 17:21). He had prayed and fasted for 40 days and defeated the strong man. He could now "loot" his house (Mark 3:22-30, NBV).

2. So to reign with Christ one must first see the devil bound. This we cannot do in our own strength. Even the Master in the wilderness called on the power of God. It is encouraging to know that there is an angel who can come from heaven and bring the key and chain to bind the evil one. However long or short one's life may be, there is a victory over Satan which all God's children can enjoy. Jesus told the disciples after His resurrection that "all power . . . in heaven and in earth" was given to Him (Matt. 28:18). John sees this power at work in the world. We can see this power at work in our hearts by the Holy Spirit. Paul wrote to the Christians in Rome, "There is therefore now no condemnation to them which are in Christ Jesus, who walk not after the flesh, but after the Spirit. For the law of the Spirit of life in Christ Jesus hath made me free

from the law of sin and death" (8:1-2). He is telling them that by the Holy Spirit the strong man of evil has been bound. Now they are free to reign with Christ.

3. There are cautions, to be sure, and these will be discussed later. But there is a gracious work of God by the Holy Spirit called entire sanctification in which the power of evil is broken. The Christian is enabled to love God with all his heart. He is free to do God's will. He is victorious in the temptations he faces. He reigns with Christ in the citadel of his heart. This work of grace subsequent to justification is described in Hebrews as "a rest to the people of God" (4:9), in which they rest from their works as God did from His. It is the peace of full salvation.

4. All that has been seen throughout the book so far that distresses and saddens has been because of the presence and power of evil in the world and in the hearts of men. Warnings are given which are ignored. Judgments come which leave men with hearts that are hard and wills that refuse to relent or repent. Suffering, tragedy, and tears mark human existence, as well as fear and terror which cause men to gnaw their tongues. The book would be a poem of beauty and joy without this darker side that evil makes necessary. But there is forgiveness and salvation. There is a book of life in which are kept the names of those who have trusted Christ for their redemption. There is an escape from the guilt and punishment of sin. And there is more. There is freedom from the power of sin. There is *an angel [with] the key of the bottomless pit and a great chain in his hand*. The truth remains: *Satan can be bound*.

The Reign of Christ Is for the Fully Committed

Rev. 20:4-6

4 And I saw thrones, and they sat upon them, and judgment was given unto them: and I saw the souls of them that were beheaded for the witness of Jesus, and for the word of God, and which had not worshipped the beast, neither his image, neither had received his mark upon their foreheads, or in their hands; and they lived and reigned with Christ a thousand years.

5 But the rest of the dead lived not again until the thousand years were finished. This is the first resurrection.

6 Blessed and holy is he that hath part in the first resurrection: on such the second death hath no power, but they shall be priests of God and of Christ, and shall reign with him a thousand years.

1. A second qualification for reigning with Christ is full commitment. As has been mentioned before, the heroes of the Book of Revelation, as far as people are concerned, are the martyrs. It would not be incorrect to say that the book was written especially for them. This is because martyrdom seemed to be widely expected. In fact, the early Christians felt that martyrdom was the supreme honor. And John saw thrones reserved for those who, having suffered with Christ, would reign with Him. He saw the souls who had been beheaded for their witness to Christ. They would not worship the beast, nor his image, nor receive his mark on their foreheads or in their hands. They had been killed. Now, John writes, they came to life and reigned with Christ 1,000 years. The rest of the dead, presumably those who died natural deaths without Christ, lived not again until the 1,000 years were past. The first resurrection is reserved for those who are martyrs for Jesus' sake.

2. In 12:11 we read that the martyrs "loved not their lives unto the death," which seems to mean they had found a love greater than life itself. It was the love of Christ, their Lord. This is full commitment. No one reigns with Christ who has not surrendered every other love. No one reigns with Christ who has not made his choice forever between this world and God's dear Son.[14] Full commitment is as much a death as though one's heart had stopped beating. It has been referred to as "dying out" or dying to the world. Paul called it reckoning the old man dead (Rom. 6:11). It is dying to a life of self-sovereignty. It occurs, if one keeps step with the Spirit's guidance, sometime after the knowledge that one has been born again. As a child of God, one bears witness to Christ by dying to this world

and living only for Christ. This life in the Spirit we will call the first resurrection.

Happy and *holy* are the words used to describe this life of full commitment. The second death has no power over the truly committed. Jesus declared, "He that believeth in me, though he were dead, yet shall he live: and whosoever liveth and believeth in me shall never die" (John 11:25-26). The second death is not cessation of physical life but the death of the soul. It is the judgment upon the sinner and rebel from God. The fear of this is gone for the fully committed. They reign with Christ. Their wills are now as His will. Their purpose is the same as His purpose. The familiar hymn "All for Jesus" spells out the essence of this commitment. It concludes with the exclamation:

> *Oh, what wonder! how amazing!*
> *Jesus, glorious King of Kings,*
> *Deigns to call me His beloved,*
> *Lets me rest beneath His wings.*

The language is from the Song of Solomon, but the truth is known by all who, because they have "died out to sin," live and reign with Christ.

Reigning with Christ Marred Only by Evil

Rev. 20:7-10

> 7 And when the thousand years are expired, Satan shall be loosed out of his prison,
> 8 And shall go out to deceive the nations which are in the four quarters of the earth, Gog and Magog, to gather them together to battle: the number of whom is as the sand of the sea.
> 9 And they went up on the breadth of the earth, and compassed the camp of the saints about, and the beloved city: and fire came down from God out of heaven, and devoured them.
> 10 And the devil that deceived them was cast into the lake of fire and brimstone, where the beast and the false prophet are, and shall be tormented day and night for ever and ever.

The strange release of Satan after 1,000 years complicates the picture. It could be explained as a return to the theme of the final conflict and triumph. This would explain what seems like a repetition of Armageddon by making the period of 1,000 years a flashback to the pre-Armageddon Church age. Nothing in the Bible or history makes such a period likely or possible. It could be explained, as has been previously noted, as a second great world battle. But how this can be when all who did not follow Christ were destroyed in the first battle is not clear.

If the inner spiritual experience of victory is viewed in this event, the release of Satan warns the Christian that reigning with Christ does not remove the possibility of further conflict with evil, if and when it is allowed to return. The *thousand years* become an indefinite span lasting as long as Satan is kept in chains. If or when he is released, one is back into the conflict. The power of evil is intrinsic rebellion. No sooner is Satan released than he deceives the nations and gathers forces to besiege the beloved city of God.

When he does, the fire from heaven destroys the armies of earth, and Satan is cast in the lake of fire with the beast and the false prophet, and they are tormented forever. Evil cannot be reformed; it must be destroyed. This vision of the final destruction of Satan seems to say that there is only one answer to evil. As long as Satan was bound, the saints reigned. When he was released, the saints were threatened. When they were threatened in the city of God, the final blow fell upon Satan, and he and his cohorts were banished *for ever and ever.*

Jesus told a story of one who had been freed from an evil spirit. The unclean spirit wandered in the dry places and found no place to stay. So the spirit returned to the place from whence he came out. He found it swept and garnished. He took seven spirits more wicked than himself, and they entered the man and dwelt there. Jesus warned, "The last state of that man becomes worse than the first" (Matt. 12:4, 5, RSV). Paul testified that he kept his body under lest, after he had preached to others, he himself might become a castaway (cf. 1 Cor. 9:27).

Some think this kind of reasoning undercuts Christian

confidence. If one is constantly on guard lest he fall, they say he is not trusting God. That is the point. Only as one trusts God and remembers that in Him alone is there certain and sure protection against evil will he remain victorious. The binding of Satan for 1,000 years meant peace and love. The release of Satan brought a renewal of rebellion and conflict, but none of it upset the reign of Christ in the *beloved city*. Wherever the return of Satan resulted in deception and rebellion, there was the powerful fire of heaven which consumed and destroyed.

The possibility of evil returning remains as long as it has not been destroyed. One should not be fooled into thinking that such a possibility does not pose a potential threat; but God, who is the Author of peace, is also the Protector of peace. He has the fire which consumes: "Our God is a consuming fire" (Heb. 12:29). A previous warning in the same letter reads: "It is a fearful thing to fall into the hands of the living God" (10:31). Neither of these statements needs trouble the Christian, for they are graphically pictured in the 10th verse of our text. God destroys evil in order to maintain the peace of the *beloved city*. Only evil need fear the consuming fire.

Again the book reinforces the theme. God is on the side of right and truth. If worst comes to worst, such as the return of Satan after 1,000 years of Christ's rule, God has the answer. He will not allow His cause to fail. Jesus said, "Fear not, little flock; for it is your Father's good pleasure to give you the kingdom" (Luke 12:32).

Reigning with Christ Includes Accountability to God

Rev. 20:11-15

11 And I saw a great white throne, and him that sat on it, from whose face the earth and the heaven fled away; and there was found no place for them.
12 And I saw the dead, small and great, stand before God; and the books were opened: and another book was opened, which is the book of life: and the dead were judged out of those things which were written in the books, according to their works.
13 And the sea gave up the dead which were in it; and death and hell delivered up the dead which were in them: and they were judged every man according to their works.

14 And death and hell were cast into the lake of fire. This is the second death.
15 And whosoever was not found written in the book of life was cast into the lake of fire.

1. In two sweeping statements John tells of the passing away of the heavens and the earth and of the general resurrection. This, declares Peter, will come about by fire (2 Pet. 3:10). Paul writes of the resurrection and the "change" at the last trump when "this corruptible must put on incorruption" and "death is swallowed up in victory" (1 Cor. 15:51-54). These passages are so brief as to leave us without any idea of how these events come about. Perhaps our minds could not grasp them even if we did know. The important truth is that these things are now past in our text. The present earth and heaven are gone. All who have ever lived now stand before God to be judged at the Great White Throne Judgment. The books are opened; all are to be judged.

2. Since the word *books* is used, there must be at least two.

a. Perhaps one book is the Bible itself, the Word of God, which contains all the truth necessary for salvation. Holy men wrote as they were inspired of God, and the words they wrote are God's words to us (2 Pet. 1:21). The final Judgment will confront men with their obedience or neglect of the clear will of God as given in His Book. The Book of God will become in the last great Judgment the Book by which men's destinies are set.

b. Another book may be the book of men's deeds, for men were judged out of *the books, according to their works.* The writer of Ecclesiastes concludes with these words: "The end of the matter; all has been heard. Fear God, and keep his commandments; for this is the whole duty of man. For God will bring every deed into judgment, with every secret thing, whether good or evil" (12:13-14, RSV). This theme is repeated in the New Testament. Everything one has done or said or thought must be faced at least one more time when the book of deeds is opened.

c. A third book was specifically identified—the book of life. Only those whose names were in this book survived. Whoever was not found in the book was cast into the lake of fire. Thus the judgment of God was complete. All have been judged, their eternal destinies announced. The world as men have known it, including the earth and heaven, has passed away. All that remain are the lake of fire, which consumes evil, and the beloved city of God.

3. Too much detail is omitted to paint a complete picture, or even outline an idea of what has happened and how in these few words that engulf a universe and history. The important truth is that all men are accountable to God. To be the recipient of His grace does not free one from accountability. Rather, the grace of God becomes all the more blessed when it is exercised in the presence of judgment. To be judged worthy of the lake of fire but spared because one's name is in the book of life is the most spectacular way for the testimony of a redeemed man to be given.

The more one has been forgiven, the more he loves. The more responsibility is laid upon him, the more he exercises himself to be found faithful to the expectations of his Savior. So to reign with Christ one deals with evil by allowing God to bind it. One commits his all and counts not his life dear. One recognizes and lives under this accountability to God, the Judge of all.

The City of God
Revelation 21:1—22:6

To fill the void caused by the disappearance of the earth and heavens John is given a vision of the city of God which takes its place. The city of man has fallen. The world in which it was built has passed away. The whole race and history of man has been judged and divided as a shepherd divides sheep from goats. The leaders of evil and all who followed them and would not repent when chastised of God have been consumed in the lake of fire. There remain the hosts of heaven and all those whose names were found in the book of life. In vision John saw a new heaven and a new earth. There was no more sea. Its disappearance probably signifies the absence of divisive factors in the new creation.

The new creation is a city which comes down from God. The writer of Hebrews pictures men of faith as those who found no continuing city on earth and confessed that they were pilgrims and strangers. They believed that somewhere there was a city worth living in, and they sought it. God was proud of them. He was not ashamed to be called their God. And He prepared for them a city (11:13-16). This is the city John saw descending from heaven—the gift of God. The first creation climaxed with a couple in a garden. The new creation is a city in which God dwells. The first couple met with God in the cool of the day. The new creation are gathered together in a city in which, a voice says, *Behold, the tabernacle [dwelling,*

NIV, RSV] of God is with men, and he will dwell with them, and they shall be his people, and God himself shall be with them, and be their God. And God shall wipe away all tears from their eyes; and there shall be no more death, neither sorrow, nor crying, neither shall there be any more pain: for the former things are passed away (vv. 3-4).

An angel, who was one of the seven that had the bowls of God's wrath, talked to John, saying, *Come hither, I will shew thee the bride, the Lamb's wife* (v. 9).

A Creation of Love

Rev. 21:1-8

> 1 And I saw a new heaven and a new earth: for the first heaven and the first earth were passed away; and there was no more sea.
> 2 And I John saw the holy city, new Jerusalem, coming down from God out of heaven, prepared as a bride adorned for her husband.
> 3 And I heard a great voice out of heaven saying, Behold, the tabernacle of God is with men, and he will dwell with them, and they shall be his people, and God himself shall be with them, and be their God.
> 4 And God shall wipe away all tears from their eyes; and there shall be no more death, neither sorrow, nor crying, neither shall there be any more pain: for the former things are passed away.
> 5 And he that sat upon the throne said, Behold, I make all things new. And he said unto me, Write: for these words are true and faithful.
> 6 And he said unto me, It is done. I am Alpha and Omega, the beginning and the end. I will give unto him that is athirst of the fountain of the water of life freely.
> 7 He that overcometh shall inherit all things; and I will be his God, and he shall be my son.
> 8 But the fearful, and unbelieving, and the abominable, and murderers, and whoremongers, and sorcerers, and idolaters, and all liars, shall have their part in the lake which burneth with fire and brimstone: which is the second death.

1. The new creation is a city of love. The first creation was marred by evil. Tempted to eat of the forbidden fruit in his desire to become equal with God, man turned his knowledge to self-conceit and built through the ages the city of man. Called by the name of counterfeit love, a harlot, the city of man merchandises love as an instrument of pleasure and self-aggrandizement. By contrast the new creation is presented in the symbol of true and pure love: *As a bride adorned for her husband.*

The purpose of the first creation, prostituted by sinful man under the aegis of the wicked serpent, is realized in the new creation as a work of love made perfect. In it all that makes love beautiful is seen. Having seen the folly of sinful self-sovereignty and having rejected it forever, its inhabitants have come to the place God intended for men by surrendering themselves to the love of the Lamb. They have found maturity and fulfillment in the community of love. As the hymn prays, their souls are now "lost in love / In a brighter, brighter world above."[15]

2. They have the victory even in sorrow and pain. God himself wipes the tears from their eyes. One wonders why there should be tears there anyway. Perhaps it is because they remember loved ones or friends who are not there. They may be weeping because they miss them. This would be understandable. Moses cared so much for Israel that he requested God to blot his name out of the book of life if his people were not spared (Exod. 32:32). Paul was so burdened for Israel he could wish himself accursed from God for his brethren's sake (Rom. 9:3). So it is not far-fetched to guess that the saints may weep in heaven for those who did not come.

These tears are dried by God. Perhaps this is done as the saints see for the first time the extent to which God has gone to redeem the lost. Again, they know fully that everything that could be done for their salvation was done. They weep no more when they understand the destructive power of sin and what it did at last even to the fairest through the years. The second death brings the harvest of rebellion and self-centered living to its final and only conclusion. When they that are within the city of love see the true maturity of evil of those that are without, they understand how much their loved ones and friends have become the total opposite of what they knew them to be and for which they loved them.

3. The city of God, a new creation of love, is all that anyone ever wanted it to be. The overcomers who inhabit it

inherit all things. The One who sits on the throne has announced that He makes all things new. Their newness implies that they are the best models possible. Every desire—now cleansed—finds its immediate and loving satisfaction. God himself, whom Haggai calls "the desire of all nations" (2:7), is with them and is their God. They are His children, the offspring of His love, the fruit of His plenty.

A City of Truth

Rev. 21:9-14

> 9 And there came unto me one of the seven angels which had the seven vials full of the seven last plagues, and talked with me, saying, Come hither, I will shew thee the bride, the Lamb's wife.
> 10 And he carried me away in the spirit to a great and high mountain, and shewed me that great city, the holy Jerusalem, descending out of heaven from God,
> 11 Having the glory of God: and her light was like unto a stone most precious, even like a jasper stone, clear as crystal;
> 12 And had a wall great and high, and had twelve gates, and at the gates twelve angels, and names written thereon, which are the names of the twelve tribes of the children of Israel:
> 13 On the east three gates; on the north three gates; on the south three gates; and on the west three gates.
> 14 And the wall of the city had twelve foundations, and in them the names of the twelve apostles of the Lamb.

1. From a vantage point high enough for full perspective which he calls a great and high mountain, John sees the city of God. It is bathed in His glory. It sparkles because it is made of things that shine from their worth. It does not need some external light to bring out its radiance; it glows on its own.

2. The city is square. No side is greater than another. Each side has 3 gates. The 12 gates are guarded by angels. These gates are inscribed with the names of the tribes of Israel. The walls have 12 foundations named after the 12 apostles. Again both the Old and New Testaments are represented.

The city is large enough to accommodate all who will dwell in it. The dimensions John gives in verse 16 would amount to about 1,500 miles in every direction—length, width, and height. Its citizens are the people of God throughout history. Ancient Israel is the offspring of the sons of Jacob. The new Israel is built on the 12 apostles. These two combine in the city of God. The people of God as a community began with the promise to Abraham, through his seed to Christ, and through Him to all who are born again. This stream of faith makes up the city of truth. Its foundation and size designate it to be a city of kept promises.

3. Paul writes, "Nevertheless the foundation of God standeth sure, having this seal, The Lord knoweth them that are his. And, Let every one that nameth the name of Christ depart from iniquity" (2 Tim. 2:19). Truth must be built on the right foundation. Having been so built, it stands sure and steadfast throughout time and eternity. Although John sees the city of God in a vision, it has its reality in time, having been built on the foundation of the 12 tribes of Israel and the 12 apostles of the Lamb.

A City of Holiness

Rev. 21:15-17

> 15 And he that talked with me had a golden reed to measure the city, and the gates thereof, and the wall thereof.
> 16 And the city lieth foursquare, and the length is as large as the breadth: and he measured the city with the reed, twelve thousand furlongs. The length and the breadth and the height of it were equal.
> 17 And he measured the wall thereof, an hundred and forty and four cubits, according to the measure of a man, that is, of the angel.

1. The angel who talks with John has a golden reed with which to measure the city and its wall. All the measurements are symbolic of its perfection. It is built by God, not human hands. Whatever the city of man was in its sins, the city of God is not. The very character of God, which is holiness, is expressed in its dimensions. This is implied in the measurement and specifically stated in the 27th verse where it is said that nothing impure will ever enter it, nor will anyone who does what is shameful or deceitful.

Only those will be there whose names *are written in the Lamb's book of life.*

What the Holy Spirit establishes in the heart of the believer when He cleanses it is brought to its fullness in the city of God. Final perfection exists as an attainable ideal for the fully committed Christian (Phil. 3:10-14). John is privileged to see the fulfillment in the city of God, "the prize of the high calling of God in Christ Jesus." The holy city is a perfect city.

2. Whatever else is meant by John's statement that the measurement of the wall is the measure of a man, he is convinced that the wonder of the city is that it is made for man. By the gracious work of the Holy Spirit man can be transformed into a citizen of the city of holiness. He can share in the nature of this city and its perfection. Having shunned the sinful ways of men, the child of God is in the world but not of it. He realizes every moment that he is out of place in the city of man. He declares to all that he is a pilgrim and finds here "no continuing city" (Heb. 13:14). But the Holy Spirit has planted within him a love of holiness; he seeks to find that rich and fulfilled life in holiness. The writer of Hebrews says that God has prepared for the entirely sanctified Christian a city (11:16). The golden measure of the angel who talks with John demonstrates that the new Jerusalem is that holy city.

3. The forgiven and cleansed man sees the city of God in all of its dimensions as the complete answer to all for which his heart and soul have longed. Having surrendered himself to the work and life of holiness, he will find in the city of God an eternal residence that complements the nature he has received in Christ. He will be at home there. As Jesus has said, it is a place for him with his Master (cf. John 14:3). Every right and holy desire is fulfilled in it. The wandering pilgrim of earth finds a home in the city of God. Though millions are there, each finds in it the full answer to all for which his soul has longed.

A City of Gold

Rev. 21:18-21

> 18 And the building of the wall of it was of jasper: and the city was pure gold, like unto clear glass.
> 19 And the foundations of the wall of the city were garnished with all manner of precious stones. The first foundation was jasper; the second, sapphire; the third, a chalcedony; the fourth, an emerald;
> 20 The fifth, sardonyx; the sixth, sardius; the seventh, chrysolyte; the eighth, beryl; the ninth, a topaz; the tenth, a chrisoprasus; the eleventh, a jacinth; the twelfth, an amethyst.
> 21 And the twelve gates were twelve pearls; every several gate was of one pearl: and the street of the city was pure gold, as it were transparent glass.

The composition of the city is one of gold and precious jewels. God had promised through the word of the prophet Isaiah, "I will set thy stones in fair colors, and lay thy foundations with sapphires. And I will make thy pinnacles of rubies, and thy gates of carbuncles, and all thy border of precious stones" (Isa. 54:11-12, ASV). Far exceeding the beauty of the harlot, the Bride of Christ is adorned with pure gold, clear as glass.

The gold and jewels enhance the beauty of the city. It is true that these have been the instruments of human pride. Evil men have sought to camouflage or color their sin with the beauty of gems. But pride is gone in the city of God. Jewels are not to cover up here but to express. It is not that gold and precious stones are evil in themselves but that they are put to use by self-centered men. In the city of God they become the fitting decoration of lives that shine with God's glory. It has been pointed out by scholars that the precious stones in the foundation of the wall largely correspond to the 12 stones worn in the breastplate of the high priest, which symbolized his holiness. The city is based on the holiness of God. It glows like precious stones or the stars of the heaven in its beauty.

The gates of the city are 12 pearls and the streets pure gold. It is almost as though the apostle struggles with words to describe the beauty he sees. If what he wrote boggles our imagination and even taxes it beyond its ability to grasp, what must it have been for the man from

Patmos to look upon and put into understandable concepts for his readers? Are there any better words or images to portray the beauty of the city built by God for His holy people, the Bride of the Lamb? The songwriter expressed it as a "land whose wondrous beauty far exceeds our fondest dreams."[16] The Negro spiritual says it rightly, "I want to go there, I do!" Our best is called "golden." So it is fitting to say that the city of God is a city of gold.

A City of Glory

Rev. 21:22-27

> 22 And I saw no temple therein: for the Lord God Almighty and the Lamb are the temple of it.
> 23 And the city had no need of the sun, neither of the moon, to shine in it: for the glory of God did lighten it, and the Lamb is the light thereof.
> 24 And the nations of them which are saved shall walk in the light of it: and the kings of the earth do bring their glory and honour into it.
> 25 And the gates of it shall not be shut at all by day: for there shall be no night there.
> 26 And they shall bring the glory and honour of the nations into it.
> 27 And there shall in no wise enter into it any thing that defileth, neither whatsoever worketh abomination, or maketh a lie: but they which are written in the Lamb's book of life.

1. What John saw transcends the forecast of the prophets and the Old Testament oracles in that there is no temple in the final holy city. None is needed, for the Lord God Almighty and the Lamb are there. Their presence makes the city itself a temple. It is not necessary to have a particular place where God's presence can be sensed and worshipped, for He is in it all. The glory of the city is that God is in her and is her Temple. With eyes and senses which now can see Him, the people of the city need nothing to remind them of His presence, for that dominates it.

There is no need for the sun or moon. The glory of God and the glory of the Lamb lighten the city to a brilliance hard to imagine. Because of that glory all the world is filled with light for the nations and kings of earth to walk in. Whatever may be the nature of the new earth, sin is forever gone, and all that are in it walk in the light of the glory of God. All honor and glory are derived from the beauty and brilliance of the presence of God with His people in the city He has prepared.

2. The gates are never shut. It is a truly open city. No one is kept there as are East Berliners behind the infamous wall. All who come are welcome. All who are there are there by choice; no coercion is needed or applied. There are no strangers. Bud Robinson once described the translation of Enoch in these quaint phrases: "God said to Enoch, 'Why don't you come over to My house and spend the night?' The Bible says they were friends and walked together. Enoch did, and since there is no night there, he has never come back." This is what John is describing. All are invited to spend whatever time they wish in the city of God. There is no night to end the days, and no one wants to leave.

3. This openness extends to everything that is good and worthwhile. There is no bigotry about the life of God. What is good and worthwhile is welcome in His city. It becomes the gallery of all that is memorable. The extravagance of poetic language should not trap us. Some very practical person may wonder how the glory of the nations and the kings can be brought when they were all destroyed in Armageddon. It was the destruction only of evil since God is not an enemy of anything of worth. If there is no other way that the good of the nations and the kings can be brought to the city of God, it will reach there in the minds of His people who have lived in the world and appropriated its good for His glory. Paul advised the Philippians, "Finally, brethren, whatsoever things are true, whatsoever things are honest, whatsoever things are just, whatsoever things are pure, whatsoever things are lovely, whatsoever things are of good report; if there be any virtue, and if there be any praise, think on these things" (4:8). By this route, if no other, the honor and glory of nations and kings can come to the city and be absorbed in its glory.

The purpose of God and the goal of civilization find common ground in the city of God. And why not? Every good and perfect gift comes from "the Father of lights" (Jas. 1:17). The nation brings back home to Him who gave it every honor. Thus the greater glory of God shines more brilliantly. There is no wasted good or beauty. The glory of the city is the totalled glory of the honor and good of earth made even more shining by the glory of God in the midst of the city.

REVELATION 22

A City of Service

Rev. 22:1-6

> 1 And he shewed me a pure river of water of life, clear as crystal, proceeding out of the throne of God and of the Lamb.
> 2 In the midst of the street of it, and on either side of the river, was there the tree of life, which bare twelve manner of fruits, and yielded her fruit every month: and the leaves of the tree were for the healing of the nations.
> 3 And there shall be no more curse: but the throne of God and of the Lamb shall be in it; and his servants shall serve him:
> 4 And they shall see his face; and his name shall be in their foreheads.
> 5 And there shall be no night there; and they need no candle, neither light of the sun; for the Lord God giveth them light: and they shall reign for ever and ever.
> 6 And he said unto me, These sayings are faithful and true: and the Lord God of the holy prophets sent his angel to shew unto his servants the things which must shortly be done.

1. A river flowed out of Eden to water the garden where the first couple lived until they sinned. When Ezekiel in captivity saw the restored Jerusalem and the temple, he saw a river flowing from it which flowed eastward, and on its banks were many trees the leaves of which were for healing. These pictures may have been in John's mind as he saw a river flow out of the throne of God and of the Lamb. It was, he said, a river of water of life. Jesus promised that if a thirsty one drank of the water He gave, it would be a river of living water. John said He was speaking of the Holy Spirit (John 7:38-39).

There is life and healing coming from God. The Holy Spirit is the power adequate for every need, and this power is always available. The dwellers of the city are sustained by it with a fresh supply every moment.

2. God's servants are busy in service to Him. They are so fully His that His name is in their foreheads. They have been redeemed by His love. They love Him, and in His love they love each other. Their service is the deepest expression of this love. There really is no contradiction between the sentence that says they serve Him, and that which says they reign with Him, for the love of God is a serving love that rules. It is the power of the meek that inherits the earth, the conquering power of a basin of water and a towel.

The prophet promised that they who served the Lord would have their strength renewed. They would run and not be weary; they would walk and not faint (Isa. 40:31). Serving-reigning love is tireless. It stoops to every depth to lift; yet it conquers all and is not exhausted in the doing of it. No night is needed for rest, for the very activity of loving service is rest in itself. No darkness distorts the configuration of the landscape, for the penetrating light of love keeps everything in perspective.

3. The idea of endlessness is not easy for the human mind to grasp. Time sequence we can understand. "Tomorrow and tomorrow" we can take in stride. But the very concept of never ending has often been threatening. What will the saints do in heaven millennium after millennium? They will serve God with their Lord in the kind of loving service which does not end or tire. It never bores. It is self-renewing, and it conquers.

4. Perhaps John realized that all of this seems "too good to be true." We reach a point in the description of the bliss of heaven when imagery fails to spell it all out. The continued repetition of its glory seems almost to take away from its reality. So John repeats the witness that all of this

he *"saw"* (v. 8). *The Lord God of the holy prophets* had sent His angel to show it all to him. *These sayings are faithful and true,* he declares. These things shall be, he avows, and sooner than one thinks. The schedule is fixed. The events move rapidly to completion. Evil will not long succeed. Habakkuk was told, "The vision awaits its time; it hastens to the end—it will not lie. If it seem slow, wait for it; it will surely come, it will not delay. . . . For the earth will be filled with the knowledge of the glory of the Lord, as the waters cover the sea" (Hab. 2:3, 14, RSV).

This then is the city of God. It is a creation of love. It is a city of truth, of holiness, of gold, of glory, and of service.

Behold, I Come Quickly

Revelation 22:7-21

Principles of Prophecy

Rev. 22:7

> 7 Behold, I come quickly: blessed is he that keepeth the sayings of the prophecy of this book.

1. Four times in the disjointed verses that close the Book of Revelation the *imminent* coming of the Lord is stated. Fourteen times in the book the fact of His coming is stated. At the very beginning and at the end the reader is told that Jesus is coming and that He is coming quickly. Now the word *quickly* carries two connotations, soon and sudden. The first must be understood in the light of an unknown timetable and a God of eternity. The latter is closer to the warning of Jesus in the Gospels. There He said that His coming will be as a thief who comes in the night. In fact, He warned, "The Son of man is coming at an hour you do not expect" (Matt. 24:43-44, RSV). So when He says, *Behold, I come quickly,* He is probably referring more to the suddenness of His return.

Jesus is coming again—and soon. If there is a delay, as we quoted Peter earlier, it is not because He is slack concerning the promise but rather that He is "longsuffering . . . not willing that any should perish" (2 Pet. 3:9). The so-called "signs of the times" have been such that every generation of Christians has felt that Christ would come in its lifetime. This itself is one reason no generation should ignore the truth or live as though it could not occur in their time. Each generation that passes without His coming means His return is more likely to occur in the next. Some have felt that, since Jesus said that no man knew "that day and that hour," it might be possible for them to know the "generation." This has led some to interpret the words of Jesus that "this generation shall not pass, till all these things be done" (Mark 13:30) to mean that the generation which sees the fulfillment of these previous prophecies will not pass until Jesus returns. Some who had strongly held this view are now with the Lord.

2. It is good to rest on the words of the risen Lord to His disciples just before He left them: "It is not for you to know times or seasons which the Father has fixed by his own authority. But you shall receive power when the Holy Spirit has come upon you; and you shall be my witnesses in Jerusalem and in all Judea and Samaria and to the end of the earth" (Acts 1:7-8, RSV). Every generation of Christians should live every day as though that were the day of His coming. This is the import of His word, *Behold, I come quickly.*

Whatever else may be the value of prophecy, Jesus told His disciples the things that would happen to them, not so much for them to know ahead of time or be able to predict, as for them to remember after it had happened that He had told them (John 16:4). This seems to suggest that the purpose of prophecy, at least as far as Jesus was concerned, was not so much to enable the hearer to predict future events as to incite to holy living and to let him know, when he sees the foretold things coming to pass, that they are part of the program of God for the ages. History cannot and will not drift beyond God's control. Thus God reveals what (not when) the outcome will be. Thus His people will know that when it seems the world has gone out of control, it really has not.

3. Throughout the Book of Revelation great and catastrophic events have paraded before the eyes of the apostle on Patmos. Some of these things could well happen in our generation, for the potential is only too graphically evident. How important then to remember the bottom line: *Jesus is coming quickly*. The earth writhes, the nations rage, and mankind seems to have gone mad. All of this John saw in these visions long ago. But he saw, too, that they were not the last word. The point of it all is that our Lord is coming to earth again in an event so sudden that it will be over before men fully comprehend what has happened.

4. The suddenness of Christ's coming should not be surprising to those who are acquainted with the Lord. He stressed this in many of His parables. If the master of a house or vineyard went on a journey, he returned suddenly and unexpectedly. People, He emphasized, either lived in a state of readiness, or they were caught short. Life is too uncertain to anticipate successfully. One cannot wait until it gets near the time to prepare. To do that, Jesus said, is to miss it. Accountability requires that one be ready whenever, and however unexpected, the moment of answer must be given.

Even more instructive is the fact that Jesus himself had a way of *showing up suddenly*.

a. When the disciples were on the Lake of Galilee and the fierceness of the storm threatened their death in the waves, He suddenly appeared. They had left Him alone in prayer, taken the boat, and started for the other side. They had not anticipated the storm or its intensity. It was too much for them until out of the wind and spray He came to them walking on the water. That's the kind of Master He is. It may not be on Galilee or any lake; but often when the pressures of life are too much and it appears that the storm will be too much, Jesus is there, just when He is needed most. The disciple on the sea and all of us in the storms of life have come to know the comfort of Jesus' appearances. We are strengthened to hear Him, as the picture of earth's last woes are ending, say, "Behold, I come quickly."

b. In the seventh chapter of his Gospel John tells of a time when Jesus stayed in Galilee because of threats on His life in Judea. It came time for the feast, and His brothers, who did not at that time believe on Him, urged Him to go to the feast in Jerusalem. They argued that, if He were the Messiah, He should show himself openly at this great religious gathering. They taunted Him with the words that He couldn't expect people to believe the things He taught if He hid out in Galilee when Jerusalem was where it all should happen. It was not because the time was ripe for such an announcement but because they thought Jesus was teaching more than He could perform that they urged the confrontation. Jesus pointed this out to them in His reply. "You go," He said, "for you are not involved in this. I will not go, for the time is not right for Me to do what you are suggesting."

But after they had gone, He went, incognito at first, and was lost in the crowd until He began to teach in the Temple yard. This was not unusual, for the Temple court was a forum for argument and discussion. It was the favorite pastime of many who came to the feast. As He taught and challenged, suddenly His identity became clear. Those who listened cried, "Isn't this the man they are seeking to kill?" Jesus answered, "Ye both know me, and ye know whence I am."

So it is with us. We leave Him behind and go into the crowd, busy with our day-to-day routine. Ideas and strategies swirl about us. There are so many conflicting ways, each of which seems right; then suddenly there is a Voice. At wits'-end-corner He is there, and His way is known. Like Saul of Tarsus on the Damascus Road, suddenly His light blinds us, and He is saying, "It is hard for thee to kick against the pricks" (Acts 9:5). He tells us the way to go, and all is changed as we obey. On the wrong road and even in the midst of confusion it makes all the difference to hear Jesus say, "Behold, I come quickly."

c. In the evening of that first Easter, the disciples were gathered in a room and had shut the door. The day had overwhelmed them. They knew that the women who had gone to the grave to anoint Jesus' body had found the grave open. His body was not there. They knew that Mary Magdalene had said that she saw Jesus alive. She said He told them to meet Him in Galilee. They knew that Peter and John had confirmed the fact that the grave was empty. They knew a young man dressed in white had said to the women that they should not seek the living among the dead. They knew, too, that the officials of the Temple and the government knew the grave was open and that Jesus' body was missing. They were huddled in the closed-in room trying to put it all together when all at once Jesus stood there among them and said, "Peace be unto you." He showed them His hands and side. They saw the scars and knew He was alive, and their fear was supplanted with joy (John 20:19-23).

One week later when they were together in that same room with the door shut, Thomas, who was not with them the first time and had said he would not believe Jesus was alive unless he could both see and put his hands into the scars, had come. Then it happened again. Suddenly Jesus was there and invited Thomas to see for himself that it was really He (vv. 24-29).

d. Stephen lay dying from the stones that were being hurled upon him. He had preached the truth to the people, and his thanks was death at their hands because they did not believe but hated what he said. Then it happened. He cried out, "Behold I see . . . the Son of man standing on the right hand of God" (Acts 7:56). Jesus had kept His promise to be with His disciples always. In time for Stephen He was there.

e. Paul was on his way to Rome. The ship had been caught in a destructive storm. It was a dark moment for the first Christian missionary. He wanted to go to Rome, to be sure, but was waylaid by men who sought His death. He appealed to Caesar and was now on his way as a prisoner. All who knew the sea and the storm despaired of life. Then it happened. He told those who could not understand his poise that the night before, Jesus had stood by him and assured him they would get to Rome even though the ship would be lost (cf. Acts 27:1-24).

f. In this book we are told that when John was in exile for his witness, alone and beset with fears, it happened. He was in the Spirit on the Lord's day and heard a voice. He turned to see Jesus in the midst of the candlesticks. He knew that, although he could not be with them, Jesus was. And now as the vision and sound of the waves beating on the rock of the lonely prison island fades, he hears Jesus say again, "Behold, I come quickly."

For John at least, the words must have brought great comfort. One could not see all that he had and not wonder how long he would be on that island, knowing all this. Would he have time and opportunity to get the message to the churches? Would they face martyrdom before they knew the triumph the martyrs would enjoy? The words of Jesus must have come as the answer to all these and other thoughts: *Behold, I come quickly: blessed is he that keepth the sayings of the prophecy of this book.*

Don't Worship Angels; Worship God in Christ

Rev. 22:8-15

> 8 And I John saw these things, and heard them. And when I had heard and seen, I fell down to worship before the feet of the angel which shewed me these things.
> 9 Then saith he unto me, See thou do it not: for I am thy fellow-servant, and of thy brethren the prophets, and of them which keep the sayings of this book: worship God.
> 10 And he saith unto me, Seal not the sayings of the prophecy of this book: for the time is at hand.
> 11 He that is unjust, let him be unjust still: and he which is filthy, let him be filthy still: and he that is righteous, let him be righteous still: and he that is holy, let him be holy still.
> 12 And, behold, I come quickly; and my reward is with me, to give every man according as his work shall be.

13 I am Alpha and Omega, the beginning and the end, the first and the last.

14 Blessed are they that do his commandments, that they may have right to the tree of life, and may enter in through the gates into the city.

15 For without are dogs, and sorcerers, and whoremongers, and murderers, and idolaters, and whosoever loveth and maketh a lie.

1. It was not a dream; it was not fantasy. All he had seen and heard would happen, and Christ would be the eternal Victor. Such a wave of relief and joy swept over him he fell down at the feet of the angel to worship him.

Why he would do this so soon after a similar experience is hard to say unless this is another memory of the same experience, or perhaps the emotion of the moment. We should understand, for we, too, forget easily and under great emotion often act almost automatically. We may call it inadvertent behavior. There may be yet another explanation. In these disjointed verses it is hard to distinguish which are the words of Jesus and which are the words of His angel.

Verse 7 begins with the words "Behold, I come quickly": so it must have been Jesus. But when John falls to worship, the angel admonishes him, "You must not do that! I am a fellow servant with you and your brethren the prophets, and with those who keep the words of this book. Worship God" (v. 9, RSV). Did John think it was the angel who had said, "Behold, I come quickly," and that the angel was Jesus? He had been told before not to worship an angel. The angel's word could indicate that the angel knew John had mistaken him for Jesus. It would be understandable at the end of so complex a revelation for such a mistake to be made.

2. The angel (or was it Jesus?) then instructed John not to seal up the prophecy but to send it to the Church, *for the time is at hand.* The truth of the book is not to be saved for some other time. Its message is relevant and it needs to be known. The angel (or Jesus) continues with the announcement that what people are when Jesus comes they will be forever. The evildoer and the filthy will remain

so. The righteous and holy will remain so as well. The implication is that there will be no time at the end for people to change. If one wants to be righteous and holy, he must become so now. The suddenness of Christ's coming means that as things are, they will remain. His coming is the end of opportunity for change. He comes at the last not as Savior but as Judge.

3. The next sentence is obviously from Jesus: *Behold, I come quickly: and my reward is with me, to give every man according as his work shall be.* He is the Beginning, who opened "a fountain filled with blood" where sinners may "lose all their guilty stains." He is the End, who brings the fair judgment of God on all who would not repent and believe the gospel. His reward is for those who keep His commandments. They will have an entrance in the gates of the city and the privilege of the tree of life. Outside the city, in the lake of fire, are all who have not repented and experienced the forgiveness of God in Jesus Christ.

The Blessed Hope

Rev. 22:16-21

> 16 I Jesus have sent mine angel to testify unto you these things in the churches. I am the root and the offspring of David, and the bright and morning star.
> 17 And the Spirit and the bride say, Come. And let him that heareth say, Come. And let him that is athirst come. And whosoever will, let him take the water of life freely.
> 18 For I testify unto every man that heareth the words of the prophecy of this book, If any man shall add unto these things, God shall add unto him the plagues that are written in this book.
> 19 And if any man shall take away from the words of the book of this prophecy, God shall take away his part out of the book of life, and out of the holy city, and from the things which are written in this book.
> 20 He which testifieth these things saith, Surely I come quickly. Amen. Even so, come, Lord Jesus.
> 21 The grace of our Lord Jesus Christ be with you all. Amen.

1. The judgment of God—life for the righteous and eternal death for the unrepentant—will come suddenly and finally when Christ appears at the end of time. Since His coming is sudden and His meting out of the judgment of God is

final, all should be warned and exhorted to repent. *This is the ultimate message of the Book of Revelation.* Jesus has sent His angel to testify these things to the churches. Men must come to Jesus while they can. This is the Holy Spirit's mission, whom Jesus sent when He ascended. It is the mission of all who are redeemed while the day of evangelism is still here. Jesus says, "Come." The Spirit says, "Come." The Bride, the Church, says, "Come." And all who hear the message should come and drink of the water of life freely.

2. In this final appeal Jesus reaffirms that He is the Promised One of the Old Testament, the Offspring of David. He is the Promised One of the New Testament, the Morning Star, the harbinger of the new day. The One who comes quickly is the Long-promised One. Like the water of life He is the answer to every need and desire of every heart. He is not only the Promised One but also the Desired One.

3. This may be an explanation of the seeming disjointedness of these verses in the close of the book. Either the angel was indeed Jesus or so one with Him as to speak not his own words but the words of Him that sent him. It may be Jesus was saying, "Don't worship me but God. I am one of your brethren the prophets, and your fellow servant." It may be called an expression of the eternal incarnation. Jesus has identified himself with men. He did so all of His earthly life. It may be that in glory He prefers to keep this identification. It may be that even now He thinks equality with God not a thing to be grasped but pefers to remain lowly of heart. The prophet Isaiah puts these words in His mouth, "I and the brethren Thou hast given me" (Isa. 8:18). The writer of Hebrews declares, "Both He that sanctifieth and they that are sanctified are all one, for which cause He is not ashamed to call them brethren" (Heb. 2:11). This passage may be an incident where those very words are fulfilled.

The above paragraph may be farfetched, but the thought it means to convey is not. In any event, the One who comes quickly is the One who loved us while we were yet sinners. He is the Shepherd who would not give up until He found us. He is the One who washed us from our sins in His own blood. He is the One who has made us to be kings and priests unto God, our Father. He is the One who has been with us always and shared of His power through the Holy Spirit. The sooner we see Him with our human eyes, the better. The more suddenly the barrier to His visual presence is forever removed, the happier we will be.

My father was a minister in the Church of the Nazarene. At one of the churches he served, the parsonage was separated from the church by a large lawn. My father had been converted in the United States Army through the ministry of a YMCA secretary. Dad loved sports and was an excellent athlete. The combination of athletics with a Christian purpose caught him. He believed also that boys were more important than lawns. So, much to the parishioners' concern, he allowed his sons and their friends to play ball on the lawn between the church and the parsonage. It suffered from this wear and tear but was the scene of some unforgettably good times. Occasionally we noticed an old man, not a member of the church, who would stand on the sidewalk to watch us at play. We soon learned that he liked boys, too, and was an expert on football. He gave us a lot of good tips about the game and even helped us patch the football when it had been torn in the locust trees nearby. Who he was and where he came from never bothered us. We were just glad when he came, and we missed him when he did not.

Now my mother was different. She loved boys, too, but she felt that love was best used in helping boys be well and strong and polite. She prayed in their hearing that they would love Jesus all their lives. One day I brought home from school a note that said I must visit the dentist. I strongly considered losing the note and probably would have "arranged" to do so but for the fact that Mother seemed to have an uncanny way of knowing when I did something like that. I was afraid that, if I came home note-less, she would sense something and ferret out the reason. So I gave her the note, but also announced that I would not go. I said I'd rather have no teeth than go to a dentist. Mother said I would go and, in order to make sure I did, she would go with me. Eventually the fateful day came, and together we went.

The dentist's office had a waiting room with a frosted door between it and the dental chair. I imagined all kinds of things. From within came strange sounds. But, since when they left, the people went out through another office to pay their bills, I saw them go in but never saw them again. I imagined the strange sounds were their last gasps for life. Every time the nurse, dressed in white, appeared, I trembled. Every time she called someone else's name, I felt reprieved. But, as it must happen to all men, at last she called my name. Mother had done her duty to deliver me to this point and when I looked pleadingly for her to accompany me inside the frosted door, she shook her head and smilingly said, "I will meet you on the other side." The words had an ominous sound. I later discovered the "other side" was the office where you went when the appointment was completed.

I walked in and sat in the chair as directed while the nurse put the bib around my neck. I grasped the arms of the chair and prepared for the worst. I heard the dentist enter and looked up at him. But when I did, all fear left suddenly, for he was the old man who frequently watched us at play. I knew he could not hurt me, for he was my friend. I relaxed, and he was through before I realized it.

This comes to my mind when I hear Jesus say, "Behold, I come quickly." My heart, which has come to know Him and respond to His love, replies, "Amen. Come quickly, Lord Jesus."

Reference Notes

Abbreviation: IB—*The Interpreter's Bible*

FIRST EPISTLE OF JOHN

1. Lloyd Ogilvie, *When God First Thought of You* (Waco, Tex.: Word Books, 1978).

2. Paul W. Hoon, "First Epistle of John," IB (New York: Abingdon Press, 1957), 12:220.

3. Ogilvie, *When God,* p. 14.

4. Ibid., p. 24.

5. Amos N. Wilder, "First Epistle of John," IB, 12:238.

6. *The Rubaiyat of Omar Khayyám,* Ed. I.

7. Ogilvie, *When God,* p. 57.

8. Paul Tournier, *A Doctor's Case Book in the Light of the Bible* (New York: Harper Brothers, 1960), p. 166.

9. Hymn, "Hallelujah! Amen!"

10. J. T. Seamands, *On Tiptoe with Joy* (Kansas City: Beacon Hill Press of Kansas City, 1967).

11. John Bunyan, *Complete Works* (National Foundation for Christian Ed., 1968), p. 133.

12. Cited in Hebrews 10:5-7 (KJV).

13. Hoon, "First Epistle of John," IB, 12:295.

14. Hymn, "I Heard the Voice of Jesus Say."

15. Charles Colson, *Born Again* (Old Tappan, N.J.: Chosen Books, 1976).

16. St. Augustine, *Confessions Book,* Chap. i (Translated by Watts).

17. Olin A. Curtis, *The Christian Faith* (New York: Eaton and Mains, 1905), p. 343.

18. Richard S. Taylor, *A Right Conception of Sin* (Kansas City: Nazarene Publishing House, 1939).

19. Alexander Pope, *An Essay on Man.*

SECOND EPISTLE OF JOHN

1. Gerrit Verkuyl, *The Berkeley Version* (James Gillick Co., 1945), p. 620.

2. Ralph Waldo Emerson, *The Writings of Ralph Waldo Emerson* (New York: Random House, 1950).

3. Hymn, "Abide with Me."

4. Hymn, "One of Them."

5. Hymn, "My Soul, Be on Thy Guard."

THIRD EPISTLE OF JOHN

1. Amos N. Wilder, "The Third Epistle of John," IB, 12:308.

2. Hymn, "In Christ There Is No East or West."

3. Hymn, "It Is Well with My Soul."

4. *The Diary of a Country Priest* (author unknown).

5. Wilder, "The Third Epistle of John," IB, 12:311.

6. Ibid., p. 312.

JUDE

1. Elmer G. Homrighausen, "Jude—Exposition," IB, 12:320.

2. Ibid.

3. Albert E. Barnett, "Jude—Exegesis," IB, 12:320.

4. Hymn, "Dear Lord and Father of Mankind."

5. Hymn, "Called unto Holiness."

6. Hymn, "Blest Be the Tie That Binds."

7. Barnett, "Jude," IB, p. 321.

8. Hymn, "My Soul, Be on Thy Guard."

9. William Shakespeare, *The Merchant of Venice,* Act 2, sc. 9, lines 182-85.

10. F. W. Boreham, *I Forgot to Say or A Gust of After-thought* (New York: Abingdon Press, 1935).

11. James Russell Lowell, *Early Poems* (New York: Thomas Crowell & Co., 1898), p. 199.

12. Homrighausen, "Jude," IB, 12:342.

13. C. S. Lewis, *Surprised by Joy* (New York: Harcourt Brace, 1956).

THE REVELATION OF ST. JOHN THE DIVINE

1. Ralph Earle, "The Book of the Revelation," *Beacon Bible Commentary* (Kansas City: Beacon Hill Press of Kansas City, 1967), vol. 10.

2. E. Stanley Jones, *Hymns for Ashrams.*

3. The writer heard this suggestion from Dr. H. Orton Wiley in a Bible study at Beulah Park, Calif.

4. Hymn, "Lead On, O King Eternal."

5. Thousand seems a figure of infinity or beyond numbering. Martin Rist suggests this. See IB, 12:409.

6. Hymn, "There's a Wideness in God's Mercy."

7. Hymn, "The Mercy Seat."

8. Hymn, "How Firm a Foundation."

9. E. Stanley Jones, *Is the Kingdom of God Realism?* (Nashville: Abingdon Press, 1940).

10. See the hymn "A Mighty Fortress Is Our God."

11. A quotation from a radio sermon by Dr. Harry Emerson Fosdick.

12. Hymn, "Ambassador for the King."

13. Jim Elliot, missionary to the Auca Indians.

14. See the hymn "Jesus, I'll Go Through with Thee."

15. Hymn, "Let Me Love Thee, More and More."

16. Hymn, "The Land of Beulah."

Bibliography

Barclay, William. *The Revelation of John*. Philadelphia: Westminster Press, 1961.

Barnett, Albert E. "Jude—Exegesis," *The Interpreter's Bible,* Vol. 12. George A. Buttrick, editor. New York: Abingdon Press, 1957.

Blaney, Harvey J. S. "Revelation," *The Wesleyan Bible Commentary,* Vol. 6. Charles W. Carter, general editor. Grand Rapids: Baker Book House, 1977 reprint.

Brown, Charles Ewing. *The Hope of His Coming*. Anderson, Ind.: The Gospel Trumpet Co., 1927.

Clarke, Adam. *The Holy Bible, with a Commentary and Critical Notes,* Vol. IV. New York: Abingdon Press, n.d.

Earle, Ralph. "The Book of the Revelation," *Beacon Bible Commentary,* Vol. 10. Kansas City: Beacon Hill Press of Kansas City, 1967.

Curtis, Olin Alfred. *The Christian Faith*. New York: Eaton & Mains, 1905.

Homrighausen, Elmer G. "Jude—Exposition," *The Interpreter's Bible,* Vol. 12. George A. Buttrick, editor. New York: Abingdon Press, 1957.

Hoon, Paul W. "First Epistle of John," *The Interpreter's Bible,* Vol. 12. George A. Buttrick, editor. New York: Abingdon Press, 1957.

Ogilvie, Lloyd. *When God First Thought of You*. Waco, Tex.: Word Books, 1978.

Seamands, John T. *On Tiptoe with Joy*. Kansas City: Beacon Hill Press of Kansas City, 1967.

Wilder, Amos. "First Epistle of John," *The Interpreter's Bible,* Vol. 12. George A. Buttrick, editor. New York, Abingdon Press, 1957.